WORDS TO WIN SOULS:

TWELVE SERMONS,

PREACHED A. D. 1620-1650,

BY EMINENT DIVINES OF THE CHURCH OF ENGLAND.

Revised and Abridged from a very scarce Collection,

BY THE

REV. THOMAS S. MILLINGTON.

"The words of the wise are as goads, and as nails fastened by the masters of assemblies, which are given from one shepherd."—ECCLES. xii. 11.

"He that winneth souls is wise."—PROV. xi. 30.

NEW YORK:
ROBERT CARTER AND BROTHERS,
285 BROADWAY.
1855.

PREFACE

The volume from which the following Sermons are selected was published in the year 1660, and is described in the title-page as "newly corrected and amended." The allusions in many of the Sermons to recent or contemporaneous events show that they were preached at a much earlier date; probably between A.D. 1620 and 1650.

The style of the Sermons is such as might often be imitated with advantage at the present day. In most of them the exordium, now so generally in use, is either very brief or altogether omitted. The Preacher makes the best use of his time and addresses himself at once to the serious business of his text, engaging the minds of his people while they are awake, and not blunting the edge of their expectation by a long or impertinent preface.

He then sets up certain divisions, which, like boundary marks, he carefully keeps in view, proceeding from one to another till he reaches the end of his discourse. Thus he loosens the parts without injuring their coherence, and, avoiding all digressions, keeps the attention of his hearers in that track to which it was first directed.

This intelligent division of the text is well likened, by one of the authors, to "unfolding a rich piece of arras, and pointing with the finger to the subjects represented;" while the earnest and sweet consideration of the several parts is symboled by "the bee that sitteth upon each particular flower and gathereth the drops of honey."

In handling the several points of doctrine, the Preacher is careful not to separate the text from the sense in which it occurs; but views it both in its first and special application (if any), and also in its present and more general meaning.

He ventures nothing on his own authority, but interprets one place of Scripture by another, and abundantly confirms every inference by the word of God, *comparing spiritual things with spiritual.*

And in applying the doctrines of his text to the hearts and lives of his people, he contrives to gather something special and appropriate for each. The experienced Christian, the returning prodigal, the sleepy careless sinner, and the hardened reprobate, each finds something fitly spoken to himself. There is a smile or a frown, a congratulation or a caution, a promise or a rebuke, for every hearer; the same fountain sends forth bitter waters or sweet, according to the taste and palate of him who drinks. Nor are the exigencies arising from outward circumstances overlooked. Rich and poor, masters and servants, learned and unlearned, each finds his own peculiar difficulties understood and his objections answered. "This is for you, and this for you;" there is an *aurea gutta,* a golden drop, in the text for each of them.

And this helps to procure attention, and to keep up the interest of the sermon, for, to use the words of good George Herbert,* "particulars ever touch and awake more than generals." To which end, also, "the preacher serves himself of the judgments of God, as of those of ancient times, so especially of the late ones; and of those most which are nearest to his parish: for people are very attentive at such discourses, and think it behoves them to be so when God is so near them, and even over their heads." He shows them God's justice and severity against the impenitent, and his mercy and forbearance towards themselves, that they may better appreciate their favourable condition as God's people, and be careful not to forfeit it by indifference or neglect. "Sometimes he tells them stories and sayings of others, according as his text invites him, for them also men heed and remember better than exhortations." †

Exhortations, however, are neither feeble nor deficient in the following Sermons. Few flowers of rhetoric are employed, but plain, earnest, forcible language, that cannot be misunderstood and will rarely be unheeded. The authors do

* Herbert's "Country Parson," chap. vii.

† Ibid.

not indeed despise eloquence:—"The wind," says one, "maketh a louder and sweeter sound in the organ pipe than in the open air; and so the matter of our speech and the theme of our discourse, when conveyed through figures and forms of art, both sound sweeter to the ear and pierce deeper into the heart"—but they decline all pomp and vanity of idle words in the pulpit, which, it is well remarked, "is no place to show our quaint and lofty strains of oratory, but our zeal for God's glory and the edification of his people." They value eloquence only as an effectual means of explaining and applying their doctrines, and judge that to be the best arrow which fliest farthest and goes most directly to its aim. The clear and perspicuous explanation of the text, the general aptness of the similitudes, and the nervous impressive language with which the lessons are enforced, have more of real and admirable eloquence than many of the finished periods of these days, when men think less and write and speak more.

The Editor would fain hope that these Sermons—the legacies of men who being dead yet speak,—may not only be the means, under God, of awakening some, and confirming others in their Christian course, but also may be found useful to many who study rightly to divide the Word of Truth, and to be thoroughly furnished unto all good works, that they may *win souls* to Christ.

CONTENTS.

Sermon IV.

THE IMPROVEMENT OF TIME; OR, THE RIGHT USE OF TIME'S SHORTNESS.

Sermon V.

ST. PAUL'S TRUMPET; OR, AN ALARM FOR SLEEPY CHRISTIANS.

Sermon VI.

CHRIST'S PRECEPT AND PROMISE; OR, SECURITY AGAINST DEATH.

Sermon VII.

THE PLATFORM OF CHARITY; OR, THE LIBERAL MAN'S GUIDE.

Sermon VIII.

THE PERFECTION OF PATIENCE; OR, THE COMPLETE CHRISTIAN.

Sermon IX.

SIN'S STIPEND AND GOD'S MUNIFICENCE.

Sermon X.

THE STEWARD'S SUMMONS.

Sermon XI.

SPIRITUAL HEART'S-EASE; OR, THE WAY TO TRANQUILLITY.

SERMON XII.

SERMON I.

THE CARELESS MERCHANT;

OR,

THE WOFUL LOSS OF THE PRECIOUS SOUL.

MATT. XVI. 26.

"WHAT IS A MAN PROFITED, IF HE SHALL GAIN THE WHOLE WORLD, AND LOSE HIS OWN SOUL?"

THE patriarch Jacob, in his vision at Bethel, saw the angels of God ascending and descending. So, from the 13th verse of this chapter, we have the disciples of Christ ascending and descending. For, first, Simon Peter had made a notable confession of our Saviour's divinity, and had received, for the further encouragement of himself and his brethren, such an excellent testimony from the Saviour as the angels of heaven might behold, observe, and embrace:—*Blessed art thou, Simon Bar-jona, for flesh and blood hath not revealed it unto thee, but my Father which is in heaven: and I say unto thee, that thou art Peter, and upon this rock will I build my church, and the gates of hell shall not prevail against it.* Which words were not only appropriate to him, but they were common to all the apostles: for, as Origen argues, Shall we think that the gates of hell prevailed not against Peter, but did against the rest? Therefore, that which was said to him was said to all: and, being such a glorious commendation,—behold the angels ascend!

But, secondly, what if the earthly mind of man dream of a Messias *temporal,* and that they should themselves be promoted to places of eminency, and styled gracious lords? This was too evidently the case with the apostles. For, if Christ warn them of his approaching death at Jerusalem, he shall be sure to meet with a check:—*Be it far from thee, Lord: this shall not be unto thee.* Oh, here is a strange metamorphose! Before, a confessor, and now a controller: there is no wisdom of the Spirit in this, and therefore no commendation; but, because Simon was somewhat too forward,—*Get thee behind me, Satan; thou art an offence unto me.* Behold the angels descend!

And surely this carnal wisdom had been able to weigh them down to the nethermost hell, had it not been curbed, and subdued, and restrained, by the wisdom of the Highest. What, not suffer? Yes; and Peter also must suffer; and all that will follow Christ must suffer; they must renounce all the enticements of the world, and mortify all the corrupt exorbitancies of the flesh, and resist all the temptations of the Devil; for, *what is a man profited, if he shall gain the whole world, and lose his own soul?*

Which words are a true description of the woful case of a temporizing professor, of a carnal gospeller; and they bring to our consideration these four generals:—

First, the excellency and worth of man's soul, which is of greater value than the whole world.

Secondly, the possibility of its loss. A man may lose his own soul.

Thirdly, the compossibility of outward prosperity. He may lose his soul in gaining the whole world.

And then, lastly, the woful bargain in such an exchange. *What is a man profited?*

Of these in order—First, of the surpassing excellency and dignity of man's soul. It is valued and prized here above the whole world. It was the plausible conceit of some philosophers that the world was a great man, and that man was a little world. A little world indeed, but, as St. Austin terms him, a great wonder! For, within this little world, there is a reasonable soul worth many worlds. To render an exact definition of the soul requires the tongue of an angel rather than of a man: it passes the ability of the wisest to apprehend its nature. These three — God, angels, and man's soul — they are unknown to us: we may more easily admire their excellency, than conceive their nature: we may argue of their operations, but we cannot attain to their knowledge.

The excellency and sublimity of the soul is

commended to us by three distinct voices—by the voice of nature, of grace, and of glory.

First, in the order of nature, it is the greatest thing, saith Plato, that we may conceive of in a narrow compass—the most noble thing that all the frame of nature affords.

View it in respect of its origin. The soul had never its beginning here. There was no voice directed to the earth, or to the water, for the production of Adam's soul; but a serious consultation of the sacred Trinity, and a breathing into his nostrils of the breath of life. Therefore, even the heathen philosopher might well conclude that the soul is not of the earth, but immortal: and, therefore, the Manichees extolled it too high, supposing it to be a portion of God's essence. Let not others abase and depress it too low, nor esteem it unworthily.

View it again in respect of the image in which it was created. Saith Plato, saith Aristotle, "The soul is most like God:" and God himself signifieth so much; *Let us make man in our image.* Therefore, the soul of man is not stamped with a Roman Cæsar, but with God's own image and superscription; and that in many respects.

In respect of the substance,—being not only a spiritual, intellectual, incorporeal, invisible essence, but explaining in some sort, by the plurality of powers in the unity of essence, the plurality of persons in the unity of the Deity.

Also, in respect of its being furnished with singular endowments; as, in the state of innocency, with perfect wisdom, and holiness, and righteousness. Yea, and even in the state of sin, some generals are still left, some broken fragments of the creation, moral qualifications, that may lead us by the hand to the knowledge of our Maker.

And again, in regard of the commanding power it hath over the body. It is to the body, as Moses was to Pharaoh, a god: it actuates it, and moves, and commands, and restrains it: whereby, next and immediately under God, *We live, and move, and have our being.*

Seeing then the soul is the immediate work and character of God himself, so excellent for the original and for the image, nature testifieth that, in these regards, it is of greater value than the whole world.

Secondly, in the kingdom of grace, the price of the soul is far above the dignity of the world; and that both in the grace of redemption, and in the grace of renovation.

For, in the soul's redemption,—its ransom mounts so high, that the whole creation is not able to discharge it. *It cannot be gotten for gold, neither shall silver be weighed for the price of it. It cannot be valued with the gold of Ophir, nor with the precious onyx. It cost more to redeem the soul* of sinful man. The precious blood of the eternal Son of God, this was the price of it. He could alone redeem it, who at the first created it. You are bought with a price; Christ hath purchased you with his own blood.

And, in the soul's renovation,—nothing is able to cleanse it from sin, but the Spirit of God. The Spirit alone can enlighten the understanding and rectify the affections, and purify the will, and sanctify the conscience, and seal up the image of God in righteousness and true holiness. And the soul thus renewed is as a garden inclosed, a spiritual paradise, where the God of heaven himself delights to dwell. It is, in the language of the Church, the spouse of the beloved: *As the lily among thorns, so is my love among the daughters.*

Seeing, then, that the universal world is not able to redeem, nor, when redeemed, to cleanse or renew the soul, let grace subscribe to that which nature concludes, that the soul is of greater value than the whole world.

Lastly, for the passage of glory, the contents of the whole universe are not able to come near the soul. Well saith St. Bernard, "It may indeed be busy and taken up with other things, but it cannot be satiate and replenished with them." And Democrates imagined that if there were millions of worlds, it were all one in comparison of the soul for blessedness: all of them together could not be weighed against the soul. The world is transitory like the dew of the morning; it fades as the grass and as the flower of the field: whereas, on the contrary, the soul of man is immortal, capable of an exceeding, surpassing, eternal weight of glory. For if, in the time of grace, we behold, as in a glass, the glory of the Lord, and are changed into the same image from glory to glory by the Spirit of the Lord, how resplendent shall the righteous be in the beatifical vision of God's excellencies! How wonderful shall that divine capacity be, that shall be capable of God himself for a perpetual residence! Insomuch that the Ancient of Days shall give to the soul fulness of knowledge and wisdom, and his sacred Spirit shall fill it with all the fulness of God, and the sacred Trinity shall be all in all to it!

Seeing, then, that the soul is capable, and is the subject, of the happiness and joys of heaven, and partner with the glorious angels in the fruition of the chief good, let the sentence of glory be joined to that of grace and nature, that the soul of man is of greater value than the whole world.

Behold, then, O man, out of the mouth of three witnesses, the surpassing excellency and dignity of the soul. It is the breathing of God, the image of God. He created it with his word, redeemed it with his Son, and, in whomsoever his grace abides, he will crown it hereafter with his glorious presence.

What then remains, but that we esteem our souls even as God values them? Let us not, with the unhallowed voluptuousness of these times, make lords of our bodies, and slaves of our souls. Let us not spend our days in providing for the lusts of the flesh. Let us not, in affectation of fair possessions, hopeful sons, good friends, and able servants, content ourselves with bad souls. "A man's soul is himself," saith Plato; and, "Oh, wretched wight," saith St. Austin, "how hast thou deserved so much ill of thyself, as, among all thy goods, to be only thyself bad! Oh, remember the sublimity of thy soul! thou knowest not what a precious pearl thou hast in thy body: like the hidden treasure of the Gospel, it is of greater worth than the whole field." I say not as he did, "Know that thou hast a God in thee;" yet, know that, in the better part of thy nature, thou art like to God; for he hath given thee a soul of his own breathing, and stamped it with the impress of his own image, and created it capable of the fruition of his own presence, in endless glory. In the consideration whereof, walk worthily of this divine inspiration. Thy soul is a spirit,—let thy thoughts be spiritual. Thy soul is immortal,—let thy meditations be of immortality; and renounce thy body, and good name, and gifts of the world, for the gaining of thy soul. *For what shall it profit a man, if he shall gain the whole world, and lose his own soul?*

So much shall serve to be spoken of the first point, the surpassing excellency and dignity of the soul. It is valued and prized here above the whole world.

Now the SECOND point is,—The possibility that a man may lose his own soul. The mention whereof causeth me to remember that passage between Christ and his disciples, where the disciples point their Master to the stately buildings of the temple, but they are soon damped, when Christ tells them that, after a while, there shall not be left one stone upon another. So, perhaps, you, who were taken with admiration at the former part of this discourse, concerning the excellency of man's soul, are somewhat damped to consider that a man may lose it. It is immortal in respect of the being of it; but, when defiled with sin, it is adjudgeable to death in respect of its *well*-being. And a possibility so to die is nothing repugnant to the immortality of the soul. The damned spirits, they are always dying and are never dead; they are always deprived of God's comfortable presence, and are never released of their hellish torments. As the apostle saith, in another case, *as dying, and behold we live;* as living, and yet behold they die. The soul expiring is the death of the body; and God forsaking is the death of the soul.

But you will say, How is it possible?

The question is soon resolved, if we ponder the causes of death. A thousand mortal maladies there are to kill the body; and there are a thousand deadly diseases to destroy the soul. There is no sin so small, but, in the rigour of God's justice and in its own nature, it may damn the soul.

When God in the beginning stated man in Paradise, he gave him a special caveat about the tree of knowledge:—*In the day that thou eatest thereof thou shalt surely die.* What, for bare eating? No, beloved, but for the sin; for transgressing even so small a commandment of so great a God. Sin alone maketh a separation between God and the soul, and so causeth the death of the soul; *The soul that sinneth it shall die.* The sin of Adam may teach us that, all the time we live in this world, there is nothing easier than to sin. There is a tree of life, and a tree of knowledge; and by eating of the tree forbidden cometh death. There is a way of felicity, and a way of destruction; there is a God of salvation, and a ghostly enemy; and by adherence to the principality of sin, a man may lose his soul.

Have we not then great reason to try and to suspect ourselves touching our standing towards God? Is there not a main necessity to seek the means to preserve us in the compass and seal of grace? It is lamentable to consider how, in bodily diseases, men can open their grief, and seek for help from some learned physician, who, after all, has, perhaps, no power to give relief. In case of law, too, we can go readily enough for advice to some learned counsel; but, alas! the soul lies wounded in the way, overladen with the grievances and pressures of sin, distracted with the affrightings of a troubled conscience, as if there were no balm in Gilead, no physician nor counsellor to afford help. There is no seeking abroad after spiritual good. A lion is said to be in the way, and Solomon's sluggard folds his hands to sleep. O let not these things be so! Be not as the horse and mule that have no understanding; neglect not the helps of your preservation in grace; but be continually watchful, with suspicion and jealousy, and *abstain from fleshly lusts that war against the soul.* The poet could say, "Thieves rise by night to rob, and steal, and slay:" and wilt not thou wake to save thy precious soul?

God, for the most part, saith St. Chrysostom, hath allotted to nature all by twos—two hands, two eyes, two ears, two feet; that if we chance to maim one, we may help to relieve the necessity of it by the other: but he hath given us *but one soul;* and if we lose that, what shift shall we make for another?—a piercing contemplation, if we had grace to consider it! Therefore, O my soul, let me cherish thee, and tender thee, as my only dependence for joy and happiness for ever! If thou be translated to heaven, then the body shall in time come thither: *this corruptible shall put on incorruption, and this mortal shall put on immortality.* But if thou be haled with the fiends to the nethermost hell, the body also shall, in time, be tormented with thee. It is altogether just, with the righteous God, that they that meet in sin should also consort in suffering. Save thyself and save all; and by woful consequence, lose thyself and all is lost for ever. *For what is a man profited, if he shall gain the whole world, and lose his own soul?* So much for the second point, the possibility of a man's losing his soul.

Come we now to the THIRD point,—the compossibility of outward prosperity: A man may lose his soul in gaining the world.

In the diversity of opinions concerning the

chief good, some there were that placed it in riches; others in honours: and, however they differed in their judgments, yet they were alike in this,—that they were both deceived. For, although it cannot be denied that both riches and honours are blessings sent from God, yet they are no demonstration of a blessed man. Lest any man should take them to be in themselves evil, they are bestowed upon the good; and, lest any should reckon them for the chief good, they are bestowed also upon the wicked. *God maketh his sun to rise on the evil and on the good, and sendeth rain on the just and on the unjust.* External blessings are but common favours, vouchsafed to good and bad. Was Abraham rich? So was Abimelech. Was David a king? So was Saul. Was Constantine an emperor? So was Julian. Salvation depends not on the multitude of riches nor upon eminency in place: the tallest cedar hath the greatest fall; and the fairest houses many times the greatest ruin: and outward prosperity, unguarded by inward sanctity, may soon lose the soul.

For, *first*, rich men are tainted with *covetousness*, which, saith the apostle, *is idolatry.*

And if you would know the reason, it is this. The more tenaciously a man loves his own, the less devotion he offers to God. You cannot live in the service of Mammon and of Christ: the mouth of the Lord hath spoken it,—*ye cannot serve God and Mammon.* If the young man in the Gospel have great possessions—if Judas carry the bag—if Demas embrace the present world, then farewell Christ, farewell Paul, and farewell soul too. So true is the saying of the apostle,—*They that will be rich fall into temptations and a snare, and into many dangerous and hurtful lusts that drown men in destruction.* He saith not, they that *are*, but they that *will be*, rich. It is not simply money, but the love of money, that is the root of all evil. Riches are good with a good conscience: but if the soul be infected with avarice, if it savour of that bitter coloquintida, then death is in the pot. The desire of worldly men is as the unsatiable thirst of the dropsy patient; there are no means that they will leave unattempted, no policy unachieved, for the accomplishment of their ends and advancing of their estates. Balaam, for a bribe, will curse where God hath blessed. Ziba, for an inheritance, will (as much as in him lieth) bring his master within the compass of treason. Demosthenes, for a little more gold, instead of pleading, will pretend he hath a cold.

There are no greedy monopolizers, wheresoever they be, in city or country, but they are like the eagle in the fable; and the coals they carry shall burn their own nests. They shall have Ahab's curse with Naboth's vineyard; and with Naaman's reward Gehazi's leprosy shall cleave to them; for, while with eager pursuit they hoard up unrighteous mammon, it is but wrath heaped up against the last day: the heap up wrath to themselves against the day of wrath.

Secondly. Great men are in danger of ambition, and a swelling inordinately on their promotion. And the ambitious man is so strangely dazzled with the beams of his own lustre, that, in the greatness of his power, he thinks of nothing but how to be most admired, and how to become yet greater. He forgetteth the Lord that made him, and God that raised him out of the mire, to set him with the princes of the people: and like that famous fool in his new coat, he knoweth not himself. So, though God hath some noble, some wise, that he hath drawn to himself, yet, by means of this impediment, not many mighty, not many noble, not many learned, are called. The gates of heaven are too strait for the swelling dimensions of ambition. There is nothing so easy to pride as to purchase a fall; and there is no fall so great as from heaven. If Lucifer long for advancement, it is a sign that he shall be cast out from heaven: if Adam desire the apple, it is a sign that he shall be cast out from Paradise: if Haman abuse his promotion, he shall be brought to the gallows. To comprise it in a word—the greater the dignity of eminence and honour, the greater the execution of pains and horror. The sum then is this:—In a world of promotion, and temporal advancement in worldly possessions and unmeasurable treasure, the covetous and ambitious man may lose his own soul.

Now for a word of application. If this be so, then, how taxable are the thousands of worldlings in this kind, that imagine the gain of this earth to be the greatest happiness! That say to the gold, Thou art my god; and to honour, Thou art my glory! that make gold their god, and mammon their mediator! Saith St. Bernard, "Yea, covetous generation, that glory in silver and gold, in that that is neither yours, nor yet precious: precious they cannot be, but by the avarice of the sons of Adam that prize them: and if they be yours, take them away with you when you go hence." Yet the children of the world are wholly for great Diana. Gods of silver and gold, multitudes of lands and revenues, and an increase of their secular estate, are all they desire. Many can complain of the vanity of this world and the deceivableness of it, but few complain of that idolatrous confidence that themselves repose in this false world. There are few that recount how, in enjoying outward things—Martha without Mary, prosperity without piety—they may lose their own souls. O let a word of exhortation prevail against this sore disease; if riches increase, beware of covetousness: be covetous for spiritual things, for immortality: hoard up your treasure in heaven.

So much for the third point, the compossibility of outward prosperity: A man may lose his soul in gaining the whole world.

The FOURTH and last is,—the woful disadvantage of such an exchange: *What is a man profited?* You may call it, not unfitly, the account of the careless merchant.

For, (a little to countenance the allegory,)

every unsatiable worldling is but a merchant adventurer; one who bartereth and exchangeth his precious soul for the deceivable riches of this world. But when God, in his judgment, transports him to his own place, the unfortunate abode of cursed spirits, then he begins, when the time is past, to cast up his doleful account, to compare his gains and his losses; and, after all the enumeration of his imaginary gain—so much by usury, so much by extortion, so much by fraudulent dealing—he perceiveth that for these things that are past and gone he hath lost his own soul for ever.

Then what is a man profited? The bargain is such that there is nothing gotten by it: nay, that is too sparing an expression; it is short of Christ's meaning, who leaves us to draw the inference for ourselves. For, indeed, it were a happiness if we could make the balance of such an account as this to be *nothing:* this were profitable for the damned, and a thing that they would most earnestly desire.

But let us see the end of this bargain in some particulars.

Suppose the case of a man that glories in the resplendency of his fortunes, and blesseth himself in magnifying his estate—a commander of kingdoms and nations—an engrosser of preferments and dignities; yet

First, death will attack him; there is no carrying his dignity and honours with him. He must, of necessity, take leave of his mammon, and then, whose shall these things be for which he hath lost his soul? Who gains by the smallness of the epha, the greatness of the shekel, the refuse of the wheat? Where is the man that gloried in his abundance and store, and thought himself the only happy man? Saith the prophet David,—*I went by, and lo, he was gone; I sought him, but his place could no where be found.* There is a lively expression that illustrates it,—*As the partridge sitteth on eggs and hatcheth them not, so he that getteth riches, and not by right, shall leave them in the midst of his days, and at his end shall be a fool.* What, not before his end? Yes, he was always a fool; but then, by conviction, his own conscience shall call him so: the confession of his own tongue shall call him so: the proclamation of just men shall declare him so. *Lo, this is the man that took not God for his strength, but trusted unto the multitude of his riches and strengthened himself in his wickedness.*

Secondly, having lost his supposed good, he loseth the fruition of God, the chief good; he loseth the countenance of the beatifical presence, the fellowship and melodious harmony of the glorious angels, and his place and portion with Abraham, Isaac, and Jacob, in the kingdom of heaven. And all for his own deservings. In his lifetime he refused God; being dead, God refuseth him. He turned his face from the poor and needy; God, in his affliction, eternally turns his face from him,—a loss so exceeding great, that whosoever descends deepest into the meditation of it, he shall not know how to find a full definition of it. For, as Chrysostom truly affirms, "though a man tell thee of ten thousand hells, all is one in comparison of this misery, to be discarded of blessedness and glory, and to be hated of Christ."

But if this be so, what shall we say to yet further misery? Having lost the chief good, he receives his punishment with hypocrites and unbelievers in the dungeon of extreme ill; a place where there is nothing but desperation and horror of conscience and a company of affrighting devils, and with all this, weeping, and wailing, and gnashing of teeth. Instead of merriment and jovial laughter, and scurrilous, lascivious songs, and wasting and abusing the creatures of God, nothing but weeping and gnashing of teeth. So that, having come into the straits of the grave, the chambers of death, the man, like the hedgehog in the fable, leaves the apples behind, and only reserves the prickles of a wounded spirit; receiving that sentence of Babylon, — *How much she hath glorified herself and lived deliciously, so much torment and sorrow give her.*

Lastly, that that is the hell of hells, that nothing may be wanting to this deserved woe, he is out of hope of all gracious means of deliverance: he must never look for the revocation of God's sentence, though he seek it carefully with tears: he must never look for the mitigation of his horror, though he beg, with the unmerciful glutton, for one drop of water. The date of repentance is out; the day of grace will never dawn again; the justice is implacable, the fire unquenchable, the worm insatiable, and all continual, without intermission, for evermore.

O bottomless depth of horror! O inexpressible torment of a forsaken soul! "What greater misery," saith St. Bernard, "than to be always wishing for that which shall never be, and for the removing of that which shall never be removed?"

Therefore the sum is this: Hath the covetous exchanged his soul for riches, the ambitious for honours; hath he lost it for the riches of Crœsus, the power of Alexander, the empire of Augustus; yet, considering the end of his life, the loss of his God, the extremity of his pain, the eternity of all, *what is a man profited?*

Now, then, for some application, and to draw towards a conclusion. Suffer the word of exhortation, brethren, and captivate your thoughts to the obedience of Jesus Christ. You, especially, whom God hath blessed above others concerning the enjoyment of outward, temporal things, if ever you be desirous to avoid the direful slaughter-house of hell, to escape those burnings and those everlasting yellings, bethink yourselves, while you have time, of some saving course *to flee from the wrath to come.*

And now, in time, cast up your accounts; take heed lest, for the love of this present world, you lose your God, the life of your souls.

There is a way which seemeth right unto a man, saith Solomon, *but the end thereof are the ways of death.* Some Babylonish garment, some Naboth's vineyard, some sweet preferment, engage the affections; but if the means be unlawful, if it disturb conscience, and prejudice the glory of God, and occasion the destruction of thy soul, then say,—What shall I do, when God shall rise up? and when he shall visit, what shall I answer? This will be the reckoning of fools at the last,—What hath pride profited us, and what hath riches brought us? Surely the gain will be no other than that Prometheus is fabled to have got by Pandora's box — a place full of torments; or what Hercules got by Dejanira's garment. Such will be the final issue of all Mammonists that live amongst Christians, and under means of better reformation and more sanctification in their ways: I say, this will be the final issue; the worm of despair always gnawing and never dying, and the flames of eternal Tophet never to be extinguished. Therefore, in such a case, if thou tell me thou knowest what thou *dost,* and what thou *gainest,* let me tell thee, thou little knowest thy *damage,* and what thou hast *lost.* Alas! what are the goods of this life when they are bought with eternal damnation? And the sweetness of imaginary gain, what proportion hath it with the bitterness of so great a loss? Riches have wings, they take their leave; honour is transitory; pleasures fly away: but the soul is the subject of immortality; and thy poor neglected soul must bide for an everlasting pledge, and pay the penalty.

O then contemn this glory that is nothing. First seek God's kingdom and the glory of it. Suffer not Heaven to stand at so great a distance from thy soul. Taste and see how gracious the Lord is, by one drop of water from that celestial fountain, by one crumb from that heavenly table; and then, as concerning the things below, thou wilt account them as dross and dung in comparison of that joy and peace of conscience. Be as Themistocles; when he saw a goodly booty, he would not stoop to take it up:—leave these things for the children of this world.

But let your care be to please the Lord, and to gain the peace of a good conscience. First seek the kingdom of God, which consists *not in meat or drink, but is righteousness, peace, and joy in the Holy Ghost.* Remember the vanity of the things of the world: remember how unable the soul is to endure Hell, and to lose Heaven, without eternal horror.

And, in consideration of this, use the world as though you used it not; and keep this text as a curb to your desires: hide it in a sanctified memory; write it on the tables of a sanctified conscience, as with a pen of iron, or the point of a diamond: *What is a man profited, if he shall gain the whole world, and lose his own soul?*

SERMON II.

SECURITY SURPRISED;

OR,

THE DESTRUCTION OF THE CARELESS.

---

1 Thess. v. 3.

"FOR WHEN THEY SHALL SAY, PEACE AND SAFETY, THEN SUDDEN DESTRUCTION COMETH UPON THEM, AS TRAVAIL UPON A WOMAN WITH CHILD; AND THEY SHALL NOT ESCAPE."

In the latter part of the chapter going before, the blessed apostle, St. Paul, revealeth to the people of Christ certain comfortable truths concerning the resurrection from the dead, and the coming of their Lord to judgment.

In the beginning of this chapter he prevents an objection that some might make. For, having fallen upon the course of the Resurrection, he well knew the curiosity of man's nature, that leaves those things that are most profitable, to inquire after such things as God hath hid; and therefore some men might say, — Since there shall be such a time and such a change, when will those times and seasons be? When shall that great day come, when all shall be brought together before God?

Of the times and seasons, brethren, saith the apostle, *ye have no need that I write unto you.* As if he should say, This is no needful, no necessary thing, for you to inquire into, or for me to tell you: rather let us fall upon those things that are necessary and useful: for neither you nor I can tell the particular time when that shall be: yet know this, that very suddenly such a time shall come, and that when the world least thinks of it.

The suddenness hereof he setteth down by a twofold comparison: First, by the coming of a thief in the night:—*Yourselves know perfectly, that the day of the Lord so cometh as a thief in the night:* and, secondly, by the travail that cometh upon a woman with child:—*When they shall say, Peace and safety; then sudden destruction cometh upon them, as travail upon a woman with child; and they shall not escape.* This latter comparison I have made choice of at this time for my text.

A little for the explanation of the words. *When they shall say, Peace and safety.* The apostle intendeth not to condemn either the speaking of peace to the children of peace, or their rejoicing in the peace they have. But that which he condemneth is, that *they* cry peace to themselves, against whom God denounceth war. Men that go on in a course of sinning and in security, and yet will persuade themselves that all shall be well with them in the end, these are the men upon whom Death shall come thus suddenly, and upon whom the judgment-day shall come thus unexpected. *When they shall say, Peace and safety;* that is, when they are living in their sins, walking on in their rebellions against God, and yet flattering themselves that it shall be well with them, then shall judgment come upon them, then sudden destruction cometh.

By destruction of the body or the soul, he meaneth not here the destruction *of their being:* for the soul, even after the death of the body, shall have a being; and the body shall be restored again to its being and parts, in the resurrection from the dead.

It were happy for wicked and ungodly men, if there should be such a destruction of their being as that they should cease any more to exist: for then, this body, the members whereof have been the servants of sin, should not be tormented in hell; and then, this soul of theirs, that hath set all the body to work in the service of sin, it would not be sensible of that anguish that shall cause gnashing of teeth. It were well, I say, for them, if there should be such a destruction: it is that which, if they might have their desire, they would wish above all things in the world. But it will be no such utter destruction as this; it shall be worse with them: it shall only be the destruction of their joy and comfort, of all their contentments, of all those things wherein they solaced and flattered themselves upon earth. All these things shall be destroyed.

Their riches, that fed their lusts, shall be destroyed; and their company, that encouraged them in sin, shall be destroyed; and all things, wherein they have delighted themselves here upon earth, shall be destroyed: the whole earth shall be burnt with fire before them. And beside this, that same cheerfulness of spirit, and that free disposition whereby they encouraged themselves in the ways of their pride, or whatsoever else it was that made them seem somebody on earth, all this shall cease, and fail them, and forsake them. There shall be no mirth, no wisdom, no courage, no friends, no wealth, no houses, no apparel, nothing to pride and delight themselves in: there shall be an utter destruction of all these things: *Then shall destruction come upon them.*

As pain upon a woman with child. This showeth the manner, the kind, of their destruction.

First, it shall be a sudden destruction: it shall not give them warning either of the time or place: they shall have no other warnings than those general admonitions that they have in the preaching of the word.

Secondly, it shall be a painful destruction; full of misery and sorrow.

And then, thirdly, it shall be an inevitable destruction; such a destruction as they shall never be able to avoid. All their wit, friends, power, strength, wealth, or whatsoever else they have, cannot put off the stroke of judgment that shall come upon them.

So, then, the meaning of the words is, as if

the apostle should have said,—When wicked and ungodly men, living in a course of sin, shall cry *Peace* to themselves, and flatter themselves in their rebellious courses, saying, in their hearts, *God hath forgotten: he hideth his face; he will never see it:* then shall a sudden, painful, inevitable destruction of all their comfort, of all their props, and hopes, and helps, fall upon them.

In the words, you have a twofold description. You have the state and condition of the men of the world, when Christ shall come to judgment:—he shall find the world at rest. As the angel that stood among the myrtle-trees spake, in Zechariah, *We have walked to and fro through the earth, and behold, all the earth sitteth still and is at rest;* so shall it be then. He shall find all the men of the world in peace, every man applauding himself in some vain conceit, in some hope and confidence or other. *They shall cry, Peace and safety.*

And you have also the consequent that followeth upon this vain flattery of themselves: *Then shall destruction come upon them.*

Thus you have the opening of the words. Let us come now to the points of instruction that may be raised hence.

Here, then, you may see, and he that runs may read it, that—They are most secure who are in least safety.

A man is in the greatest danger when he is in the least security; his judgment is nearest when he least thinks of it, when he least feareth it.

This is the main thing that the Holy Ghost

would have us take notice of here. At that very time, not before that time, they shall cry, Peace: not after the time, when they have done it, and repented of it; but just at the very time when they are in the midst of their sins, applauding their own estate, living under the power and guilt of sin,—then cometh the destruction upon them, and they shall not escape.

That we may make this point clearly understood before we come to prove it, give me leave, first, briefly to tell you, what we mean by that security which is upon men, even in their chiefest dangers. Know, therefore, that there is a twofold security: there is a holy, spiritual security; and there is a sinful, carnal security. There is, first, a holy and spiritual security (and that even in this state whereunto we are fallen), which consisteth in a man's reconciliation with God, being at peace with him, having obtained remission of his sins, and his favour, through Jesus Christ: so that God is pleased with him in his Son, hath received him into the covenant of grace, hath interested him in all the promises, and is become his God by a covenant for ever.

Now here a man may be secure, yea, and he must be so, in a spiritual manner. Confidence upon the goodness of God in Christ, upon the promises of God in the Gospel, is that which is requisite in every Christian; it is that which God commandeth. *Fear not*, saith he, in one place: and again, *Trust in the Lord with all thine heart.* The Scripture is full in calling for such a security as this; that men should lay aside all carking and distracting cares when once they are in the covenant of grace; that thenceforth they should mind nothing but duty, and not be troubled about success.

This was the kind of security that David had and rejoiced in: — *I will both lay me down in peace, and sleep, for thou, Lord, only makest me to dwell in safety.* This it is that the Lord commandeth to the people of Israel: — *Come, my people, enter thou into thy chambers and shut thy doors about thee: hide thyself, as it were for a little moment, until the indignation be overpast.* He would have them secure themselves under his protection, and in his ordinances. This is such a security as draweth men nearer to God, bringeth them to further acquaintance with God, keepeth them in a constant communion with God, causeth them to walk in God's presence, &c. This is a good security.

But then, secondly, there is a sinful, carnal security: that is, when a man, yet living in a course of sin, beareth up his spirit against all fear, either of judgments threatened, or of judgments approaching unto him, under a vain hope of I know not what mercy in God, and of I know not what assurance from men; and upon worldly conceits and flatteries, either from others or from his own heart. Here is now a sinful, carnal security; not warranted, but condemned, in the word of God. This is the security that is ever an ill prognosticator and forerunner of some heavy judgments to fall upon that person in whom it is. This is the security that we have now in chase.

We will make it then appear, that it is an infallible sign of God's judgment upon a person or a people, when they cry peace to themselves, and are secure, and no way troubled at their estate, though God is at war with them, and with their evil ways.

You shall see instances and examples of this. Look for it in particular persons, and in states and kingdoms, and you shall generally find that, before the destroying judgment came upon them, they have been given up to this security whereof we speak, this crying of peace upon a false ground.

See it in Agag: *Surely the bitterness of death is past.* But was it past? Nay, at that very time it was upon him; for the very next thing we meet with in the story is, that *Samuel hewed Agag in pieces before the Lord.*

Ye have it in Belshazzar. Wondrous secure was he, carousing and quaffing in the holy vessels that were taken out of the temple of the house of God which was at Jerusalem, amongst his princes and nobles, his wives and concubines, as if there would be no change of his estate, no translation of his empire. But what? Was it so? Nay, at that very time, *In that same hour came forth fingers of a man's hand, and wrote . . . . . upon the plaister of the wall of the king's palace, ...* MENE, MENE, TEKEL, UPHARSIN.

. . . . . *God hath numbered thy kingdom and finished it. Thou art weighed in the balances, and art found wanting. Thy kingdom is divided, and given to the Medes and Persians.* And immediately, *in that very night, was Belshazzar the king of the Chaldeans slain.* He was taken away from all his comfort and jollity.

See this also in the rich man. *Soul, soul,* saith he, *take thine ease; eat, drink, and be merry:* and why so? Was it because his soul was indeed in safety, being washed in the blood of Christ? Far from it: but *take thine ease, thou hast much goods laid up for many years:* thou art well provided against a hard winter, against a dear year, now take thine ease. Well, what of this? Had his soul any whit the more ease? Had he many years to enjoy that which he had laid up for many years? Nay, mark the answer of God: *Thou fool, this night thy soul shall be taken from thee; then whose shall those things be which thou hast provided?*

It is ordinary, as Job noteth of worldly men, thus to flatter themselves. *They spend their days in wealth, and, in a moment, go down to the grave.* They spend their days in wealth: this it is that they resolve upon, while on earth; they will be merry, and enjoy their wealth and worldly contentments to the height, and want for nothing: but, in a moment, while they are in the midst of these thoughts of raising a happiness to themselves out of their worldly estate, in the midst of these thoughts they go down to the grave.

So it is also in nations and states. See it in the case of Sodom and Gomorrah. They were eating and drinking, and building and planting, and marrying and giving in marriage, till the flood came upon the one, and fire and brimstone upon the other; till sudden destruction came upon both, according to my text. See it again in Jerusalem. Their prophets were flattering them, and crying, Peace, peace. According to the word of Jeremiah the prophet,—*They have healed the hurt of the daughter of my people slightly, saying, Peace, peace; where there is no peace. Nay, they were not at all ashamed, neither could they blush: therefore they shall fall among them that fall: at the time that I visit them they shall be cast down, saith the Lord.* Mark the prophet's cry,—*Peace.* It had been well done of the prophets, to cry peace to those Israelites that, in truth, were at peace with God; but they cry peace to them, to whom there was no peace. What then? did the people reform? did this make those that, before, were rebellious against God, come in, and accept of the conditions of peace, and forsake their sins, and turn to God? No such matter: nay, though their sins were reproved, by Jeremiah and by other faithful prophets, yet they were not ashamed: though they had committed abomination, yet they could not blush: they stood it out; they remained in their impenitency. Well, what of this? therefore, saith the Lord, *they shall be cast down*, they shall cease to be a people.

See it also in Babylon. The Lord observeth her boasting. *I am,* saith she, *and none else beside me. I shall not sit as a widow, neither shall I know the loss of children.* But mark what God saith: *Hear now this, thou that art given to pleasures, that dwellest carelessly; these two things shall come upon thee in a moment, in one day,—the loss of children, and widowhood.* All thy props, all thy stays, shall be taken from thee; yea, and that in one day, in a moment, when thou least thinkest of it; suddenly thou shalt be husbandless and childless.

Nay, this is that which the Lord speaks of Romish Babylon. She had heard of the pride and boasting of old Babylon, and she would fain be like it. *I sit as a queen,* saith she, too, *and am no widow, and shall see no sorrow.* She stands upon her outward hope, and pomp, and glory, as worldly-minded men do, specially when they come to greatness and eminence. Well, what will the Lord do? *Therefore shall her plagues come in one day; death, and mourning, and famine; and she shall be utterly burnt with fire, for strong is the Lord God who judgeth her.*

Thou sayest, I sit as a lady; I shall see no change. Well, saith the Lord, thou shalt indeed be famous for something,—even for such judgments as shall fall upon thee, above all other places: there shall be famine, and death, and burning. And this shall happen to her, when all outward means, that should bring it to pass, seem to fail. When this Babylon shall seem to advance herself above all other churches, when there is nothing but strength and might on her side, then shall God do it; for strong is the Lord that judgeth her.

God shall deliver his Church and people from the adverse party, when it seemeth to thrive most against them; when men are taken off from self-confidence; when they are in fear, and weakness, and have none to fix their eyes on but God, then will God do this for his Church. He saith plainly, that Babylon shall be burnt with fire; and that at a time when it shall plainly appear to be impossible, except He put his strength to the work. Thus, ye see, the security of a people or nation is an infallible sign of judgment about to fall upon it.

And it must be so, and there is great reason for it: if we consider either the causes of security, whence it cometh; or the concomitants that accompany it; or the fruit and events of it; it must be, that great judgments must befall men and places, when they are under this carnal security.

First, look to the causes. Whence is it, that men that are not at peace with God, yet flatter themselves that they shall do well? It proceedeth from that unbelief and infidelity that is in the hearts of men: therefore they flatter themselves, and pride themselves, in things that will not hold them up in the end. I say, *infidelity* is the cause that men are so secure.

Did men believe the word of God, that every

threatening that goeth out of the mouth of God, against any particular sin, should certainly fall upon the head of the sinner, durst they go on in a course of sinning against God? Durst they add drunkenness to lust—one wickedness to another? No, certainly. In that measure a man hath faith; in that measure he feareth God, and his judgments that he hath threatened.

See it in Noah: *By faith Noah, being warned of God, moved with fear, prepared an ark.* He believed the word of God was faithful, that had threatened a judgment upon the world: he believed the word of God that commanded him to provide an ark, for the safety of himself and his house, and therefore he feared the deluge to come, *and prepared an ark.*

So, likewise, Josiah, when he read the book of the law, and saw what was threatened against the sins of the people, his heart melted within him. And why? Because he believed that this was the word of God; and he believed that God would be as true as his word: therefore, his heart melted within him at the sight of those sins, wherein the people had continued so long a time. Nay, it is made a description of a believer, that he *trembleth at God's word.*

On the other hand, what is the reason why infidelity doth presently bring judgments upon men? The cause is apparent. Infidelity draweth men from God; an unbelieving heart departs from the living God; and when a man departs from God's presence, God pursueth him with his judgments. All the judgments of God are upon that place where God's presence, in his graces, is not. *If I go,* saith David, *to the uttermost parts of the earth, thou art there: if I go down into the deep, thou art there:* and how? Not only as an observer, but as a punisher,—an avenger to pursue and to execute judgment, when men flee from God. Now unbelief is a drawing of the soul from God to the creature; therefore it provokes God: it sets up an idol in the heart of man, and idolatry exceedingly provokes God; and, therefore, he bringeth judgments upon it.

Beside that, mark the threatening of the word against this:—*When a man heareth the words of this curse, and blesseth himself, and saith, I shall have peace, though I walk in the imagination of mine heart, to add drunkenness to thirst: the Lord will not spare that man; but then the anger of the Lord, and his jealousy, shall smoke against that man; and all the curses that are written in this book shall lie upon him.* When shall that be? When is it that the wrath of God shall smoke? At that very time and instant when he flattereth himself, with his vain conceits, that he shall have peace, though God threaten judgments,—then the wrath of God shall fall upon him.

You see, then, it must needs be a grievous forerunner of a judgment upon a place or city, or people or nation, when they remain impenitent in their sins, and yet cry, *Peace.*

Look, in the *second* place, to the concomitants; and it will also appear from them, that security in men's hearts must, of necessity, bring a judgment upon a land. For, what is it that accompanieth this carnal security, but a disrespect of God in all his attributes? When a man heareth the word and the judgments of the law, warning him to take heed of wrath, and the Gospel alluring him to repent, and is nothing moved, but still flattereth himself, and goeth on in his sinful course, this is a slighting and despising of God himself. God's power, wisdom, justice, truth, all are despised. Yea, and his mercy, and patience, and long-suffering are especially slighted, when a man hardeneth himself in sin by a feeling of security.

Wherefore do men shut their ears against all exhortation to repentance, but because they presume upon the continuance of God's long-suffering towards them? Mark how the Lord takes notice of this: the forbearance and long-suffering, the goodness and mercy of God, should lead thee to repentance; and therefore God hath forborne, all this time, that he might bring thee to repent; but, if thou wilt not repent, then,—*after thy hardness and impenitent heart thou treasurest up wrath against the day of wrath.* Thy daily going on in sin, and despising the long-suffering and patience of God, doth but add wrath to *the day of the revelation of the righteous judgment of God.*

So it is, likewise, when God warneth a man by his patience towards others. We see God hath been merciful to many sinners, and this often hardeneth us in security. Why may He not be merciful to me, too? He gave them repentance, after many sins committed; why may He not do so to me?

Mark what Solomon saith;—*Because sentence against an evil-doer is not executed speedily, therefore the heart of the sons of men is fully set in them to do evil.* This they presume upon—this they venture upon: God hath been thus to others—patient and long-suffering—and why may He not be so to them? *Yet surely I know,* saith Solomon, *it shall not be well with the wicked, neither shall he prolong his days.* Why? *Because he feareth not before God.* They are not awakened by the example of his judgment on others; they are not allured by his patience and long-suffering; it doth not make them to fear Him, therefore it shall not go well with them in the end.

Thirdly, look to the end: What is the consequence of this carnal security? What follows upon it? Where there is carnal security, there must, of necessity, be an increase of sin, and, consequently, a hastening of judgment; for the more sin hasteneth to ripeness, the more judgment also hasteneth upon the sinner. God hath set unto particular men a certain limit or stint, and it is not known to them what that stint is:—*The iniquity of the Amorites is not yet full.* They were a sinful people all that time; but, the nearer they came to the fulness, and stint, and limitation, that God intended to be the immediate forerunner of the judgment, the faster judgment hastened upon them. So, for particular persons, there is a certain stint limited. Let every man look to it. The adding of *one* sin more may be thy uttermost stint, the filling up of the measure of thine iniquity, that shall bring the stroke of judgment and destruction upon thee.

Thus, you have seen the reason and the truth of this assertion, that when kingdoms, or states, or men, running a course of sin or impenitency, cry peace to themselves, then judgment and destruction is coming upon them. Let us now come to make some use of it. What doth this teach us to think of ourselves—of the estate of this land wherein we live—of these times wherein we are fallen?

What can we expect, when we consider to what a height of sin we are come, how impenitent men are, how obstinate, and hard-hearted, and stiff-necked against the voice of God in the Gospel, but—destruction to come upon us?

If we look upon the sins of men, we may perceive a general ripeness for judgment. When the sins of the Amorites were full, judgment came upon them. How near the sins of this land are come to that fulness, we know not,—we have cause to fear. We see, in other countries, the shaking of the sword over us;* it hath not yet awakened us to fear God. At home, we have had the voice of the prophets, the ministers, crying unto us from day to day, to return, lest

* See Note, p. 41.

destruction come upon us; but it hath not brought us to turn again from our sins. We have seen the mercies of God upon particular persons and families; but it hath not awakened men to walk faithfully in their places. We see no reformation; there is rather an increase of sin. And what can we expect is yet wanting, but one sin? and, when that is come, then cometh sudden destruction. What is that sin? Security.

And is not security already begining to prevail amongst us very generally? May not the angel of the Lord return that answer, as he did in Zephaniah, *All the world is at rest?* Go into the streets, the houses, the shops of men: every man is at rest: no man is troubled about his estate, nor affected with God's displeasure, either against himself or the land we live in. See, is not the land as secure as was Laish, or worse? They were secure, because they did not hear of the danger—of the purpose of the Danites against them; therefore their security was not altogether so culpable and blameworthy. But I will tell you what our security is: nay, the Holy Ghost hath told us to our hands, and that judgment that is threatened against a man that goeth on in sin, seems to be a judgment executed against us at this time:—*Thou shalt be as he that lieth down in the midst of the sea, or as he that lieth upon the top of a mast. They have stricken me, shalt thou say, and I was not sick; they have beaten me, and I felt it not.* Is it not thus with us, in these dead and secure times that we live in? And shall we say that we are not asleep? Hath not the Lord sent the destroying angel among us, that hath smitten thousands in our streets?* And yet we have not felt it. Shall we say that we are not in danger? We are as a man that sleepeth on the top of a mast at sea. As a man in the midst of the waves, in a dead sleep, like to one drunken; we feel nothing, we are not aware of our danger. Truly we have little cause to be secure; we have little cause to flatter ourselves with vain conceits of peace and continuance of prosperity, if we look well about us. Where is any man that takes occasion, by what he hears abroad, or sees at home, to enter into the reformation of his own house, of his own heart? It may be some men will say: This is an unjust charge that you make against us. We are not so secure as you speak of: you shall scarce come to any man's table, but they will be talking of the judgments that are stirring: you shall scarce meet a man in the streets, but he will leave other occasions, and tell you how ill it goes with the churches beyond the seas: you shall scarce meet with one in the field but all the time is taken up with discourse of the evils at home, or troubles abroad; and is this a sign of security?

Alas, beloved, this is to be asleep in the midst of the waves. Every man is in the midst of danger, and yet he is secure.

How shall that appear?

* Allusion is here made to the plague of the year 1625, when 35,417 persons died in London alone.

I will prove it by demonstrations and signs that may convince you, before the Lord, that we do indeed add this to the rest of our offences; that, in the midst of our sins and impenitency, we are secure; and, therefore, that destruction is coming upon us.

The *first* sign shall be this. When men profit not by the judgments of God. Certainly it is an evident sign of a deep sleep in sin, when neither the afflictions that are upon others, nor yet those which are upon ourselves, do any good to us.

Look how God hath smitten others. Hath he awakened us? You will say that that child is bold and secure who seeth his brother beaten before his eyes, and yet goeth on in the same fault. You will say that that is a secure malefactor that seeth such a person executed, before his face, for a theft, and yet goeth on in the same felony. And must we not say that we are a secure generation, when we can see our brethren, in other countries, how they have suffered,* and yet go on in those very sins for which we think

* The preacher here alludes to the Protestant Church in Germany, which had suffered severely under the Emperor Ferdinand II., a zealous Romanist; and which was only preserved from total annihilation by the intervention, under God's providence, of Gustavus Adolphus, king of Sweden. Shortly before the date of this sermon, James I. had sent a feeble armament in aid of the Protestant Elector Palatine; and it was the refusal of adequate supplies for this enterprise that caused the first quarrel between his successor, Charles, and his parliament.

the hand of God is upon them? We can talk of their sins, of their unrighteousness, and injustice. We can talk of their neglect of the Lord's day, and other holy duties; and for these, we judge them smitten of God. How is it then that we, ourselves, are like them? How is it that we go on in unrighteousness, in profaning the Lord's day, in neglecting the house of God? Have they found such sweetness in these sins that we walk on in the same? Is it a pleasant and comfortable thing, to be driven from God's house, and from our own houses, and to be a reproach to all the world? If we think that the hand of God is upon them for these sins, how is it that we are not awakened? I remember Daniel, in his prophecy, taxeth Belshazzar for this:—*Though thou knewest* how the hand of God was upon thy father for this and this, yet thou hast done the like, and *hast not humbled thine heart.* So may I say:—You have known what God hath done to your brethren in other countries: yet you do still the same, yourselves, for the which they have been punished. Is not this security?

Look again, and we shall see also a general neglect of those judgments of God, which have been upon ourselves. Hath not God smitten this land—this city especially—with the pestilence? And may we not say, we have been smitten, and yet have not felt it? Is not this security and a dead sleep? Look upon yourselves, upon your houses, upon your dealings, your company, your conversations. See if there be any reformation, since there was such a mortal calamity as drove you from the city, and frighted you from your own houses, and from the house of God. Well, these are fearful presages, that, when former judgments prevail not, worse are coming. *I have given you cleanness of teeth, and want of bread in all your places,* saith God; *yet have ye not returned unto me.* What then? *I have smitten you with blasting and mildew, yet have ye not returned unto me.* What then? *I have sent among you the pestilence, after the manner of Egypt, yet have ye not returned unto me.* And what then? *Therefore, thus will I do unto thee, O Israel; and because I will do this unto thee, prepare to meet thy God, O Israel.* As if he should say:—I have tried you, and found you obstinate, and rebellious: and since you will stand out against me, notwithstanding the judgments executed upon others, and afflictions upon yourselves, see if you can stand out against my last stroke! You have escaped some lesser judgments upon your own bodies: you have escaped the pestilence already; but you shall find it a hard task, when God biddeth battle, to escape his last stroke, if you will not now be reconciled and come in and seek his face. This is the first demonstration, whereby it appears that we are sinfully secure; which is a forerunner of judgment, because we are not awakened by the judgments of God upon ourselves and others.

Secondly, another sign is this: the contempt

of God's ordinances, the slighting of the prophets. This is an evident proof that we are under this carnal security of which I now speak.

Mark how the Lord describeth a people whom he meant to destroy. *They refused to hearken, and pulled away the shoulder, and stopped their ears, that they should not hear. Yea, they made their hearts as an adamant stone, lest they should hear the law, and the words which the Lord of Hosts hath sent in his Spirit by the former prophets: therefore, came a great wrath from the Lord of Hosts.* A great wrath,—what is that? *Therefore it is come to pass, that as he cried, and they would not hear; so they cried, and I would not hear, saith the Lord of Hosts.*

Beloved, little do you know what time and ways God hath to make you cry and roar, in the anguish of your hearts, because of judgments and afflictions, if you will not hear, now that God striveth with you, and crieth unto you, with the voice of his Spirit, in his prophets, from day to day. When men will not hear God speaking to them in his word, it is always a forerunner of judgment. In the sixth of Micah, God challengeth his people, and telleth them that he hath used many means for their reclaiming, but nothing would do them good: Well now, saith he, *Hear ye the rod, and who hath appointed it.* As if he should say, There is no more dealing with you by word; but I must come with the rod, and with judgment. Is it not thus with us at this day? May not the Lord say of us, as he did of the people in the time of Jeremiah,—*They have forsaken the law which I set before them, and have not obeyed my voice, nor walked therein;* and then, what follows?—*Therefore, thus saith the Lord of Hosts, the God of Israel; Behold, I will feed them, even this people, with wormwood, and give them water of gall to drink: and I will send a sword after them till I have consumed them.*

Do not many cry out now, as they did of old, *What is the burden of the Lord?* Where is it that the ministers have not been threatening judgment, and telling you that God is coming out to be avenged upon a sinful nation? Have they not been crying out thus, this seven, ten, twenty years; Where is that burthen of the Lord? Well, you shall find what it is, when the day of the Lord cometh, a day of blackness and terror: it hasteneth; and this very security is an evident sign thereof. Even as in the days of Noah, that preacher of righteousness, and in the days of Lot, they would not believe their words, but they seemed unto them as if they mocked: and then came the judgment of the Lord upon them.

If this be not the estate of the land at this day, what mean the complaints, the heaviness of the spirits of the prophets? what mean their tears, and cries, and prayers, because of the obstinacy and hard-heartedness of the people, that will not be drawn from their sins by any means? When all this crying and calling will not awaken, this is a second sign that we are in a deep sleep of security.

Thirdly, another evidence is, the vain confidence of this land. It is a sign of carnal security, that we are all in a dead sleep, when we have such idle confidence, and vain dreams, that delude and deceive men.

What do men rest on to secure and persuade themselves of immunity from wrath? Certainly this; that we have the ordinances of God amongst us:—Oh, the temple of the Lord, the temple of the Lord!

Alas! had not the people of Israel the ark? and yet the Philistines took the ark, and slew the sons of Eli. Had they not the temple? and yet the Lord sendeth them to Shiloh for an example:—*I will do to this house, which is called by my name, wherein you trust, as I have done to Shiloh:* that is, I will utterly destroy it; *there shall not be left one stone upon another, that shall not be thrown down!* Had not the churches of Asia the golden candlestick? and yet they are now tributary to the Turk. The ordinances of God, beloved, are means to increase and hasten a judgment, when we shut our eyes and will not open them, but choose to walk in darkness.

Oh, but you may cry, there were never so many preachers before, nor so many means: there seems to be a new spring of the Gospel: there are men enough that come daily, furnished for the ministry, and are zealous, and forward, and powerful prophets, and the like; and this is a sign that much good is intended towards us, and that no judgment shall come.

But do we not read, that immediately before

the seventy years' captivity there were more prophets than in many years before? Why should we rest in such things as these?

But, nevertheless, we have many good people, that are full of prayers, and tears, and they shall deliver the land.

It is true there are many, blessed be God, and we have cause to wish that there were many more; and to say, as Moses said to Joshua, when he would have had him forbid Eldad and Medad, that prophesied in the camp of the Israelites, *Would God that all the Lord's people were prophets, and that the Lord would put his Spirit upon them!* So we, of such godly men that walk with an upright heart, Would God that there were many such! But yet, are not these as lilies among thorns; a few good amongst many bad? are not these the objects of reproach and contempt amongst an unrighteous generation, that are cried down most by the world, that are most opposed and injured by all men? Are not these they that support the land by their prayers, and hold up all by their standing in the gap? May we not rather fear, that God will avenge the quarrel of his servants upon an ungracious and ungrateful people, amongst whom they live?

What shall we speak of other things? Did not Bozrah boast herself of her situation, that she dwelt in the clefts of the rock? Saith God to her, *Thou that holdest the height of the hill, though thou shouldest make thy nest as high as the eagle, I will bring thee down from thence.*

It is idle talking, that our island is situate in the sea, and well protected; judgment can leap over the sea, as the pestilence hath done already: this is a vain thing; and yet, if you hearken to the discourse of most men, you shall see that it is this that keeps them secure.

What mean these idle dreams and vain conceits, that when we go on in an unreformed condition, and in a course of sin and impenitency, yet we fear nothing, because we have the ministers, and the ordinances, and the people of God amongst us; because we are convenient for situation, and such-like things! These are vain things: they will do us no good at that time; and, for the present, they show our security, our horrible security.

Fourthly, take another evidence; and that is, the abounding of the sins of the land. Were it possible that, at such a time as this, of shaking the rod, of unsheathing the sword over us, when judgments are upon the nation, that there should be such abundance of sin in all places, if men were not in a deep sleep? How doth drunkenness stagger and reel in every street! How doth pride vaunt and boast itself in every church and assembly, though it be cried down never so much! Alas, beloved, are these times to pride ourselves in vanity? Are these times to run after the sensual and sinful courses of an ungodly generation? These are times when God calleth for fasting and brokenness of heart. *Put off thy ornaments from thee*, saith God, *that I may know what to do unto thee.* Men generally do so abound in wickedness and ungodliness, that we may rather conclude, as it is in the Revelation, that the time is now come too near. It is evident and apparent, that sin is increased since the sickness: it is apparent that our sins are aggravated, though they are daily cried down. And now, at this time, as if we would defy God to his face, and call upon him to hasten his judgment upon our land, upon our families and persons, every one strives, as it were, who shall outdare him most in our excesses, in our impenitency, in hardening ourselves in a course of sin. These things convince us of our security.

There are many more that might be named, if the time would permit. But put these together, and they may show us our wretchedness. When we consider how little we have profited by judgments, how little we have profited by the ordinances, how full of vain confidence and idle dreams we are,—how, notwithstanding all these, we still abound in wickedness, and there is no reformation of our hearts and lives; what may we not conclude against ourselves?

If ever men were drowned in a drunken security, we, of all people under heaven, are so at this time. For, of all people, we are in a manner the last. God hath spared us to the last. We have had warning by judgments inflicted upon others, for many years together. It hath come nearer to us by degrees. It began afar off, in Bohemia, and then in the Palatinate, and in

Germany. The Lord would have us see how he cometh to us by degrees, by steps, that at the last he may win us to repentance. But where is the man that yet gets out of the bed of security, that cometh out of his sleep, to meet the Lord; that comes with a broken heart to beg for forgiveness of his sins past, and to seek for mercy for the time to come?

Well, now, since it is so, that we are convinced by these signs that we are in a carnal and sinful security, we see (so many of us, at least, as are children of the light and of the day) what cause we have to be awakened, and to do that for others which they will not do for themselves; to be more earnest in prayer, more frequent in humbling our souls for our sins and theirs, that God may lay aside and cast away his judgments and displeasure, that either are to be feared, or else already lie upon us.

Is it not a fearful thing, that when the lion roareth, the beasts of the forest tremble; yet the God of heaven roareth against the world at this day, and the proud hearts of men do not tremble before him? Shall the beasts of the forest be afraid of the lion, more than we poor worms of the earth, of the mighty God of earth and heaven? But this is the horrible atheism and infidelity that is in the hearts of men,—they believe not God's power and justice, nor his threatenings.

I beseech you let every man be exhorted to stir up his soul to this business; to awaken himself in his own particular person. Consider that there are others that are awake, that may bring you sorrow enough: be you awakened to prevent those miseries. Satan is awake to tempt you. Your adversary, the devil, goeth about, seeking whom he may devour. Satan is busy and watching to make you his prey; watch you therefore, and pray that you enter not into temptation.

Your own corruptions are always awake. The concupiscence and depraved disposition of the soul is awake still, to further every evil motion, to draw you aside by its temptations. Therefore saith the apostle, *I beseech you, as strangers and pilgrims, abstain from fleshly lusts, which war against the soul.* Do as men in war, when they know that they have a waking enemy against them: be sure to keep your watch. Beloved, you cannot but know that your corruptions are always awake; you may perceive it even when you sleep, in your dreams: take heed that you be not sound in a spiritual sleep, that corruption prevail not over you.

Besides these, the enemies of the church are awake; Scribes and Pharisees, men who teach their own inventions, who bring in their vain superstitions and doctrines of Antichrist, are awake to turn men from the faith, to prevent the faith of many. Oh then, be you awake, that you may be at peace with the Lord of Hosts, the God of armies, that laugheth the devices of the ungodly to scorn, and hath all power in his hand to keep you safe.

Again, consider the evil of this security you

are in, when you cry Peace, peace, to yourselves, in the midst of God's displeasure. It is an evil disease, a spiritual lethargy; it takes the senses from the soul, and not only overcometh it, but preventeth men from seeking a cure.

And, as it is an evil disease, so it causeth much evil. It is that which driveth away the Spirit of God. It is the counsel of the Apostle, —*Grieve not the Spirit: quench not the Spirit.* When we neglect the motions of the Spirit, the Spirit withdraweth itself. Doth not your own experience tell you this? Consider a little, what motions you have had; how God, by the voice of your conscience, and sometimes by secret incitements, as it were a spur upon your hearts, hath moved you to duty, and to leave your sins. How have these moved you? You have had purposes, it may be, to perform those duties, to walk in the ways of God, to please him in all things: the neglect of those purposes hath driven away the Spirit; and it may be, God now leaveth you to final hardness.

Again, it letteth in Satan. *When the unclean spirit is gone out of a man, he walketh through dry places, seeking rest, and findeth none; then, he saith, I will return unto my house whence I came out. Then goeth he, and taketh with him seven other spirits, more wicked than himself, and they enter in and dwell there.*

Alas! how many men there are that, for a fit, have altered their course, and have thought to become new men, yet rushing upon former occasions and temptations to sin, they have grown secure and careless, and now Satan hath gotten stronger hold of them, with seven spirits worse.

How then shall we escape from this mischievous security? How shall we come to be awakened? I will tell you some helps for this.

First, I will propound *sobriety* as a main help. Would you be watchful, and kept from spiritual slumber,—take heed that you keep yourselves sober. I speak not of sobriety as it is opposed to drunkenness, though that is one thing; *Be not filled with wine, wherein is excess, but be filled with the Holy Ghost.* As if he should say—You cannot be filled with the Holy Ghost and with excess of wine. Persons that take liberty in excessive drinking, certainly they are destitute of the Holy Ghost, and so of life and salvation. But I mean a further sobriety: that is, as it is opposed to worldly-mindedness. Take heed that you plunge not yourselves too much in the world and worldly pleasures and cares: for these are against the rule of sobriety. Be sober in your diet, in your apparel, in your gaining, in your spending, in your mirth, in your company, in every thing: that is, moderate yourselves and your affections in these things. A man may soon grow to such a drunkenness, by excess in worldly affections, that he may be in a dead sleep, neglecting God's judgments and his own estate; as we see men that plunge themselves overmuch in worldly business do. It takes away the thoughts of those things that concern our spiritual good.

I say not that you should leave off the business of the world; for every man must continue in the calling that God hath set him: but I say, moderate your affections to the things of the world. Do worldly business with heavenly minds, in obedience to God: do them with waking hearts, to repent for the sins of your callings, and to avoid them for the future. And what I say of labouring in your callings, I say of pleasures, and of everything else: we should be watchful and sober. As St. Peter saith, *Be sober, and watch.*

Secondly, if you would be free from security, which is a forerunner of judgment, be sure to keep yourselves in exercise. A man that would keep himself awake must busy himself in some exercise or employment. What exercise should a Christian use? The exercise of grace, and the duties of obedience. Be sure to keep yourselves in the exercise of all the advantages that God giveth you in your lives, for the employment of your graces. In difficulties and straits, exercise your faith. In provocations to anger and discontent, exercise meekness. In crosses and troubles and afflictions, exercise patience. In the miseries and wants of others, whether spiritual or corporal, exercise mercy.

And what I say concerning grace, I say concerning duty. Keep yourselves in the exercise of prayer and reading and meditation and conference; some one thing or other, some holy employment or other, that may keep the soul waking. For, I tell you, you shall find that, whensoever you let fall spiritual exercise, you will, at that very instant, fall into carnal security in some kind or other.

Thirdly, would you keep yourselves from this dead sleep of security, then keep your spirits in fear. Sorrow and grief make a man heavy; but fear keeps a man waking. When Jacob feared Esau, he kept a watch that night. Samson feared the Philistines, and it wakened him out of his sleep. Fear makes a man watchful. In that measure that the fear of God prevaileth, security is expelled. Keep fear, therefore. *Happy is the man that feareth alway: but he that hardeneth his heart shall fall into mischief.* Mark how he opposeth the hardening of a man's self, in carnal security, to the fear of God. Keep your heart in a constant fear. Reason thus;—*How can I do this great wickedness and sin against God?* Will not God be offended and displeased? Shall I go on in this vanity? Would I have the judgment of God find me in this company? Would I have it seize upon me in this employment, in this business? Fear, lest God should strike thee in such an act, lest death should seize upon thee in such a place, and let that make thee keep a constant watch against the snares that are in those places.

Fourthly: Keep good company. Company, you know, is a good means to keep men awake. *Two are better than one; and woe to him that is alone,* saith Solomon. I say *good* company; for there is a company that will infect you. *Make no friendship with an angry man, lest thou learn his ways, and get a snare unto thy soul.* So keep not company with drunken and swearing persons: these are the devil's instruments to keep a man in carnal security. No; keep company with those that have a charge given them, to exhort one another daily, *to provoke unto love and to good works.* Keep company with the saints, and make use of all opportunities to provoke others to good works. That is the fourth help.

Fifthly: Keep God always in your sight. It is a good way, for a man that would keep himself awake, to fix his eye upon some object. Fix your eye upon this main object, God; remember that his eye is always fixed on you. *Am I a God at hand, saith the Lord, and not a God afar off? Do not I fill heaven and earth?* Can a man hide himself from God in any secret place? Think, in thy chamber, in thy parlour, in thy shop, in thy house, in thy friend's house, in the street, in the church, in whatsoever place thou art, that there God is also.

If a man had but always some one before him as a witness, he would not venture upon many things that he now doth. If a malefactor should see the judge before him; if the child had always his father's eye upon him, or the servant had always his master sitting about him and above him, he would serve him busily, at the least with eye-service. Now set yourselves in the sight of God, that sees you in the dark, hears you in your most secret whisperings, knows every action of your life and every thought of your heart. This will be a means to keep you from security.

I will add but one more help: consider thy latter end. The night is now coming upon us. If we were told, any of us,—*This night thy soul shall be required of thee,* I think there is none that heareth me this day, but he would certainly keep waking this night. But it is not bodily waking we plead for, but spiritual waking,—a waking from sin—a waking to repentance. And we tell you that death is now at the door, ready to seize upon you. We speak not only to you that are aged, that are at the brink of the grave; but also to you that are young. Death may seize upon you and strike you this night: be awakened now to repentance. I remember what God said to the Church of Sardis:—*Be watchful, and strengthen the things that remain.* That church was asleep, as many of us are, at this day. God cometh to awaken you now, as he did them, that that little goodness you have left, may be renewed and confirmed. You that are quite out of the way of grace, and go on in a course of sin, sit now down and humble your souls: get into a secret corner, wherein you may confess those many provocations whereby you have provoked God all your days, and resolve to amend, if the Lord spare you. Begin now; delay it no longer; it may be the last night; take this warning now; be awakened to repentance.

It is appointed unto all men, once to die; and after that the judgment. The judgment of every man is immediately after death; I do not mean in regard of time, but in effect. Man falls asleep in death, and wakes to judgment. So, I say, this may be the night of thy death, and the morning may be the day of thy particular judgment. Judge yourselves now, that ye be not judged of the Lord. Bring yourselves, as prisoners, before the bar: arraign yourselves, as malefactors, before the judge; bring out the particular bills of indictment against yourselves, whereby ye have provoked God: *agree with thine adversary quickly, whiles thou art in the way with him.* There is yet mercy; the day of grace, and opportunity of repentance and turning unto God, yet lasteth: therefore do it now. You know not what a short time you have, whether you be young or old; you know not what sickness you may have; you may be deprived of your reason, and senses, and never regain them until the morning of your judgment: therefore now, while health and reason and sense are afforded, take time, and make use of time, lest your security make good this text upon you:—*When they shall say, Peace and safety, then sudden destruction cometh upon them, as travail upon a woman with child; and they shall not escape.*

SERMON III.

FAITH'S TRIUMPH
OVER
THE GREATEST TRIALS.

HEB. XI. 17.

"BY FAITH ABRAHAM, WHEN HE WAS TRIED, OFFERED UP ISAAC; AND HE THAT HAD RECEIVED THE PROMISES, OFFERED UP HIS ONLY-BEGOTTEN SON."

THIS chapter speaketh in commendation of the faith of many of the Patriarchs; and Abraham is brought in among the rest. There are two things observable, which Abraham's faith strengthened him to do: one was to give up his country; the other was to give up his son.

By faith Abraham, when he was called of God to go out into a place which he should after receive for an inheritance, obeyed; and he went out, not knowing whither he went. To leave our friends and our parents, to take our journey we know not whither, to live among we know not whom, to part with good land for a few good words, this were not an easy thing: sense derides it; reason condemns it; but faith can see more in God's promises than sense can understand; and

Abraham will leave his country, when God calls him.

The second thing he is to part with is, his son—his only son. He must sail against wind and tide: he must overcome, not only the arguments of sense and reason, but also the pleadings of natural affection. God had given Abraham a son in his old age,—the child of many prayers, and an heir of life, according to the promise: and now God suddenly calls upon Abraham to give back his son—his very son Isaac.

Now, what doth Abraham do? Doth he expostulate with God? Doth he murmur? Doth he repine? No, he *offered up Isaac*. As if he had said, Lord, what is it that thou callest for? Is it for my only son Isaac, the son of my love, the son of thy promise, the son of my age? Verily Lord, thou shalt have him; it is true I love him well, but I love thee better: I got him by believing, and I shall never lose him by obeying: though I am a father, yet Lord, thou art a God: without thee, he had never been born; and though I kill him, thou canst quicken and raise him again. I shall never lose my Isaac, though I offer up my son; for thou hast said, *In Isaac shall thy seed be called.*

Now the parts of these words are two:—first, we have Abraham's great *trial;* and then, we have his *triumph.* Abraham was tried, when God commanded him to offer up his son: he triumphed, when by faith he obeyed the command. From these two parts I shall collect two propositions. The first is this:—that strong and great trials may befall strong and great Christians. And the second is this:—that faith will make a man acquit himself, even in the greatest trials.

Abraham's trial was very great.

He was to part with his only son, the child of promise, the child whom he loved. He was an old man, and could not hope that another would ever be born to him. And not only this, but he was to kill him, to slay him, and to offer him up, with his own hand: the tender father must take away the life of his tender child. No one could impose such a trial, but a God; and none could answer such a trial, but an Abraham.

For the full and clear opening of this point, I desire now to show you wherein the strength of a trial may consist; and also, why God is pleased to lay strong and great trials upon strong and great Christians.

One thing that may make a trial great is the goodness and kindness of him that deals with us; as, when any near relation shall seem to turn against us: when a dear friend shall prove a bitter enemy. For a man to meet with trouble and sorrow, when he expects all mercy and tenderness of love, this doth cause singular affliction. Abraham had often heard God's voice in blessing, but now it was to bring him sorrow and distress too great for utterance. For a Christian to find scorn and hard usage from the world, this is but an ordinary thing; but when he looks to heaven, and receives from God such frowns and rebukes as fetch tears from his eyes and from his heart, this is the sorest wound of all.

Again, the strength of a trial may consist in the nearness of the object we are compelled to lose. For a man to lose his money is something; but to lose a child is much more. For David to lose his servant, is not so much; but when he loses Absalom, then he cries out, *O Absalom, my son! would God I had died for thee; O Absalom, my son, my son!* Yet David had many sons; and Abraham had but one. God is pleased many times to try his servants, by taking away the delight of their eyes, and the joy of their heart, and the hope of their lives.

A trial is also the more severe as it is more sudden. When the prophet saw the cloud ascend out of the sea, being warned of abundance of rain, he hastened to escape. So, if a person have fore-notice of a cross that will befall him, he may be somewhat armed and prepared; he may be able, in some measure, to bear his trial. But Abraham had gone on hoping and delighting in his son Isaac, until the day when God called him suddenly to sacrifice this only child; to be, himself, the murderer of his son.

Now the reasons why God layeth such strong trials upon strong Christians may be these. First, grace will be obscure, and will scarcely show itself, unless there be trials. To St. Paul there was given a thorn in the flesh, a messenger of Satan, to buffet him; lest, when he was lifted up to the third heavens, he should be exalted above measure. He was oppressed with trials and temptations, that the grace of God might the more appear in his deliverance. They who have much grace, have also great conflicts: the soul is thus kept busy, and hath little leisure for glorying or admiring its own fulness.

Again, God is wise in all his actions; and so he proportioneth the affliction to the strength of him who is to bear it. A little blast is enough for a tender plant; but an oak, well grounded, may endure the strongest winds. A poor, weak Christian, will be cast down by a little trial; but one who hath enriched himself with the promises of God, who hath had experience of his goodness, and who standeth by faith, he can endure a hard storm, he can bear great trials. The more his grace is exercised, the more he gaineth: *he goeth from strength to strength.* He can say with Job, *Though He slay me, yet will I trust in him:* he can go through a great fight of affliction, and his faith will make him conquer all.

I come now to the second proposition, and that is this:—that faith will make a man acquit himself in the greatest trials. Faith will enable a man to give back his dearest comfort again to God. Though Isaac lie in Abraham's bosom, though he lie at Abraham's heart, yet Abraham's faith will take him thence, and present him to God who gave him. Faith can take a mercy, and be thankful; and faith can part with a mercy, and be content. Paul had learned how to abound, and how to be in want; and this was the lesson of faith. If God give him any mercy, he is cheerful; if the Lord take away any mercy, he sits down with contentment, quieting his soul in patience. If God give him any mercy, he is not swollen with pride; if God take away any mercy, he is not cast down with sorrow. Lord, I am unworthy of the least of all thy mercies, saith Faith: dost thou call for this blessing back again? here it is, Lord, do as thou pleasest. Like an honest debtor, he saith, If thou wilt spare me a little, I will thank thee; but if thou wilt have all, here it is.

There is a double manner of acquitting ourselves: there is a yielding to necessity; and there is a pious, cheerful, submission to God's will. A man who wants a lively faith, may acquit himself in a trial; for when he sees that floods of tears will not help him, he resigns that comfort, he parts with that blessing, that he can keep no longer. But faith presents the comfort to God again when he calls it back: Abraham offers up Isaac with his own hand: God, saith he, is the Lord who gave him; and now God calleth for him again, and he shall have him. Thus faith acquits the soul in great trials, and makes a man to sit down with much patience in great losses, to submit to God's call and to God's appointment.

Now, the reasons why faith can thus prevail may be these:—

First, Faith can exalt God's will, and submit our wills to God. Remember this. God is the author of mercy: when he will, he gives us; and when it pleaseth him, he takes it from us. It is well to have abundance, saith Nature; and Sense—We cannot do without it. No, saith Faith, I will yield to God's will. It is good to enjoy this, saith Sense. It is better to part with it, saith Faith, when God calls for it.

Secondly, Faith can give God the glory of all outward comforts. This is a great means of quieting our souls, to find out the right owner of our comforts. God is the God of our bodies, of our souls, and of our comforts. We are but tenants at will; and whatsoever our outward estate may be, faith overlooks all and submits all to God, and receives it by God's permission, and hears, as it were, God say—I must do what I will with mine own. Faith makes a man acknowledge—Nothing is mine own; my child is not mine own; my riches are not mine own. Faith resigns every thing as God's due: faith renders unto God the things that are God's.

Thirdly, Faith can make the soul acquit itself in great trials, because faith finds no loss by submission. All our unwillingness to part with any comfort doth arise from infidelity. Either we stubbornly desire to have and hold our comfort, contrary to God's will; or else we fear some damage will redound to ourselves, in parting with such a blessing. But faith sees safety only in obeying God's command and yielding up all into His hands, who is the father of mercy and God of all consolation. Thus we see Abraham, being put to it about his only son, he gives up his child, his Isaac. And God bestows Isaac upon Abraham again: nay, he gives him a further degree of blessing, confirmed with an oath; *In blessing I will bless thee; and in multiplying I will multiply thy seed as the stars of heaven.* This is ever true: faith makes a man give back a blessing, with this conviction,—that either God will restore the comfort to him, or else he will give him more, or a better, for it.

A fourth reason why faith makes a man acquit himself in all trials is, that faith can find all hopes made up in God alone. Faith doth look upon God as a most ample and universal good, a good that answers for all others, that abundantly makes up all losses. Many broken pieces of comfort must concur here to make up our outward good: our children, our friends, our health, our riches, many of these are compounded together to make up our good below: but God is all this in himself, and much more than this, to faith. What is it thou findest in a husband, a wife, a child, or a brother, that thou mayest not see in God? What is there in riches, that thou mayest not have much more in God? A friend may counsel and direct thee, but he cannot deliver thee: a child may comfort thee, but who can comfort thee so much as God? Faith sees more in God than in all outward blessings. God and his favour, God and his gracious countenance, these alone support the Christian, these make up his comfort. In the want of all things, faith can comfort itself more abundantly in the favour of God.

A fifth reason why faith can make a man triumph in great trials is, that faith knows upon what terms we possess those outward comforts that we are called upon to resign. We possess them upon moveable titles. Here we have no abiding city. Our place and being here is but for a short time: all the creature is but vanity; it is of a shifting nature, and therefore it is said of riches, *They make to themselves wings:* riches are soon gone, honour is soon gone, life is soon gone. All our comforts are of a changeable nature, and that whereon we set our affection may be taken from us in a moment.

Thus I have opened these two points. There are now two uses that I will make of these two propositions.

The first use is this:—since great trials may befall Christians, then let us prepare for great trials; forasmuch as such afflictions and crosses may befall us.

There are two things that a man should always provide for: one is, while we live, to provide for death: the other is, while we are in prosperity, to provide for affliction. Our outward condition is but a shadow; it hath a natural aptness to change. *Man is born unto trouble,* saith Eliphaz, *as the sparks fly upward:* as if trouble were his natural sphere, wherein he is to move.

Thou canst not assure thyself of life, no not

for a moment, nor of any of these outward comforts. Thou mayest get assurance from God that he will save thee; thou canst not get assurance from him that he will never try thee. Abraham was sorely tried, and Job, and David, and Daniel, men greatly beloved: so mayest thou be tried: the things nearest thy heart may be taken from thee in a moment. What is life, but a shadow? What is honour, but a blast? What are the things in which we pride ourselves so much? They are but as Jonah's gourd, which perished in a moment, and many times cause us sorrow and affliction. The loss of them is often a greater grief than the want of them: the staff on which we lean too strongly breaks and pierces our hand. What is the wise man's verdict of all things under the sun? He concludes they are all vanity, nothing but *vanity and vexation of spirit:* how little then are we to expect from them! how needful is it that we be ready and provided for a change!

For when these changes do befall us, when they strip us of our usual comforts, verily we are put to it. It is not so easy to bear the loss of a dear friend, or to give up wealth and honour, as it may seem. We may be very bold before affliction comes, but when adversities and trials fall upon us we are soon ready to faint. It is with us as with a ship: when the sun doth shine, and the seas are calm, and the wind fair, then she goes on pleasantly in her motion; but when the storm cometh, what can keep her steady?

In our easy days, in our days of peace, in our calm estate, then we can hold our heads well enough; but in our losses and crosses we shall hardly bear up, unless the Lord do mightily support us.

There are in the world some insensible persons, who are like the rock, that nothing can break; who are so hardened, that though God do scourge them yet they feel it not; though God threaten them, they fear not; though God's hand be even upon them, they regard it not. To such persons it is all one whether God bless or whether God curse; whether he speak by his word or by his rod; they feel nothing, they fear nothing.

But there is another sort of persons, who are sensible persons; sensible of God's love, and sensible of God's anger: they know that God is good and wise, and that he doth not strike off our comforts from us but upon some special cause. Now, say they, to stay upon God: it is the Lord, let him do what seemeth good unto him: God doth not deprive me of such a comfort but he seeth it best for me.

Beloved, it were good to learn this lesson: else it will cost thee something, in a near trial, to acquit thyself by faith. To submit to God's chastisement, to kiss the rod, to judge the sin, to bend the soul, to better the life, this were an excellent lesson for us in all our trials and afflictions.

Secondly, since faith is that which will make

a man acquit himself in great trials, then get faith, use faith. If there were no other reason but this—that faith is able to support us in our days of trial and to give us comfort in our greatest sorrow, this were motive enough to make us labour for faith; the day of trial being so common and we apt, every moment, to fall into some affliction.

Faith gives us comfort and assurance under every trial: it can eye God as our God: and though the storms be very great, yet God can quiet them. Faith assures the soul that God will put an end to the trial: for though there be changeableness in the outward condition, yet there is safety and stability in God. Though a man may look with a dull eye upon his loss, yet if he can look upon God with the eye of faith as his God, the absence of the creature cannot so much trouble him as the presence of a great and glorious God can comfort and support him.

Again, faith works in us submission to God's will: it fashions the heart and the mind to the condition; it makes us stoop to our burthen, and that contentedly, knowing that God will not lay more upon us than we are able to bear. *I became dumb*, saith David, *because thou didst it.* Zacharias was made dumb because he *believed not;* but David was dumb because he *believed* in God: unbelief procures dumbness as a judgment from God; but faith makes a Christian dumb from complaining: it quiets the soul from murmuring against God: it doth not make a person dumb so as not to pray and to praise God, but dumb in complaint.

Moreover faith, as it is an active grace, to enable the soul for the performance of duty, so is it also a passive grace, to strengthen the soul to suffer and bear affliction. *To you,* saith the Apostle, *it is given, not only to believe, but also to suffer for his name.*

Faith will call in strength enough to bear affliction. God is pleased to exercise a Christian with great trials; but faith carries the soul along through all. Faith bears God's trials with God's own strength. There is no cross nor affliction, but faith can find support in the promise of deliverance. Faith makes a man see the affliction, as it were, come out of the hand of the Lord—out of the hand of mercy. Faith discerneth God's purpose of love in the chastening he inflicteth. Faith sees all things measured out by God himself, and taketh with patience the portion allotted to him. Faith enables a man to conquer himself; it silenceth all murmuring and makes the soul to bear its cross with patience.

SERMON IV.

THE IMPROVEMENT OF TIME;

OR,

THE RIGHT USE OF TIME'S SHORTNESS.

---

1 COR. VII. 29, 30.

"BUT THIS I SAY, BRETHREN, THE TIME IS SHORT; IT REMAINETH, THAT BOTH THEY THAT HAVE WIVES BE AS THOUGH THEY HAD NONE; AND THEY THAT WEEP, AS THOUGH THEY WEPT NOT; AND THEY THAT REJOICE, AS THOUGH THEY REJOICED NOT; AND THEY THAT BUY, AS THOUGH THEY POSSESSED NOT; AND THEY THAT USE THIS WORLD, AS NOT ABUSING IT: FOR THE FASHION OF THIS WORLD PASSETH AWAY."

THAT I may briefly open out to you the sum of that I have to deliver out of this scripture, I desire you, beloved in the Lord, in few words, to take notice of the drift and scope of the holy Apostle in this place; and that is this. The Corinthians, as it appeareth in the beginning of this chapter, had written a letter to St. Paul, wherein they did propound to him divers cases of conscience, and did entreat him that he would send his judgment concerning those points. Some five or six, we may gather, they did write to him about: one was this;—Whether he thought it either a lawful or a fitting thing for a man to marry? Another was, Whether, if a man were married, his wife and he might not separate themselves one from another? A third was, Whether, if one of them being a believer, and the other an infidel, it were lawful or convenient for the believer to remain a yoke-fellow to the infidel? These, and divers other cases of conscience, they entreated St. Paul to resolve for them.

Now the Apostle, in the beginning of this chapter, writeth an answer to every one of these questions that they propounded. To some of them he answereth thus: Indeed I cannot give an absolute determination what is to be done, but I suppose this and this is best. To another —I advise such a thing: I cannot directly determine the will of God; but I have received mercy to be accounted faithful; I think also that I have the Spirit of God; and if you would know my opinion, it is this. And so he giveth divers doubtful answers to their questions; only he telleth them that which seemeth fittest for each occasion.

When he hath done all, he cometh to this that I have read, *But this I say, brethren,* &c. As if he should say—The answers I have given you may not be enough to resolve your doubts, because I say only, this is my *counsel,* or this is my *opinion:* but in this I am peremptory; that is, that ye be mindful that *the time* for all these questions *is short; it remaineth that they that have wives, be as though they had none; and they that weep, as though they wept not; and they that rejoice, as though they rejoiced not.* In this matter I do not say—I suppose, and I think it fit, or I give my advice, or for the present occasion it is fit to be thus; but herein I am confident and resolute, that you should be *as if not* in all things. This is the drift of the Apostle; that he would bring in one thing wherein he is confident, after the resolution of divers questions wherein he could not be so confident.

So, then, the words I have read contain two general things:—

First, the Apostle's preface to his exhortation: —*But this I say, brethren.*

Secondly, the exhortation itself:—*The time is short,* &c.

The first general thing in the words is the Apostle's preface:—*But this I say, brethren.*

And in this I would note but two things: *first,* how confident, and earnest, and resolute a faithful minister will be, when he cometh to a point that mainly concerns his people. In all other things the Apostle giveth them his answer, so as it might seem he had not fully resolved their questions. I give my advice, saith he; and again, I suppose this. But now, when he cometh unto the right use of the world that it be not abused, and the thought of heaven that they might set themselves about it, he useth no *ifs* and *buts;* he setteth it down resolutely and positively: *Brethren, this I say;* this you must do.

And I would note in this preface, *secondly*, the appellation or title that he giveth the Corinthians,—*Brethren:* as if the Apostle should say, I am putting you now upon such a duty, that if I could not give you the term brethren, I should hope little to prevail with you. To come and tell a young gallant that is in the midst of his ruffe, and his jollity, and pleasures, *the fashion of this world passeth away;* and I would have you use these things as if you used them not: I know he would not receive it. Or to come to an old soaked worldling, whose mammon and penny is his god, whose thoughts run altogether upon his wealth, and to tell him that he should use the world as if he used it not: or to come to another that is newly married, and it may be hath made a goddess of his yokefellow for a while, and to tell him that he must be as if he had no wife: I should have little hope to prevail with these. But you are *brethren;* and because brethren, you know the good things of God, you are acquainted with things concerning eternal happiness: therefore, as long as I can call you brethren, I am bold to put you upon the duty.

So, *Brethren,* this is my preface to you. I shall anon speak to a point that I shall have little hope to prevail upon with many in the congregation. When I come to speak of the immoderate use of the world and all the blessings in it, it may be that both your ears will be stopped against it. But as many of you that are brethren, that have given up yourselves to God and have taken him for your portion and his word for your guide in all things, I hope *you* will bring willing and yielding hearts to resolve what is delivered out of the word of God, you will embrace it and endeavour it during all the course of your lives. And so this will suffice for the preface.

I come now, SECONDLY, to the exhortation: *It remaineth that they that have wives be as though they had none*, &c.; wherefore? because *the time is short;* that is the ground of this exhortation. I will begin with this, and afterward proceed to the exhortation itself.

The word translated "short" signifieth in the original, time "cut off;" and the Apostle here alludeth, as the best expositors agree, to seafaring men that have almost done their voyage, and begin to strike sail and to lower down the yards, and are even putting into the harbour, and preparing to unlade their goods. So, saith the apostle, *the time is short.* As if he should say:—If a company that are going out on a long voyage should strive who should be master, and who be master's mate, and who should have this or that office in the ship, I could not greatly blame them. But when they are almost at home, when they are within sight of the shore, when they begin to strike sail and to go themselves out of the ship, then if they should fall a quarrelling for places, and contend and use all the friends and means they could make, it were a ridiculous folly. So it is with us. Timc was when the world was but beginning, and then when a man came into it he might say, By the course of nature, I have a matter of six or seven or eight or nine hundred years to go on in my pilgrimage, before it will be ended: and then when a man might live perchance to see himself the father of a thousand children, and might come to people almost a whole country, then I say, if a man should greet the world he might be excused. But brethren, God hath so cast out the time of our age, that as soon as we begin our voyage we are ready to strike sail presently. We have but a little time to continue, and much work to be done for another life: therefore, for us to stand striving about wives and children and estates, to cry out concerning afflictions and inconveniences, when we are ready to strike sail and even to go out of the ship on to the shore, it is a mere folly. These things are not worthy the while: heaven is the thing we should look after. Therefore let us be moderate in all temporal affairs.

Brethren, the serious meditation of the little and short time that we have to remain here below, should be a great means to cut us off from the world, and to put us upon thoughts and actions concerning heaven. I might give you a world of Scripture to prove this; but you have proof enough in the text.

The time is short, saith the Apostle, the time is contracted; you are ready to strike sail: therefore forget the things that are behind, and look forward: set not your hearts on those things that you are about to leave for ever.

We know that all things that a man can enjoy in this world, they die as soon as ever his time is gone. Mark it: all things here below, let a man dote never so much upon them; let him have wife, and children, and beauty, and credit, and pleasures, and learning, and whatsoever else, if his glass be out, if his time be gone, there is an end of all those to him. Now the soul of man careth not for that happiness that hath no continuance at all in it: yea, the rarest things that mortal men seek, if they should know beforehand that they should enjoy them but a little time, the soul would not care for pitching upon them. If a man were offered the goodliest woman for his wife that ever lived in this world, and if God should send him this message,—There, take her; I bestow her freely upon thee; but to-morrow thou shalt die: who would care for marrying? To be a king, we know, is simply the greatest thing that men seek after in this world; yet, among the Grecian cities, as that of Sparta, because one was to have the kingdom but for a year, and then to lay down his crown and become a private man, all the wisest men of the city strove not one half so much to be king as we to get great places. Why? because they knew that that honour was but for a year, and that would be gone presently; therefore they cared not for it. So the Apostle teacheth in this place. Thou that hast a wife that thou lovest mightily, thou that hast pleasures in which thou takest full content, why doest thou so? We are ready to strike sail; we have but a little time to continue. So that, because all the blessings of this life, let them be never so many, never so great, yet they all die with us when our time is ended; therefore, he that could but seriously think that he hath but a little time to continue below, will never let his heart be violently set upon them.

Another reason why the meditation of the shortness of our time should be such a marvellous means to take us off from the things of the world, is this: that we shall find work enough in this short time for things that more concern us. Now the very nature of our soul that God hath put into us is this, that a man cannot intend, earnestly and violently, two things different in their nature, at the same time. Let a man, for a certain hour, be earnestly engaged about some business, and though there may be a great many other things that he could find in his heart to think upon, yet the soul intends that one mainly and can find no time for the other. This is our case. We have but a little time; but in that little time, admirable is the work we have to do before it be spent, if we would give a comfortable account.

What have we to do?

I tell you in a word. The main and needful thing of all that we have to do in this little time here allotted us is, to learn and practise how to shoot the gulf of hell,—how to make our peace with God,—how to get his favour in Christ,—how to have the corruptions of our soul cured and healed,—how to grow up in grace, and to get sure evidence against that day when all shall stand naked before him, that then we may be found in Christ. Have I ever heard that I have a great work to do, and that I have but a little time to do it in? Surely then, if I think seriously of it, I cannot find in my heart to let my soul pitch earnestly upon the things below. Beloved, our time here is the only time we have to make heaven sure. It is the most precious thing that ever we have in the world. Now if a man have such a precious thing, and but a little of it, will he go and spend it for toys and baubles?

This is a thing that the Emperor Caligula is laughed at for in all stories. There was a mighty army provided, admirable and strange and all trimmed; and every one expected that with it the whole country of Britain should have been conquered; and so it might have been. But he employed his soldiers to gather a company of cockle-shells and pebbles, and so sailed home. Had not every one cause to laugh at the folly of this emperor? Verily such a fool is every man; and so we should acknowledge, if we would but weigh this:—God hath given thee but thus much time; it may be twenty years, it may be but a day or two more: in this time, he hath furnished thee with that which may be a means to conquer heaven itself. Now if thou lay out this little only about wife or children, or to purchase a little of the things that are below, is it not the greatest folly that may be?

Suppose that a servant hath a great deal of work to do, and knoweth that he must give an account to his master thereof, and that if all be not done that should be done, he can never appear with comfort before his master; and he seeth also that the sun draws low, and the day hasteneth to an end: do you think that this servant can find time to play? If a man have much to write and but a little paper to write in, he must write small and thick and close as ever he can. So it is with every one of us. I warrant you there is not any soul of us, but he shall find so many thousand things to repent of, so many graces to obtain that he stands in need of, so many evidences for heaven to get that yet he hath not got sealed, so many particulars concerning a better life, that a man may wonder that ever any one should find one half day to attend to anything else.

Oh that we had learned this excellent lesson that the Apostle here teacheth the Corinthians; what wondrous happy people should we be!

You shall find evermore in the Scripture, the Spirit of God putting the neglect that is amongst men, and their carelessness of heaven, and all the wickedness of their lives, upon this—the not serious meditation of that small time they have to continue below.

If a man come and speak to the worldly-minded with these words that St. Paul useth to the Corinthians, they will say:—This is true, and a good point to be pressed upon a man that is in a consumption, or one whom the doctors have given over, to tell him that he cannot continue a week, that his time is short. But for our parts, we are but in the beginning of our voyage; we are (it may be) but twenty years old; we began but the other day to be furnished with our stock for trade; we are but newly entered, and do you think that we are already striking sail? Or another, that hath lived forty or fifty years in the midst of a full trade, that hath got something in the world and beginneth now to enjoy the goods he has laid up; do you think that he is about striking sail? Thus people put it off. Alas, what is all thy time, what is thy whole life? Is it not a vapour, a dream, a tale that is told—like a ship that saileth by and is gone almost in the twinkling of an eye? If thou have no more time of life here, but only while a little sand is running out of a glass, while a ship is sailing out of sight, while a short tale is told (God saith it is no more), wilt thou account that thy voyage is not yet near its end?

I beseech you, beloved, often think, at home, of this point. Say within yourselves, How long, Lord, am I to continue below? and what is there for me to do before I go out of this world?

But the truth is, men dare not think of this: and the Devil laboureth for nothing more in the world than this,—to make them put off the serious consideration of the brevity of their lives, and to persuade them that they have longer time to continue here than they have: because he knows the truth of this that I have spoken, that the meditation thereof will stir them up to make clear all reckonings with God, before they go hence and be no more seen. You may find this to be true in your own experience. How loth men are to entertain thoughts of their latter end! Go to one that lies sick of a consumption, and he will tell you: The doctors say that I may live, and I doubt not but I shall get up again: such a one hath been brought as low as I, and he is recovered, and why may not I? I once knew one that, when the physicians came and told him that he must die,—Good Lord, saith he, what a deal of work have I to do! I have all my seed to sow, all my evidences to seal, that my soul should be saved, &c.! Such thoughts should enter into us now. Pitch on them seriously; buckle to them soundly.

We may learn this point of wisdom from the Devil himself: he, because he knoweth his time is short, is so much the fuller of rage and malice, and plies his work with so much the more eagerness. *Woe be to the inhabiters of the earth and of the sea! for the Devil is come down unto you, having great wrath, because he knoweth that he hath but a short time.* So should we do. Think with thyself: *The seventh angel* will come ere long, and *swear by him that liveth for ever and ever, that there shall be time no longer.* But God will have an account for the time that is past: and what if the angel should come now, and swear that, for some of us, there shall be no more time, after this week or this day! Put the case, —it may be thine, or mine, or any one's case,— that God should say:—Go fetch such a man: I will give him no more time; it is true I gave him some; but now his voyage is at an end, his sail is struck. Then we should be called at once to go and give an account to God. What have you done with all your time? will God say; I must have a reckoning of it. And then cometh, Imprimis, so much time in drinking; so much time in revelling; so much time in dressing myself every day. And then God shall say, Were these the things I gave you time for? did I bestow time on you for to be spent about your miserable bodies? No, it was that you might serve me and gain heaven. Beloved, how could we answer to these things?

It is good and profitable seriously to consider of this betimes. Say to thyself, I have not long to live; after a while I must go hence and be no more; I must give an account and a reckoning unto God of all that I have done, whether it be good or evil.

So much for the ground whereon the Apostle resteth his exhortation. I come now to the exhortation itself. *It remaineth, that both they that have wives be as though they had none; and they that weep, as though they wept not; and they that rejoice, as though they rejoiced not; and they that buy, as though they possessed not; and they that use this world, as not abusing it.*

In a word, I take the meaning of the exhortation to be somewhat as follows. Brethren, you are ready to cast anchor: trouble not yourselves: be steadfast: gird up the loins of your minds: let your care be greatest for heaven. As for these things that are here below,—if you have wives, be as though you had none; think, as soon as you are ashore you shall have none. If you are sick or under any cross or affliction, be as though you wept not: suppose you be as a fellow that is fain to ply the pump all day,—as soon as he is ashore he is free. If you rejoice, if you be in prosperity, if you be as the master of the ship that hath great preferment, be as if you rejoiced not: why? you are almost come ashore; your preferment will soon be at an end: therefore be as if not in all these things.

I will briefly open the meaning of each part of this exhortation, and then put all into one point of instruction, and so come further to apply it unto you, as God shall enable me.

What, therefore, is the meaning? *First: Let them that have wives be as though they had none.* Now a man that hath a wife hath two things that another hath not that hath no wife.

The first is, he hath a great deal of joy and comfort. He hath a second self, a loving yoke-fellow; one in whose bosom he can pour out his heart at any time; one that he can make partaker of all his contentments; one that is willing to help him to carry all his crosses. So in a wife, supposing her to be a good wife, he hath that comfort that another knows not of.

Secondly, he that hath a wife hath a great many cares that another hath not. He hath a great deal of fear lest he should leave her in distress; a great deal of care how she, and the children that are begotten of her, should be provided for when he is gone: so that, as St. Paul saith, he cannot but care for the things of the world, how he may give content to his wife.

Now what is it to be in this as if he had no wife? It is this. In all contentments that come by a wife, to use them as if he had none at all: that is, to be moderate; not to glut himself and to think,—Now I am a happy man, I need no more: God hath given me such a yokefellow and I have abundant joy in it: but to moderate his heart in this.

And for the other thing, for care and thought how to provide for her and her children, to do his best like an honest man, and then to be at peace in his mind as if he had no wife and children to provide for; to leave all to God; to go on in his calling in obedience to God, and let God do what he will. This is to have a wife as if he had none: to be as moderate in the enjoying of the contentments that come by his wife, to be as moderate in cares required for a wife, as if he had no wife at all to joy in, none to take care for.

For the *second; They that weep, as though they wept not.* One man rejoiceth and glorieth exceedingly in his happiness, that he hath a wife: another complaineth—No man is so full of crosses as I; every day one cross after another: no man hath such children, such a wife, such an estate, so poor, so afflicted, so weak: ever groaning and complaining. Now to such saith the Apostle, *Be as if not, in weeping.* That is, let the thoughts of the nearness of the shore make you so contented, as if there were no cross at all lying upon you. For (I still follow the same metaphor) he that is the poorest man in the ship, he that doth nothing but dress the sails and ply the pump, and, it may be, is beaten withal and poorly fed, yet in the midst of all these hardships he thinketh,—I shall by and by cast anchor, and though I work hard, yet one hour more will make me free. So it should be with us in all our afflictions, as if not: that is, we should always remember this: Death will soon come and end all: I am sick in body; I am crossed in my good name, in my yoke-fellow: well, death will end all these: I have but a little while to tarry in this world, and short things cannot be tedious.

Thirdly: He that rejoiceth, as though he rejoiced not. That is,—in all the contentments of the world, in all the joy a man hath in the things below, in his estate, in his credit, or in anything else for which the world accounts a man happy, let him remember that these things will soon be gone. Let him be as the master of the ship, who thinketh with himself—All these are under me; I can command them, and punish them if they disobey: yet I am now near the shore and shall soon be out of the place I am in, and lose all authority and power; let me, therefore, moderate myself. So let us, in all worldly contentments, be so moderate as if we should take our leaves of them and they of us.

And so, *fourthly—for them that buy, as though they possessed not.* That is, for a man not to enlarge his heart as his estate increaseth: but if he have so many pounds, and therewith maketh such and such a purchase, let him not be too much wrapped up in his possession; but let him live and carry himself in his thoughts as if he had nothing but food and raiment.

And then, *lastly*, cometh in the main of all the rest: *They that use this world, as not abusing it.* By world, St. Paul means all the good things of the world: all that I have already named, and all else that you can think of,—wife and children, prosperity and adversity; everything on the right hand and on the left; all cometh within the compass of the world: use all these things so. But especially he aimeth at worldly businesses, the things we are exercised about. Do them as not abusing them: as not letting your hearts be too much set upon them: but be temperate and moderate in all, that you may ever be fit for that greater service that God hath to employ you in.

This, then, is the point I would have you observe and consider. That in wife, children, prosperity, crosses,—a believer must be in them *as if not;* as if he were not in that condition. And this duty I cannot better explain to you than by such a comparison as this. Look how worldly men use the things of heaven: so let a heavenly man use the things of the world.

To instance a few duties in which this comparison may apply. Suppose it be the duty of prayer: bring me out a true believer and a worldling; let them both be put upon this duty of prayer. The true believer, his heart, before he goes to prayer, is full of care that he may pray aright, full of fear lest he should not carry himself as he ought when he is in the duty; his heart is violently bent to it; it struggleth and striveth that he may do it so as may please God. When he hath done, he hath much joy and comfort if he have carried it well; and much sorrow and grief if he have carried it ill. Thus a religious heart carrieth itself in this duty. Now a worldly man doth the duty too: but how? as if not: that is, he hath none of this care before he cometh to it; he hath none of this trouble when he is at it; he hath none of this perplexity when he hath done, if he have miscarried in it. If he be able to come off, it is well enough, though it be performed in never so ill a manner. Why? his mind is after other things: he intends greater matters, as he thinks: the minister hath taught him to pray, and he can say his prayers, and so he doth the duty; but still, *as if not.*

Or again, suppose a man whose heart is set upon mammon; put this man to recreation. He may, perhaps, find time to play at bowls or cards or tables with a friend; but how? He cares not for the game for its own sake: he whiles away the time and occupies his hands, but this is not the thing his heart is set upon: that which giveth him contentment, and on which his mind resteth all the while, is his commodities, his wealth, his trade, his merchandize, his business in the world.

Just so, beloved, it must be with every true believer, in the using of all the things of this life: that is, without care, without fear, without perplexity, without distraction; and if they come on pleasantly, so: if they fail, so: he must be pleased if he have them, and content if he want them; and howsoever these things fare with him, his thoughts must be carried higher and better. To think thus,—I am a servant of God; I have a calling here; I will follow it in obedience to God; I have a wife, I will use her as a wife should be used: I have children, I will have a care of their education. But I must not come to be distracted about my calling, about my wife, and children, and servants, and good name, or anything that is here below. I am here to-day; it may please God, I may be gone to-morrow; my heart's desire must be to be content with this,—that God is my all-sufficient portion. If

I be in prosperity, to be *as if not:* if in affliction, in the midst of sorrow and trouble, to carry myself so as if God freed me from all: to feel that I can lose nothing if I lose not God's favour; I can gain nothing while He is mine.

And this point that I have now opened out, namely, that *a true believer must be as if not in all the things of the world,* though it is plainly laid down by St. Paul in the text, yet for the better confirmation thereof I will add to that two or three other plain passages of Scripture. There is one eminent place for this purpose in the Epistle of John. Saith the Apostle: *Love not the world, neither the things that are in the world; if any man love the world, the love of the Father is not in him.* Now he that must thus use wife, children, credit, friends, good name, prosperity, *without loving them,* it is likely he useth them *as if not;* for love is the great wheel that setteth all the faculties to work: therefore the Spirit of God doth directly forbid all Christians to love the world, or the things of the world: the Scripture absolutely enjoineth that we should not love them: that is, that our hearts must not be fixed on them.

Another place, likewise, is this;—*Set not your affections on things below.* Now, as I said before, if a man use or do anything that his affections are not upon, that he doth not love and joy and delight in, that he doth not take care for, and the like, certainly that man useth it as if not: and thus must every true believer use the things of the world; so that he must not set his affections upon them.

Other Scriptures I might give you to make good this point; but it is proved already. Two or three arguments I will add to make it plain *why* every true believer must be as if not in all these things.

First, because all the things in this world (which are contained in the text), they are all but empty, poor things to a believer. To another man, who makes them his god, in his conceit, they are full; but to a true believer these things are well known to be but empty things. I need give you no better proof to make this evident, than that which followeth in the text: *for the fashion of this world passeth away.*

The *fashion* of the world: what is that? It is a show without a substance; such a fashion as is in a comedy or stage-play, where all things are but for a while, to please the eye. A man, it may be, acts the part of a king, that is no better than a beggar or a varlet. So all things in the world are no better than shadows, and empty like a piece of a stage-play: and no marvel therefore if believers, that know this, use them as not.

Secondly, another argument why believers must, in all these things, use them as if not, is because they are none of a believer's; and being none of his, it is mere folly for him to set his heart upon them. How are they none of his? you will say. First, because these things are below, they belong to the men of this life, whose treasure is in the earth; but the treasure and estate of a believer is laid up in another life: he is but a stranger and pilgrim here below; and therefore they are none of his. And then, likewise, they are none of his, because he hath resigned them all up to God in the day when he made the bargain for Christ. For when we come to be Christ's, we must sell all to buy that pearl; and in selling all, we sell not only our corruptions and lusts, but wives, and children, and credit, and pleasures, and all. We have them now no longer to have and to hold, to do what we will with them; but we return all to Christ, and have them as copyhold, to be tenants at will to that great Landlord: we have only a little title in them. The children of the world are, truly, no better off than we in respect of this: they cannot hold or enjoy the things they value longer than God leaveth them in possession, but the believer hath voluntarily given up all to God, and is resolved to live as if he had nothing else but God for his joy and hope.

And if it be so, that every believer hath no more to do in this world, but merely to use and employ that which belongeth not to him, but is lent to him for a time, so that he can properly call nothing his own, but God and Christ; then, certainly, he must use all these things as if not. Conceive it thus. A traveller goeth a long journey: he cometh at night to his inn: when he is there, he is wondrous glad of his table, of his meat and drink, of his fire, of his bed, and everything; and he is wondrous welcome: but he doth not so delight in them as the host of the house, who is living there, and is the right owner, and hath the whole estate. No, he only resteth there for the night, after his weary journey; but on the morrow,—"God be with you," and then he is gone.

So a worldly man, he may say,—Here is my estate, here is my stock, all that I have is laid up here: but a believer saith,—I am now in my journey; I am here only as a pilgrim; my home is in heaven: and while I am passing through my pilgrimage, if I have a piece of meat in my hunger, and a cup of drink in my thirst, and clothes in my nakedness, there is all that I need care for.

Thirdly, the last and main argument, to prove that every true believer *must be as if not*, in all things of this world, is, that if he be any otherwise in them, he will be so entangled that he shall not be fit for the service of God. And this third argument will be of the greatest force to a true believer. For the other two, you will say,—If they be none of mine, why should I meddle with them? and if they be empty, why likewise should I desire them? but now, thirdly, if I meddle with them, they will directly make me that I shall not be a Christian; they will hinder me from the service of my God. This will make a believer carefully to look about him.

The Apostle saith directly, that *none that*

warreth entangleth himself; that is thus: suppose a man to have received press-money to go a soldier; will he be so mad as lay out his money upon a farm in the country, when, upon the command of his captain he must, upon pain of death, follow presently to a distant land?

Beloved, he that entangleth himself with the things of the world and of the flesh—if his wife, his pleasures, his reputation, or anything have taken up his heart; or if sorrows and afflictions drink up his spirits and eat up his very soul,—when God calls this man now to come to prayer, to come to the church, to hear his word, to fight against his lusts, or to do any duty, alas! his head, his heart, and all, are eaten up with his farm, with his oxen, with his wife, with his crosses and afflictions, so that he is altogether unfit for any service that God hath called him to. Therefore, saith St. John, he that entangleth himself with these things below, he cannot possibly have the love of the Father dwelling in him.

This shall suffice for the clearing of the point. I have spent the more time in it because I would fain lay as good a foundation as I might, that the application may take a deeper impression in your hearts.

We that live in the country, when we come up by occasion into the city, and here see all men so full of trouble, every man so toiled in his work, so full of business, and so little time taken for anything else, then we learn how easily we may be so taken up with worldly things, as not to look beyond them; then we see how that such a point as this that St. Paul speaketh of may be of special use to all believers. *Be in all these things as if not.*

Shall we resolve, as obedient children, to carry this point home, and examine, in deed and in truth, whether we be in these things as if not? Alas! what shall I say? I remember a story of one Thomas Lennot, a learned Englishman, who—reading once, in the fifth, sixth, and seventh chapters of St. Matthew's Gospel, how our Saviour saith, *Ye have heard how it hath been said of old, Ye must do thus and thus; but I say unto you, Love your enemies, pray for them that curse you, do good to them that hate you and persecute you,* and so goeth on, enjoining strange duties to flesh and blood,—broke out into this exclamation,—Oh Jesus, either this is not thy Gospel, or we are not Christians! Truly, beloved, I would to God a man might not have just cause to say so in this point: that when he cometh and readeth this of the Apostle, *It remaineth, brethren, that he that hath a wife be as though he had none; he that buyeth, as though he possessed not; he that useth this world, as not abusing it,* &c. I say, I would to God he may not break out and say,—Oh Paul, either thou art not the writer of this, or we are no Christians!

We talk and profess in words, that we purpose to do it; but if we come to the deed and the truth, it is clean contrary: we are not at all moderate in the use of these things. In matters of heaven and in things that concern our everlasting welfare, where God would have us *take the kingdom of heaven with violence,* where we should cry out, as the horseleech's daughter, *Give, give,* and never say, It is enough, we are even like children that go to school, that care not how little they have for their money. In hearing, if the sermon be but half-an-hour, we think it enough; and in prayer and conference, a little will serve the turn. Like the Jesuit that, when he thought he had a vision and a revelation, he was terrified and cried out, Enough Lord, I have revelation enough; so we in matters of religion, Enough, Lord. But turn us to wives, to children, to clothes, to honours, to preferments, to riches, to ease, to pleasures, and the like, there we are as the horseleech's daughter, that crieth Give, give, and can never have enough. Brethren, is not this true?

But methinks I should bring you some particular instances to convince you of thus; and I would to the Lord I could convince your hearts that it is thus with you. Suppose now, a man comes and meets with a citizen in his business, and saith to him, How have you spent this day? Truly, he will say, I am so full of business that I have not time so much as to eat my meat. But I hope you have been at prayer with your family; have you not? Alas, he will answer, I cannot get so much as a quarter of an hour's time. Do you call this, *as if not,* brethren?

Come to another that hath a wife,—all his care is for her; Oh my wife and children; if I should die and leave them poor, what would they do? when I sleep I dream of them: when I awake in the morning my thoughts are of them. Is this to be as if you had no wife or children?

Another is ever complaining and mourning: Oh I have such crosses, I am so full of affliction; I have lost such and such friends, and such and such an estate; and though I go to church, and hear such and such comfortable doctrines one after another, and all telling me of the all-sufficiency of God, of the comforts and joys of the Spirit, of the good things that are laid up in heaven, yet, like Rachel, I can never be comforted under my losses and trials. What shall we say to these things? Do you think the Lord speaks not as he meaneth? or that when the Apostle saith here, absolutely and determinately, thus and thus you must do if you be Christians, we may yet do contrary to all this, and think that we are God's people?

I know you may put it off, many of you, and allege many things: We have callings, and we must follow our callings; if God bring me in employment, blame me not if I follow it; and I know not how I should live, if I busied not myself thus and thus.

But *be not deceived; God is not mocked.* If thou findest, in the midst of thy trading and merchandizing and whatsoever calling thou art of, thy heart daily gathering toward heaven; that thou canst say, Blessed be God for this and other commodities, but Christ is my real treasure: this is good. And then, in these things, if thou hast a care to use them aright, as well as to get them and to thank God for them, and that thy project is, how thou shalt do good with that thou hast, that thou art always saying with thyself—Lord, how shall I do good with so much money that I have gained by such and such a bargain? then, God forbid that I should blame thee, though thou be full of business from morning to evening. But alas, there are many good people and godly, that have hope that they serve God, yet if they go home and examine themselves thoroughly, their own consciences will tell them, that in the things of this world they are not *as if not;* but rather that they have been overcareful, and too full of distractions in business.

And so for matter of joy. If a man have a little pleasure or preferment given him and his heart is so up that he knows not where he is,—he is so transported that he hath clean forgot himself,—this cannot stand, this is not to be *as if not;* and therefore I beseech you, in the fear of God, think of it.

Now if a man would know how he should come to have his heart in a good temper, to be in these things *as if not;* in one word let me tell you that rule of St. Paul. In all things be filled with the Spirit, and then thou wilt not take thought much for other things: if once you let your soul be filled with the things of a better life, then wife and children and wealth and pleasures or anything else, will not draw away your hearts.

Get a good hand-fast of Jesus Christ; work out your salvation; be sure that you are believers upon good grounds, and that you have the graces of the Spirit of God in you, in deed and in truth; that you are really new creatures.

And then, often think of the rare things that are provided for you in another life. What! to have God to be your Father, and angels your keepers; to be children of God, and companions of angels! Weigh these things daily, and then you will be *as if not,* in all these outward and worldly things: and until thou dost this and thinkest withal of that I have formerly said, that thou art ready to strike sail, I will never believe that thou wilt be as if not.

And now a word or two as to the spur which the Apostle useth; and it is necessary he should use such a spur, for it is a very hard lesson.

If you would be as if you were not, consider this, — *the fashion of this world passeth away:* that is, it is even such a fashion as is on a stage: all these things below they are but as the acting of a comedy or a scene, which, it may be, is done in half an hour; and though it make a fine show, yet in truth there is no substance in it. It is but a fashion, and even that fashion passeth soon away.

Our life is but the acting of a part in a comedy; and even as in a scene or play, things that have a glorious, glittering show to the eye, if you look closely upon them, are of little or no value; so in all the outward things thou possessest, thy contentment in wife or children or credit or pleasures, thou dost but act a glorious part: it may be thou hast a goodly outside, fine clothes, rich apparel, an outward representation of comfort; but look through them, and there is no such matter.

And then this poor appearance, this vain fashion, *it passeth away;* it is suddenly gone. As a man hath but a little time to tarry in the world, so all the things he enjoyeth in the world are wondrous inconstant. As it is in a play, he that now acts the part of a king, it may be next he will act the part of a beggar; or as it is with some of your delicate fashions, that while you are speaking of them the fashion is spoiled; even so the fashion of this world, it will not continue.

This is the sum of that I desire you to take notice of, that if you will not be persuaded by me, or by the Spirit of God in his unworthy minister, to use the things of this world moderately and to carry yourselves as you ought in crosses and afflictions; yet know this, that the fashion of these things will shortly be spoiled: and if they be all inconstant, what a folly is it to set thy heart upon them!

We may learn this wisdom from the foolery of our English nation, esteemed now the idlest people of the world for changing their fashion. They will never make clothes twice of one fashion;

but one gown of this fashion, and another of that; and though he be never so good a tailor that makes it, yet he must make no more of the same fashion, but the next term they will come to another. Learn, I say, this wisdom from that foolery. Now the Lord giveth thee comfort in thy wife, set not thy heart too much upon her; the next season the fashion may change. Now thou art rich, let not thy heart doat upon thy riches; it is but a fashion, a show, it passeth away, and to-morrow thou mayest be a beggar: — to-day, a man; to-morrow, none.

But if thou wouldst keep the fashion, get the fashion of grace; get a right to heaven, an interest in God; and be content, in God's name, to follow his fashion: if God will have thee to be in the fashion of a humble, dejected man, be content with that fashion. If, anon, he will have thee on the top of the wheel of prosperity, thank God for it, and take heed of abusing the things thou enjoyest. Remember, the things of this life are inconstant: as a flower, as a nosegay, that seemeth as a dainty, fine thing, but while we are smelling at it and praising it it withereth away, so is it with all these things.

I would I could tell how to speak home to your souls; and yet I know that that little I have spoken, if it be entertained with faith, if you believe it to be the truth of God, not as the speech that a man makes to you, but as the speech of St. Paul, an inspired apostle of Christ, who sets it down by the direction of God, that thus it is; I say if you lay down this as a truth that comes from God, and seriously think with yourselves,—I have but a little time to tarry here below, and when I am out of the world I shall live for ever in heaven or in hell. While I do enjoy the things of this world, God will have me to be *as if not* in them; and there is good reason why, for they are shows and not substances; grace and the favour of God is the only thing that is substantial; riches and honour and worldly contentments, they are but shadows; like one in a play, that is but a peasant under the coat of a king, these have but only outsides, under them there is no such matter;—this, I say, being seriously considered and faithfully received, may, through the blessing of God and your own prayers to God to teach you this, be a means to moderate you in the use of all those things that are here below.

SERMON V.

ST. PAUL'S TRUMPET;

OR,

AN ALARM FOR SLEEPY CHRISTIANS.

ROM. XIII. 11.

"AND THAT, KNOWING THE TIME, THAT NOW IT IS HIGH TIME TO AWAKE OUT OF SLEEP."

THE holy Apostle, in this chapter, delivers a number of precepts and general rules for conduct, and enforceth them with sundry reasons. Among them all, the words that I have read are the principal, both precept and reason enforcing them. Considering the season, it is time that ye arise from sleep.

These few words may be called St. Paul's trumpet to rouse the sluggish Christian. They were the occasion of the conversion of that famous instrument, St. Austin, as he saith in the eighth book of his Confessions, in the last chapter. He reports that when the time of his conversion drew near, he was in a marvellous great agony and conflict, beset with a number of temptations, whereby Satan would still have detained him in the spiritual sleep he was in. Being in this marvellous conflict, he could not but go from his chamber to his garden, and there he prostrated himself on his face before the Lord and earnestly and ardently called upon God. And in his prayer, as himself records, it seemed to him that he did hear the voice of a child speak to him:—*Tolle lege: Take up the book and read.* Hereupon, running back again to his study, the book being open, the first place that he cast his eye upon was this verse: *Now it is high time to awake out of sleep.* "And," saith he, "with the end of the sentence, I found an infused life." He found, in the reading of this sentence, grace, as it were, infused into him, turning him from dead works to serve the living God.

This place of Scripture hath been famous in the Church as the means by which one famous disciple received his conversion. I would to God that the Lord would bestow the same blessing among some of those who not only hear these words read, but also have them expounded in their ears.

For the understanding of which, we are to inquire,—

First, What is meant by sleep? *It is time to awake out of sleep.*

Secondly, What is meant by arising, or awaking, out of sleep?

THIRDLY, Who they be that must arise, or wake out of sleep.

For the FIRST of these, What is meant by sleep? Sleep, in Scripture, is threefold,—natural, moral, and spiritual.

Natural sleep is that spoken of by David. *I laid me down and slept; I awaked, for the Lord sustained me.* This natural sleep is the rest and restitution of nature.

Moral sleep is natural death: this is the death and dissolution of nature of which the Scripture speaketh:—*They that sleep in the dust of the earth shall awake:* and again,—*When Stephen had said this, he fell asleep.*

Spiritual sleep is the sleep of sin and security: this is the death and privation of grace in the soul, as the other is the privation of life in the body. Of this our text speaketh: It is high time to awake out of this sleep.

Now the state of sin and security is compared here to the state of sleep, because there are many resemblances and likenesses between the state of a sinner and of a sleepy man; for what effect sleep hath on the body, the same effect hath the sleep of sin in the soul. I will show you this in a few instances, and then pass on.

First, They that sleep, saith the Apostle, *sleep in the night.* This is the same that he aims at here: *It is time to awake out of sleep;* because *the night is past.* The night is the time to sleep in: and so, those that sleep in sin, it is because they are in the night of sin: there is a darkness around them; the canopy is spread over them; the sun of grace and the day of salvation shines not upon them: their eyes are closed up in darkness, as it is with a sleepy man.

Again, when a man goes to sleep, he puts off his clothes; he lies naked, exposed to all dangers. And so, when a man is in the sleep of sin and security, he wants his garments; he needs to be clothed with Christ's righteousness and holiness; he lies naked, exposed, and open, to all God's displeasure and to all the arrows of God's wrath. He is in the same condition as the Israelites, when they had made a calf, and Moses came and found them *naked unto their shame among their enemies*. He is destitute of God's protection, and wanting that garment, that armour of proof, that righteousness, that Christ giveth to his people.

Again, a man naturally lays himself down *willingly* to sleep; he is willing to take his rest. So it is in the sleep of sin: every natural man is willing to lay himself down to sleep in sin, to take his ease, and to rest in sin. There is no man but hath a natural inclination to sin, though none have a ready will to do good.

And again, as sleep surpriseth a man suddenly, ofttimes before he is aware, or before he can remember himself, where he is or what he is doing; so the sleep of sin, it oft surpriseth a man before he is aware. This we see even in the disciples of Christ; bodily sleep surprised them even when they intended to watch: but the sleep of their minds and souls was much more; for that was not a time to sleep if they had known what they were about.

Again, further: The sleep of the body binds up the senses and makes a man unconscious of that which is good or evil. Offer a kingdom to one that sleepeth, and it moves him not; threaten him, draw a sword, offer to stab him—he shrinks not; he is not sensible: a man that continueth in sleep, where you left him there you shall find him still. So it is also in the sleep of sin: it binds up all the spiritual senses, so that a man that is in this sleep, he wants a seeing eye and a hearing ear; he sees nothing, he apprehends nothing, he knows nothing of God; he feels not how good God is to him: offer him the kingdom of heaven, and grace in the means,—it moves him not: threaten him, draw out the sword, the weapon of God's wrath, against him,—he fears nothing: though he may even feel its point in some temporal or bodily affliction, it rouseth him but for a moment; he sinketh again in sin, as one who foldeth his hands still to sleep. As he is insensible in these courses, so he is immovable: look, where he was at the first, there you shall find him still: he is altogether as a dead man while he continueth thus in sin and security.

To conclude this point; The sleep of the body deludes a man with many vain dreams and foolish conceits; false joys and false fears and false hopes. So the sleep of sin in the soul hath the same effect; it feeds a man up with false joys and false hopes; it casts him down with false fear, where no fear is. A man in the state of sin, he fears the face of man, the hand of man, and the word of man: he fears not the eye of God, nor the word of God, nor the mighty power of God. So likewise for false joys: a man that is a beggar dreams that he hath gold enough, that he rolls and tumbles in it: and thus do beggars in grace, those that have not a rag of righteousness upon them, dream that they are rich and increased in goods, and that they have need of nothing; not knowing that they are all the while poor, and beggarly, and naked. Spiritual sleep filleth a man with false conceits and hides from him all the true occasions of joy and fear.

A man sometimes, when he goes to sleep, he thinks not to sleep long, but to take a nap and awake by and by: yet it may be, he sleeps beyond his compass, and sometimes he wakes no more. So it is with a man in sin: he hopes to wake; he thinks to sleep but a little; but sometime he sleeps long, and sometime he never wakes at all. So we see how aptly the Spirit compares the state of a man in sin to sleep. This is the first thing in the meaning of the words.

Now the SECOND thing is, What is meant by arising, or waking out of sleep? It is for a man to do in the matter of Christianity, as a man that awakes out of the natural sleep of his body. There are three things that a man doth, when he awaketh. *First,* there is an opening of the eyes and a beholding of the light: and this is likewise the first thing in awaking out of the sleep of sin and security. A man must labour to open his eyes, to behold the light of God's word, and that shining grace that the Lord propounds to him in the Scriptures. He must open his eyes to behold the light, and that will discover such objects to him as will then keep him awake. Men sleep in the night because they are in the dark and no light shineth around them; but in the day-time they see many objects that keep their minds a-stirring and awake. So, if we would keep awake from this sleep of sin, let us open our eyes to behold the light of grace, and in the light of the Scriptures we shall see objects that will help to keep us waking. We shall see God's mercy and God's displeasure, things that the carnal eye cannot see, nor the ear hear, nor the heart conceive. We shall see them in their beginning and degrees (though the full degree cannot yet be conceived), and this will help to keep us waking.

Then, *in the next place,* when a man hath opened his eyes to see the light, there must be a rousing of the senses. This awakes a man, when his senses that were bound up by sleep, are loosed, so that now he is able to see and to move and to talk. Now what is it that unbinds the spiritual senses of a man in this sleep of sin? Only faith in the Son of God that opens the eyes of them that were dead in sin: this restores new senses and new life, so that they are able to walk in the ways of God, and to move in the actions of godliness and Christianity. Therefore the second thing that a man must do, to arouse himself from sleep, is to get faith in his soul, that he may suck virtue from Christ; and so get his senses loosed, that he may see and taste and feel the goodness of God, which, without Christ, he cannot attain.

Thirdly, and *lastly;* a man must get out of his bed, that he may completely shake off sleep, when his eyes are open, and his senses loosed. That is, by repentance, and by ceasing to do evil, he must get out of the bed of sin. Therefore, when the Apostle exhorts to *rise out of sleep*, these are the three main things that he intendeth. First, to get the true knowledge of God, to see those objects that may allure and draw our minds; and then to labour to get faith in the Son of God, whereby our senses may be unbound: and then to get out of the bed of sin by repentance, to cease to do evil and learn to do well. This is to awake out of the bed of sleep.

THIRDLY: who are they that must arise out of sleep? Every man: for so the Apostle plainly expresseth it: *Awake, thou that sleepest;* whosoever thou art that sleepest, awake; it is now time to rise out of sleep. Now all men may be divided into these two classes,—the natural man and the regenerate man: and both of these sleep.

The natural man is in a fast, dead sleep; you shall as soon get a rib out of his side, as God did out of Adam when he was asleep, as wake him: you shall sooner drive a nail into his temples, than disturb him. He is in a fast, dead sleep; in the sleep of death. He is as a man in a lethargy, that never wakes. Therefore, this man hath need to arise, to be called upon, and to be roused out of the sleep of death. *Awake, thou that sleepest, and arise from the dead, and Christ shall give thee life!* Arise, as Lazarus arose out of the grave at the call of Jesus, thou that art in a dead sleep!

But not only are the natural men in a dead sleep; the regenerate also are asleep: they keep not themselves so waking and so watchful, as they ought to do. Therefore the Apostle applies it to himself and to all the saints:—*It is time for us to awake out of sleep.* He puts himself in the number: for he that is most wakeful had need to be yet more so, and to rise still out of sleep. It was the voice of the Church; *I sleep, but my heart waketh.* Even the Church herself, that was waked already in great part, yet confessed that she slept: her sleep was not so dead nor so fast as formerly; yet she slumbered. So it is said of the wise virgins, as well as of the foolish,—*They all slumbered and slept.* And so the disciples themselves, by the side of our Lord, even when a temptation was near and the tempter was upon them, they fell fast asleep and were not able to watch with Christ, no, not one hour.

Thus we see, brethren, that those also who are regenerate, those that have received the greatest measure of grace, and are in the highest form, (for who was higher than St. Paul?) they themselves have need to be called out of sleep; it is time for them to awake out of sleep, though they be waking persons. Even those that have received grace to believe and obey and be watchful, in some measure, even these must be called out of sleep.

Therefore, this is the counsel that is given to the Church of Sardis, that had received some grace, and was in some measure watchful: saith the Holy Ghost to that church,—*Be watchful, and strengthen the things that are ready to die.* He tells them before,—*Thou hast a name that thou livest, and art dead:* that is, thou art almost dead; there is but little life of grace left in thee, wherefore strengthen the things that remain. Thus we see the difference between the calling of the wicked and of the godly in their sleep. The one is called from sleep, to stand up *from the dead;* the other, to strengthen the things that *are ready to die:* and thus we see the persons who must wake.

The point thus opened, we are next led to the consideration of that woful sleep that oppresseth the world, and after that, to the sleep that oppresseth the church of God.

First, to consider the sleep of the wicked and unregenerate, those that are in the dead sleep of trespasses and sins. Even as the prophet observed in his time, so now—who doth not see all the world at rest and at ease? Like Lachish, that secure people, crying *Peace, peace,* to themselves, and fearing nothing till they be awaked. There is nothing but security among all classes.

First of all there is, everywhere, a numerous generation of idolators: they are fast asleep in the bed and bosom of that Babylon that hath enchanted and bewitched them with the cup of her fornication. They have laid themselves down to sleep in her lap, as Samson did with Dalilah, until like him they lose both their locks and their lives; and all the means that God hath used for a long time, the light of grace, the light of knowledge, the ministry that hath been so powerful and so plentiful, cannot pull them out of her lap. They trust themselves to her keeping, and so sleep in a treacherous security. But the Lord hath threatened, not only Jezebel, that whore and strumpet, by which he means Rome, but also all those that commit fornication with her, to cast them into a bed of sorrow: he will cast them upon a bed of little ease, and he will slay her children. The conclusion of this fearful sleep shall be death.

So, likewise, there is a generation of unclean adulterers: they are asleep upon the foul bed of voluptuousness and immorality. Blow a trumpet in their ears; ring a peal of ordnance against them, that is able to make the stones quake and the rocks to break asunder; tell them that *whoremongers and adulterers God will judge;* nay, let the world follow them with a cry of infamy, and reproach, and shame; yet all this awakes them not: they will scarce open their eyes, except it be in the twilight, as Solomon saith, to seek food for their lusts; until God cast them upon the bed of shame and sorrow and scorn and curse, from which they shall never rise again. It is a lamentable thing that a man's conscience, hearing this, should not apply it to his heart; that he should dare to shut his eyes, and dare still to cast himself on his bed of wickedness, not thinking what will be the issue of it.

And so, likewise, there is a monstrous generation of drunkards—monsters against nature, for no unreasonable creature so much extinguisheth the noblest gifts of nature as they. These cast themselves upon the bed of surfeiting and excess, where no covering is large enough to hide their shame. Let a man speak to them and advise and counsel them, there is no hearing of him while they are at their feasts or in their cups. Nay, let God speak to them, and pinch them in their bodies, in their strength, in their estates, let the Lord make them feel the smart, be their dangers never so near, they will not forsake their abominable course. Though they be, as Solomon describes them notably, in most extreme peril, yet they will not be roused: as he that lieth *in the midst of the sea, upon the top of a mast. They have stricken me, and I was not sick; they have beaten me, and I felt it not: when shall I awake? I will seek it yet again.* He will follow his cups still.

The like may we say of a number of Sabbath-breakers, that cast themselves upon the bed of profaneness and atheism; sometimes, for form and fashion, they will come to the temple, perhaps, and listen a little to the word spoken; but presently you shall see that they cast themselves fast asleep, as Eutychus, who, when at midnight Paul was preaching, fell from the loft and was taken up dead. But there is this difference, that was at midnight, these will do it at mid-day. So little have men gained of instruction, and of the knowledge and fear of God. They can scarce keep their eyes and their ears open, to hear one quarter of what God saith to them for their own good.

What shall I say of those unjust, injurious, usurious persons, whose jaws are as knives to cut those that they deal with? Those that use injustice in their weights, in their wares, in all that they touch; that use any manner of deceit, for the defrauding of their brethren; and then cast themselves upon the bed of their mischief, and solace themselves in their present unjust gains and unlawful riches.

Let a man speak to these, and tell them their estate, out of the Scripture; alas! they hear not. Deal with them as we deal with men in a swoon; rub them and chafe them, pinch them and wring them, if it be possible to make their consciences feel; alas! such a man dies in our hands; there is no life to be got in him. All that we can get from such a wretch, so bound up in his own self-love and his temporal wealth, is a rude repulse, a brush or a blow. This senseless man lays about him, he knows not upon whom: the love of riches hath blinded his eyes, and closed them in a dead sleep.

In one word, when I consider the secure course of the multitude of men amongst whom we live, it seems as if they had found that cave of sleep which the poets feign and speak of; a place very fit for these persons; a cave of sleep, as they describe it, where sun never shines; a place far remote from all company, where the houses have no doors, for fear the hinges should wake them, where they suffer no cocks, nor clocks, nor nothing that may hinder them from sleep. For the generation of men that I speak of, they are a kind of people that are loose, and lazy, and sleepy, and lascivious, that will not endure any clocks nor bells, nor any artificers that use tools and hammers, to knock and disturb them.

But why do you speak these words? They seem strange to us. What have we to do with such people?

Yet you, yourselves, shall say that they be true in the application.

For do we not see most men, except only a few, whom the Lord hath taken into his own teaching, that they cannot abide the place of the sunshine, the place where the light of grace shineth? Do we not see them absent themselves upon every occasion from the house of God, and from the means and ordinances of grace? And do we not see that they cannot abide the society of godly men, of religious people, who fear God, and deal truly with them, in exhortations and admonitions and loving rebukes? They will none of these. How ready and willing are they to chase away, if it were possible, all the Lord's servants and prophets, that they may not cry against their sins, that they may not awaken them, nor come near them. And for the ministry of the law, which Jeremiah calls *a hammer, to break the hard heart,* and to knock and rap the sleepy soul, it is an intolerable thing. They cannot endure this hammer, they cannot abide these dogs that bark against their sins: whereas dumb dogs, that can neither bark nor bite, they can like well enough. Somewhat they would have, some apology for religion; but they choose an outward fashion, and flatter themselves with smooth things; and those men that speak against their sins, that discover the true state of their lives and souls, these they cannot endure. Now tell me if these men live not in a carnal sleep—if they are not dwelling in the cell and cave of darkness, where they desire to sleep for ever.

But, to come from these natural men, let us consider, in the *second* place, that not only are these unregenerate worldlings cast into a dead sleep, but that even Christians are also overcome with sluggish indolence. Is it not a wonder that the disciples of Christ, that men so near to the side of their Master, that men in the midst of danger and temptation,—is it not a wonder that they should not *watch one hour* with Christ?

Let us then, that are infinitely behind the disciples in grace, beware much more of a careless security: let us rate ourselves for the heaviness and dulness of our hearts.

But because men are baptized and hear sermons, &c., they will not believe that they are asleep: let us therefore consider whether they that hear the word, and are professors of the life of grace, and are already awakened, may not be, notwithstanding all this, in so dangerous a state of indifference that it may rightly be called sleep.

Observe then, that this is one mark of a man that is asleep,—he hears not, he understands not the things spoken to him. And so it is with the sleepy heart and conscience: it hears not, or it understands not that it hears. It is one judgment upon wicked men that the Book of God is clasped to them: they read and hear, but they discern not: if the book be open, yet their heart is clasped fast, and they get no good by it. And this is not the least part of the misery upon the saints—that the book is not so open to them, nor do they so understand and discern that which is in it, as they might.

We hear the word, many of us, many times, and we seem to receive it; but yet, who is he that may not find in himself, that the sleep and security of his mind and soul make him not much to attend and regard it? And so it comes to pass, that God's word that we hear hath no effect upon us: we are overpowered by the sleep and sluggishness of earthly cares, instead of maintaining that we hear, and framing ourselves according to it.

Again, a man that sleeps, you shall know it by this; he doth not mind his ordinary business; he neither troubles his head nor his hands with it; his business sleeps with himself, for while he sleepeth he can do nothing else. So hereby we may know ourselves to be in the sleep of sin, when we give not our serious thoughts to God, and to the practice of piety and godliness: this is an argument of sleep and slumber in us. The mind of man should intend the principal thing for which God hath put us in the world; and when we give not our thoughts to God, and mind not the things of God's kingdom, it is a sign we are asleep. When we move not, nor stir our hands and our feet in the way of God's commandments, it proceeds from this sleepiness and drowsiness; whereas would we be wise for ourselves, and awake as we should, *we should neither be idle nor unfruitful in the work of the Lord;* we should ever be doing something that might glorify God and further our own reckoning. But this is the sign of a sleepy person; in the main and principal things his heart is not upon them; his hands and feet move not in the ways of God; he works not to the principal end for which he came into the world.

Once more, you shall know a sleepy man by this; he knows not of the passing of the time, but so much time as he sleeps he wastes: it is as the time of death to him: for what is sleep but the shadow of death? Even so it is with many of us, that profess the teaching of grace. Alas! how do we waste time insensibly, and pass away the time without profit! Some feast away the time, others play it away, and spend it in amusement—days and weeks and months together—as if we had received time only for recreations, and sports and pleasures; and not rather that we might further our repentance and our reckoning, and help the servants of God, and get oil in our lamps and faith in our souls, and patience against the time of trouble, and assurance of a blessed inheritance, when we shall be turned out hence. Time is given us for these ends, and yet we, silly as we are, devise pastimes to ourselves, as if our life did not pass away as a *weaver's shuttle!*

Alas, brethren, we may speak to the shame and sorrow of many that have exchanged their care of godliness for sensual indulgences; that have exchanged their seeking of God, in the appointed means, for company and good fellowship and drunkenness. Let the Lord's mariners come to such, and say: *What meanest thou, O sleeper? arise, call upon thy God:* why dost thou not do thy *first works?* why art thou lazy? And they will grow angry, as Jonah was, who thought he did well to be *angry unto death.* This is the misery of many that live under the teaching of the Gospel, in the light of the Gospel: they cannot bear to be awakened from their slumber.

To draw to a conclusion. The consideration of this point serves to rouse, and to raise us from this sleep and security, this slumber that is in the best of us. And know, my brethren, I speak not now to those that are out of the church, and those that are notoriously wicked and scandalous, and rebellious to good counsel, but I speak to those that live in the bosom of the church, that possess goodness and godliness; yea to those that are disciples, and are near the side of Christ: let this exhortation be to them, to raise and rouse themselves out of this sleep. *It is time,* saith the Apostle, *to awake out* of sleep. The sum of this exhortation I will propound, and so conclude.

First, consider how unprofitable a man, a Christian man is, when he is asleep. What is a man when he is asleep? But that there is hope of awaking, and coming again to the actions of life, he is no better than a plant, that hath nothing but being and nourishment. A waking beast is more profitable. So, when we sleep and slumber, and toss ourselves in dead security, how unprofitable are we to God's glory and to our own selves!

Secondly, consider, when a man sleeps in sin, how unfit he is for any Christian duty and exercise, for the main parts of godliness and Christianity. How unfit is a sleepy man for the actions of life and of his calling. And how unfit and unable and indisposed is a man that sle
sin, to the actions of spiritual life.

There be some main parts and branches of our general calling to which this sleep makes us unable.

The first of them is the exercise of godliness, the main duty in the profession of a Christian. For how can a Christian exercise himself in his praying, in his hearing, in his reading, while he sleeps? If these duties be done coldly, what are they worth? Actions that are done in a man's sleep, they come to nothing. So a man that sleeps in sin, let him do never so many good actions, they are of no value.

A second main branch of our Christian calling, is the spiritual combat to be maintained against our corruptions. Now, alas! how unfit is a sleepy man, either to expect or to repel an enemy. When he is asleep, he lies open to all disadvantage. Sisera himself, a strong and noble captain, was so weak that a silly woman, Jael, slew him when he was asleep. Therefore we know this part of our Christian calling cannot hold, as long as we sleep in sin.

Another part and duty of Christianity is to expect our Master's return, to wait for the coming of our Lord, that we may enjoy that sweet blessedness that he hath promised. Now, how unfit must a sleepy man be to prepare and watch for his Master's coming, and to set things in order. Thus we see in these particular main duties of Christianity, they cannot be performed by men that are asleep, and therefore we had need to wake ourselves. If we will either honour

God or profit ourselves; if we will be fit to do service to God, or to his church; we must keep ourselves awake, and bestir ourselves in the exercises and duties of Christianity.

Thirdly, consider, while we sleep and are secure, the enemy never sleeps—he is then most watchful against us. We may sleep, and think we do well to take our ease, but Satan sleeps not. We have a watchful enemy to deal with.

And then he hath some advantage by our sleeping. The enemy sows tares *while men sleep:* he comes into the field of the heart, where the word of God, the good seed, is sown, and what doth he do there? He sows a crop of thorns, and they make the heart of the believer like the field of Solomon's sluggard: *I passed by the field of the slothful, and lo, it was all grown over with thorns,* &c. Thus is the heart that is neglected, of a man that is sleepy and secure in sin. When do robbers and thieves assault the house? In the dead of the night, when they may take men at advantage, in their first sleep. Shall thieves and burglars watch at midnight to break the house and cut men's throats, and wilt not thou watch to save thyself?

Further, consider, as the enemy never sleeps, so God's mercy never sleeps. God's mercy is ever watching over us to do us good; and it watcheth to keep us watchful: for what should all the mercies of God do to us, but to keep us watchful? Our God that we serve is not as Baal, the god of idolaters,—*Peradventure he sleepeth, and must be awaked.* No, no, the Strength that keepeth Israel neither slumbers nor sleeps. Therefore let not Israel slumber nor sleep: because God watcheth over his children, let them watch with him, and keep themselves near to him.

And if this will not move thee, then consider, as God's mercy sleeps not, so God's judgments sleep not. The Apostle saith of those that were led away by false teachers, *Their damnation sleepeth not.* God's judgments are always waking: thou mayest sleep on both sides in sin, but God's judgment sleepeth not. And thou that art the Lord's, if thou sleep, know that correction and chastisement sleep not, and they will awake thee: thou wert better to awake by slighter means.

To conclude all, consider that we are all going surely to meet the mortal sleep of death; and if, when that meets us, our consciences shall tell us that we have also a spiritual sleep within us, that we carry a spiritual sleep to meet that mortal sleep, what a miserable and mournful state will that be. When the heart of a man or woman that is about dying shall speak aloud, and witness against his master,—Oh thou that hast been a sluggish and sleepy Christian, thou that hast had good means, but hast not kept thy watch,—thou wouldest sleep in spite of the exhortations of the word, and now thou shalt sleep the sleep of death for ever.

How many are there who, when they come

to grapple on their death-bed with that mortal sleep, cry, Oh that I had but one day, but one hour more, that I might awaken and strengthen the things that are ready to die, and that it might be better with me than it is! But alas, now their short day is passed, and one perpetual night cometh, and it is too late to awake out of sleep.

Therefore, let not time go, but know that that mournful day must come upon us; we must meet that mortal sleep. Let us labour to shake off spiritual sloth and drowsiness of soul, and to make our peace in the meantime, that conscience may witness with us, and for us, at the day of judgment. Let us labour to be watchful, and to be ready for the Lord, and to have our accounts settled, that when he cometh and reckoneth with us, we may not be found wanting.

SERMON VI.

CHRIST'S PRECEPT AND PROMISE;

OR,

SECURITY AGAINST DEATH.

JOHN VIII. 51.

"VERILY, VERILY, I SAY UNTO YOU, IF A MAN KEEP MY SAYING HE SHALL NEVER SEE DEATH."

IT is not long,* men and brethren, since Death rode in triumph through this city, and did bear down all before him: he locked up your houses, pulled down your windows, and made the wealthiest among you put upon them the semblance of bankruptness, by locking up their doors, and turning their backs to their houses, and running away: so it played the tyrant then. There died thousands a week; and the grave, that always crieth *Give, give,* was almost choked with carcasses. Death served himself so fast, that the prison could scarce hold the prisoners: it might

* This sermon appears to have been preached in London, in the year 1626, when the plague, which in the preceding year had carried off no less than 35,450 persons, had mercifully been removed.

almost have been said then of this city, as once it was said of Egypt, *There was not a house where there was not one dead.*

Now, it hath pleased God to show you more favour, and men die but by scores. Death goeth his old pace, and takes away a few, secretly, without public observation: but death is amongst you still, and will be so long as sin is amongst you; and therefore it can never be unseasonable for me to speak, and for you to hear something that may arm you against this last enemy; which, though he make not such a stir in these times of less mortality, yet he will certainly take us all away, one or two at a time: and who can tell but he may soon be among the fewer hundreds that die now, as no man could tell whether he should be among the number of the thousands then?

Death is always an enemy, and always fighteth against us: and though he urge us not always with like fury and violence, yet it is a part of wisdom in us always to hear and to practise that which may secure us against the danger of death. And this is the lesson that the text teacheth us; a lesson that we ought to learn in our days of ease and comfort, that we may be able to practise it when the time of our last contest draweth nigh,—*Verily, verily I say unto you, If a man keep my saying he shall never see death.*

Wherein I pray you, first, to take notice who speaks the words:—the Author of truth; the Destroyer of death; He that hath vanquished it, and overcome the uttermost of its assaults; *Our*

Lord Jesus Christ, that hath overcome death, and brought life and immortality to light, he it is that giveth us this direction for the avoiding of the hurt of death.

Then, observe the manner of his speaking; *Verily, verily, I say unto you:* with an affirmation, earnest and redoubled. He never affirmed anything untrue; therefore that which he speaks is an undoubted verity. He never spake anything rashly; therefore that which he affirmed so earnestly is a weighty thing, and of great consequence. And, in the third place, observe that which I shall alone insist upon, the matter of his direction. This is here comprehended in a proposition which hath two parts — an antecedent and a consequent. There is a duty to be done, that is the antecedent; and there is the benefit that followeth upon the duty, that is the consequent. If a man keep my saying, he shall never see death.

You see now the only and perfect remedy against the evil of death; that is, to keep the word and saying of Christ. If any would know by what means he may be secured against the terrible of all terrible things (as one calleth death), here is a sure and certain rule for him; and he need not doubt it, for it cometh from the mouth of Christ: let him keep his saying, and death shall never do him harm.

I will first interpret these words unto you; and then make them good by Scripture and reason; and then apply them; and at the last commit myself and you and all to the blessing of God.

The saying of Christ, or the word of Christ, is the doctrine of his Gospel; which is so called, because he is the author of it, and the worker of that salvation which it declareth to us.

Now this doctrine of the Gospel hath two parts—the first acquainting us with our misery; the second, with the remedy. For as the bond and acquittance both specify the debt, but to different purposes,—the one to tie the debtor to the payment, the other to absolve and acquit him; even so the Law and the Gospel both declare the misery of man,—the one to tie it fast upon him, the other to loose him from it. The physician inquireth of the sickness, but only for the cure's sake. The judge passeth sentence of condemnation, and so doing, largely rehearseth the crime and punishment due to the offender: the pardon, likewise, makes mention of the fault and of the punishment, but to a different end. So the Gospel declareth man's misery, and borroweth so much of the law as may prove our wretched estate, and then showeth us that which is the main and principal part of it, the remedy of our souls.

And this first part of the Gospel St. Paul succinctly delivereth in a few words: *All have sinned and come short of the glory of God.* All have sinned, in such a manner and degree that they are fallen short of life eternal; for *the soul that sinneth it shall die.*

The second part of the Gospel is concerning

the remedy whereby a man may be helped against this misery; and for that purpose it showeth who helpeth us, and how he helpeth us, and also what is to be done by ourselves that we may obtain and enjoy this help.

The person that helpeth us is the Son, manifest in the flesh: the Son of God, taking our nature upon him, and clothing himself in the similitude of sinful flesh: the Eternal Son of the Father, assuming the very nature of man into the unity of his person. He being thus, in the same person, God and man, is the sole Redeemer; neither *is there any other name given under heaven whereby we must be saved*, but by his alone.

Again, it showeth us by what means he saveth us: as the Apostle speaks plainly enough in the next verse to that I spake of before, *being justified freely by his grace, through the redemption that is in Christ Jesus*. To the intent that he might free us from the wrath of God and the danger of eternal death, he vouchsafed to be *made sin for us;* he satisfied the justice of his Father by enduring the curse of the law, being born *under the law*, that he might suffer its penalty, and so make atonement for the sins of the whole world. Thus Christ, by this perfect satisfaction made to his Father, and by that perfect righteousness whereby he was subject to the law for our sakes, hath absolutely and fully delivered us from the power of sin and of death, and hath performed the work of our redemption; by the merit and value of which we are delivered and redeemed from this death, and from all other evils that cross our eternal happiness.

And, thirdly, the Gospel showeth us by what means we may become partakers of this happiness and redemption in Christ. It telleth us of three conditions to be observed by us as members of the covenant of grace; which conditions, if we faithfully keep them, we shall assuredly enjoy the promised mercy of God in the Gospel of Christ.

The FIRST condition is repentance; the SECOND is believing; and the THIRD is our new obedience. All and each of these is plainly expressed in the word of God.

FIRST: As for repentance, it is that wherewith John the Baptist began his preaching. It is that that our Saviour commanded his apostles to declare to the Jews,—*Repent, for the kingdom of heaven is at hand.* It is that which himself preached at the first, as St. Mark witnesseth. It is that which St. Paul began with when he came to the Athenians, saying,—*God now commandeth all men everywhere to repent.* This repentance is that which the Lord requireth absolutely of the sons of men, as a condition of the new covenant, the covenant of grace, and without which they cannot possibly be made partakers of the same.

And this repentance hath *four parts;* every one of which is so needful, that without it the rest are little worth.

First, lamenting for our sins, and being sorry

for our iniquities; as David said of himself, *I will declare my iniquity; I will be sorry for my sin.* And so the Apostle St. James expresseth it,—*Be afflicted, and mourn, and weep; let your laughter be turned to mourning, and your joy to heaviness.* Therefore Christ was sent to preach glad tidings to the prisoners and captives, and the opening of the prison to the prisoners, and to bring the oil of gladness to those that mourn in Sion. A man must first be a mourner in Sion, one that smiteth on his thigh, and saith with Jeremiah, *Woe is me, for my hurt, my wound is grievous!*

Secondly, to this sorrow must be joined acknowledgment and confession of sin to Almighty God, for so witnesseth the wise man,—*He that covereth his sins shall not prosper; but whoso confesseth, and forsaketh them, shall have mercy.* And St. John telleth us, *If we confess our sins, he is faithful and just to forgive us our sins.* So you see, confession, as well as sorrow, are absolutely required to obtain remission. A man must even arraign, and as it were, indict himself before God: he must plead guilty, acknowledge his trespasses, whatsoever they be, and judge himself worthy to be destroyed for them, or else he repenteth not, though he should weep his eyes out with mourning and lamentation. Many persons weep and groan for the effects of sin, who have no real sense of its sinfulness. Many feel or fear its consequences, who forget their own guilt and offence against God.

The *third* thing requisite is, a firm purpose of amendment of life. Whosoever will have God to accept his tears, and bend a favourable ear to his humiliation and confession, he must so acknowledge what evil he hath already done, that he put on a steadfast purpose of doing so no more. This direction our Saviour Christ giveth to all whom he pardoneth,—*Go, and sin no more.* St. Paul also teacheth,—*Let him that stole, steal no more.* There must be, I say, a settled purpose and a fixed determination in the soul of every man to cast off those transgressions that he hath confessed, and to return to them no more; at least no more to allow those sins that he hath acknowledged.

Lastly; there must be added to the former three, or else these will avail nothing, an earnest supplication to God for mercy and forgiveness, through the mediation of his well-beloved Son Jesus Christ. We must specially and particularly prefer our thoughts and desires to the Son, begging mercy at the Father's hands, for his sake alone. We must both pray for forgiveness and believe that we shall have it. So David, after the numbering of the people,—*I have sinned greatly in that I have done; and now, I beseech thee, O Lord, take away the iniquity of thy servant.* Thus did David when he renewed his repentance, and thus must all men do when they begin to repent,—*Have mercy upon me, according to the multitude of thy mercies, and blot out my transgressions.*

These are the parts of repentance; and this

is the first thing required at our hands, as the condition of the covenant of grace, without which we can never obtain life eternal. And this repentance consisteth, as I have shown you, of sorrow for sin, and acknowledgment of it to God, with a firm purpose of amendment, and earnest petition for pardon, for the sake of our Lord Jesus Christ.

And this is such a doctrine as the law, the covenant of works, never taught to the sons of men: nay, verily, it will not admit it: the law scorns, as it were, to admit repentance; for it absolutely excludeth all sin—and repentance implieth sin in all degrees and kinds. If thou hast once broken the law, repent or not repent, amend or not amend, be sorry or not sorry, thou shalt never be pardoned nor forgiven. It is a rough and stern schoolmaster, that will whip and scourge offending children, though they crave pardon and promise amendment never so earnestly. It is a rough creditor, that will throttle the debtor and cast him into prison, though he confess the debt, and be never so importunate in asking favour and patience.

But the covenant of grace, it is a sweet doctrine—a comfortable doctrine. Thou hast sinned, O man, and broken the law, and fallen from the favour of God, and all possibility of salvation in thyself; but come, be sorry for thy sin,—acknowledge it to thy Maker,—resolve to run on in it no longer,—cry to him for pardon, and he will graciously forgive thee.

This is a sweet doctrine you see, full of comfort and consolation: yet it is a doctrine that doth honour, as well to the justice of God, as to his grace and love. The Lord could not prescribe other conditions for receiving us to favour but that we should repent. What judge would so abuse mercy as, having passed sentence of death upon a malefactor, yet to pardon him and save him from the halter, if he be not sorry for his crime nor yet entreateth for mercy and favour, and neither confesseth that he hath offended nor promiseth never to do so again? There is no mercy and pardon for such an one, because mercy must not oppose justice. The blood of Christ, if it were shed a thousand times over, could never corrupt the justice of God: it may satisfy it, but not corrupt it; and the justice of God would be corrupted if it should admit an impenitent and hard-hearted sinner to favour. It were a violation of justice to bestow remission of punishment and an everlasting reward upon him who would never leave his sins, but still go on to offend God and trample under foot his authority. The blood of Christ is of that value that it satisfieth the justice of God, and so causeth him, upon the penitence and humiliation of a sinner, and on those conditions alone, to receive him again to grace and favour.

The SECOND part of the condition required on our side, for the obtaining of life by Christ, is Faith. This we are taught everywhere. *Believe in the Lord Jesus Christ*, saith the Apostle to the trembling jailor, *and thou shalt be saved:* and our Saviour teacheth, *This is the work of God, that ye believe on him whom he hath sent.*

This believing on Christ is, I suppose, nothing else but a staying and resting and depending and relying upon the merits and satisfaction of our blessed Saviour, by the virtue of which to obtain remission of sins and eternal life and all good things promised in the new covenant by God. He that goeth quite out of himself, forgetteth all his own actions, casteth behind him whatsoever seemed good in him, and wholly claspeth on Christ and cleaveth to him, stays on him, rests on him for the remission of sins, and for the favour of God, and for grace and salvation, this man believeth in the Lord Jesus: and this man performs that duty which makes him one with Christ, that causeth him to become a member of that mystical body whereof Christ is the head, and that causeth him to be one with the Father, and to be the child of God; for *by faith are we become the children of God.*

This faith in Christ the law doth not teach, the former covenant would not accept. What, to bring to the law the righteousness of another—the satisfaction of another—and to trust upon that to be entertained and received! The law rejects such a plea. Thou must pay thyself, in thy own person and with thy own goods; thou must yield perfect obedience to the law, and fully accomplish it in thy own person: it will not receive payment of another for thee: it will not accept satisfaction of the righteousness of another on thy behalf.

But, oh! the sweetness of the doctrine of the Gospel. If we have a treasurer that is able and willing to pay the debt, that will tender and make payment of it, it is one that will not, under the new covenant, be refused. He is not ashamed to call us brethren, and as a brother, he redeems and ransoms us. He giveth us the means of discharging the burdens, so that we only give him the glory, and be not so absurd as to mix any action of our own to that payment that he hath made, fully and completely, for us. This is a doctrine of sweetness and favour and great compassion, that though we cannot do it of ourselves, yet God hath promised and engaged in the covenant of grace to accept us if our surety will do it for us, so that we give our surety the glory of being a perfect and able paymaster, and rely wholly on his satisfaction.

The LAST part of the condition on our side is, that we yield new obedience to the law, perfectly to obey it; to which we are tied by the former covenant.

But now this is the obedience of the Gospel, a thing far different from the obedience of the law that was formerly required in the old covenant: there a man was tied and bound to obey perfectly, fully, completely, without any defect: in a word, he must *pay the uttermost farthing:* he must do his duty, his whole duty, in all the parts and degrees, with all fulness of perfection, absolutely, without any defect or want, without any imperfection at all. An impossible labour for corrupted man; a service that none cculd ever reach to, all having lost those abilities that God gave man at the first. But then cometh the sweet Gospel, the doctrine of grace and favour, of tender compassion, and saith thus,—*If ye be willing and obedient, ye shall eat the fat of the land. If ye, through the Spirit, do mortify the deeds of the body, ye shall live: but if ye,* though never so much in appearance, under the covenant of grace, *live after the flesh, ye shall die.*

Ye see, then, that new obedience is required, absolutely, as a condition of the Gospel, for the obtaining of everlasting happiness, for the escaping of death: and St. John saith,—*If we walk in the light, we have fellowship one with another, and the blood of Christ purgeth us from all sin.* So that this walking in the light and new obedience, is absolutely required of all those that intend to be made partakers of Christ and his benefits. They must give up their souls and bodies as instruments of His glory, and not serve sin any longer in the lusts thereof. They must not give their members as weapons of unrighteousness to sin, but live as becometh them that are one with Christ; mortifying all the lusts of the flesh, and quickening themselves, or being quickened by him, to practise all good things required in his word, and to obey all his commands, which were first written in Adam's heart, and then in tables of stone. This new obedience is the same, in substance, that was required in the former covenant; but now with a gracious acceptation of *endeavour* after perfection, instead of perfection itself. The former tied us to the obedience of all that was required in all fulness, and then promised acceptance; but the obedience that the Gospel requires is a striving to this perfection in truth and sincerity; a desiring and labouring after it, which if we do, it promiseth acceptance through the perfection of Christ, in and by which our imperfections are done away.

Now, brethren, you understand what this saying of the Lord Christ's is, by virtue of the keeping of which we can alone be secured from the hurt of death.

What is it to keep Christ's saying? It is to inform our judgments in the understanding of these truths, and to assent to them as truths; to practise and follow them; to do the duties which we have heard; to practise the doctrines of repentance, and faith, and new obedience.

I confess our Saviour doth include all in this —*Repent and believe the Gospel:* but for the more clear explaining of it, we make new obedience a thing of itself, and not included in the doctrine of repentance. For obedience is the acting and fulfilling of that whereof repentance is a resolute wishing and desiring. A man cannot possibly rest on Christ for salvation till he hath so asked pardon, as he resolveth amendment; and when he hath this resolution and relieth on Christ for the pardon of his sin, then from him he receiveth power to amendment of life, and so his purpose cometh to action and his desire to execution. Herein only is the difference between repentance and faith, and obedience; obedience springeth of repentance, and is brought about by faith.

This, then, is the doctrine of the Gospel, the saying of Christ; and to keep it, is to know and believe and to follow it: as Christ saith, — *If ye know these things* — there is one part of the duty, — *happy are ye if ye do them,* — there is another part; for they can never be done except they be done as known.

Let us say somewhat now of the second part of the proposition: viz. the benefit that followeth upon the duty of keeping Christ's saying, and for the obtaining of which the duty is necessary: — *he shall never see death.*

What is it to see death? and what death is meant here?

To see good things, in the Scripture phrase, is as much, oftentimes, as to enjoy them, to have the benefit and commodity of them, to receive them, to entertain them; *Without holiness no man shall see God;* that is, no man shall enjoy God: *Blessed are the poor in spirit, for they shall see God;* that is, they shall enjoy God.

On the contrary, to see a thing that is termed evil, is to be annoyed with it; to have the hurt of it lying upon a man, and pressing him down; as they (in Jeremiah) said, *Let us go into Egypt, where we shall not see sword nor famine;* meaning that they should not suffer those evils: so, by seeing death, is meant suffering hurt and damage from death.

And by death is meant both *natural*, and, as we may term it, *supernatural*, that is, *eternal* death. For the keeping of Christ's sayings so freeth men from the latter, as that they never come near it; and it so freeth them from the former, that they never can suffer harm or loss by it. The first death, which is the separation of the body from the soul, is no death, if it separate not from God; which it can never do if a man keep the sayings of Christ: therefore, though his body be taken from his soul, yet he seeth not death so as to have any hurt by it; he feeleth no ill by it; nay, it is good to him, for it is a passage from misery to rest and felicity.

Thus ye have these words interpreted to you, as faithfully as I know how.

And now I will make proof of the doctrine thus explicated: namely, that thus to keep Christ's sayings, to know and follow the doctrine of the Gospel, is the only sure way to escape the danger and hurt of death.

St. Peter acknowledged as much when he said to the Lord Jesus Christ that he had *the words of eternal life;* for then, he that keepeth those words is certainly safe against the hurt of death. So the angel spake to the apostles whom the Pharisees had imprisoned, when he brought them forth of prison, and bade them speak to the people *the words of this life:* for since Christ's doctrine is the word of life, it must needs follow that the keeping thereof is a perfect antidote against the poison of death. And St. Peter, when he gave an account to the rest of the apostles of his going to the Gentiles, said, that an angel appointed Cornelius to send for him, that he might speak words to him, whereby himself and his house *should* be saved: and those words which cause a man to be saved, you know, will give him freedom enough from death.

The point being thus proved by express texts, I come now to show two reasons for it. The first reason is delivered by the Apostle St. John, in the first epistle and second chapter, where he saith,—*Let that abide in you which ye have heard from the beginning* (that is, the doctrine of the Gospel which Christ taught,—the *sayings* of Christ): *if that which ye have heard from the beginning shall remain in you, ye also shall continue in the Son and in the Father.* He that hath fellowship with the Son and with the Father can never see death, for God is the Fountain of life: therefore those that are one with him, and continue in him, cannot see death; no more than he can be overwhelmed with darkness that is where the sun shineth fully, no more than the body can be dead as long as it hath communion with the soul. Those in whom the word of Christ remaineth and stayeth, they are assured that they shall remain with the Father and the Son; and therefore, being united to that that is life—God the Father and the Son, it is impossible that they ever should be hurt by the first death, or at all taste of the last.

The second reason is, that the word of Christ freeth him in whom it remaineth from the power and hurt of sin, bringing to him both remission of sins and sanctification; and being free from sin, the cause of death, it is easy to conclude that he shall be freed from death itself. Let a man's debt be satisfied, let the favour of the prince be obtained and a pardon granted, the prison shall not hold him long, he shall never be brought to the place of execution, but when his gyves are knocked off he is set at liberty: so, when we are freed from the power and guilt of sin by the work of the Spirit of God, it is impossible that death should lay hold upon us, as his prisoner, to carry us to the dungeon of hell, and to hold us under the wrath of God, and that fiery indignation of his which causeth hell to be hell. Therefore, certainly, the words of Christ are an undoubted truth, and we must rest upon them without distrust or wavering,—*He that keepeth my sayings shall never see death:* for the knowledge, and believing, and obeying the doctrine of Christ, is the only way to escape the hurt and ill of death itself.

Let us make some application of this doctrine to our souls.

First, to stir us up to a right hearty thankfulness unto Almighty God, who is pleased to cast our times and days into that age, and those places, where the doctrine of the Gospel, this *saying* of our blessed Saviour, is so clearly and plainly and evidently laid open to us, so frequently and earnestly pressed upon our souls; where the Lord cometh to declare unto us the way of life, where he scoreth us out a path that will bring us quite out of the clutches and danger of death: this is the happiness of our present age and place wherein we live. The grace and mercy of our loving God hath so disposed of us that we do not live in times of Paganism and ignorance, when there was no news of Christ; nor yet in places of popish darkness, where the doctrine of the Gospel is so mixed and darkened with tricks and devices of man that Christ cannot clearly be seen. It is our happiness, I say, that we do not live in those places and times where either paganism or popery, with their darkness, covered Christ from men, and caused them that they could not clearly see him nor hear him, and so not keep his sayings. Now grace is offered; light is tendered to us: we may be saved, we may escape the danger of damnation, if the fault be not solely and wholly in our own carelessness and wilfulness and neglect and abuse of the means that God hath afforded us.

The heathen men that have not heard of Christ cannot possibly attain to life, as far as we can judge by the Scripture. And it is very difficult for the Papists, that hear so darkly, and are told of the doctrine of the Gospel with so many sophistications, to come to the knowledge of salvation. But for us that have the saying of Christ so plainly and carefully taught and revealed unto us, we may be saved and may easily see the way to obtain forgiveness of all our sins. So we go beyond them in blessings, and ought to exceed them in love and thankfulness.

Oh, blessed be the name of the everliving God, that beside the peace and plenty and other temporal benefits wherewith he hath crowned this unworthy nation of ours, he hath added this blessing of blessings, this king of favours, to give us so clear a revelation of the doctrine of salvation by faith in Christ alone. Blessed be his name, and let your hearts say *Amen* to this thanksgiving; and let it be one part of your endeavour this day to give solemn praise for this unspeakable mercy of his, in making you live in the days of light, and in the bright sunshine of the Gospel; and you shall thus prove yourselves to have begun to keep Christ's saying, if you be thankful for his making of it known unto you, and for writing it in your hearts.

Next, I beseech you, let me take boldness to reprove—I fear, a great number of you—of a sin, whereof I will make it appear that you are guilty. Men there are that make large promises to themselves that they shall never be damned; they shall not go to hell; they hope death shall not have power to drag them from this world to the place of darkness.

Dost thou hope so? Come, render a reason of thy hope. To hope without ground is to deceive one's self with extreme folly. As for example — there are a number of prisoners in Newgate, or in some other prison: if these should hope for some man of great wealth to pay their debts and to save them from hanging, would they not be arrant fools, except they could show some ground for their hope, and some reason for their expecting such a kindness? Thou that hopest thou shalt never see death, come, answer God in thy conscience,—Dost thou keep the saying of Christ, or no? Where is the knowledge of the doctrine of the Gospel? Dost thou believe that which concerns thee touching *thy misery*, and so apply that to thyself to make thee a penitent sinner? Dost thou believe the doctrine concerning *the remedy*, and so apply that to thyself to make thee perfect thy repentance, by being not only grieved for sin but taking boldness to confess it and to ask pardon, and by framing thyself to amendment of life and new obedience? Dost thou, I say, know this doctrine, and so know it as to practise it? Then hope and spare not: the more thou hopest the better thy hope is; and the stronger and surer it is the more thou glorifiest God and the more it shall comfort thee.

But oh, unhappy man, if thou findest not in thyself the care and power, in some measure, to do these things, cursed be thy hopes because they be disgraceful to Almighty God, tending to make him a liar and an unjust person, and because they are dangerous to thine own soul, tending to rock thee asleep in the cradle of security.

Cursed be those unsound and sandy-built hopes of most men, that never yet applied themselves to confess and lament their sins; that never applied themselves to crave pardon and to resolve upon amendment; that never studied to throw themselves into the arms of God's mercy in Christ for pardon; that never intended to *mortify the deeds of the body* and to *subdue the flesh* with the lusts thereof: and yet they hope they shall not be damned. Thou mayest as well hope that the Devil shall come out of hell into heaven, as that thou shalt go out of earth to heaven. If thy hope be not grounded upon the workings of these graces, making thee sad and penitent and careful to rest wholly upon Christ for salvation, leading thee diligently in the study of newness of life; except, I say, thy hope be thus grounded, it is the vainest thing in the world, and it will never do thee good at thy last hour.

Brethren, give me leave to tell you that there are two gospels in the world: the Gospel of our Lord Jesus Christ, and the gospel of Beelzebub—the gospel of the Devil that comes from hell and tendeth to bring men thither. Christ's Gospel is, *Repent and believe and obey, and be saved.* The Devil's gospel is, *Say* you believe, make yourselves imagine that you have faith, and then never care for repentance nor obedience, and you shall be saved. Christ's Gospel is summed up thus by the prophets,—Return to him and live. But the Devil's goeth thus,—Assure thyself thou shalt live, though thou care not for repentance.

Oh, let not the Devil beguile you with that false, counterfeit gospel of his ; whosoever leaneth to it shall find it, like the author of it, a liar ; and when he hath trusted to it, that confidence and hope of his shall be as the spider's web ; the besom of destruction shall sweep it and him down to the depth of hell. Death shall have dominion over him, and carry him from this present world to the region of darkness into eternal torment. He shall see death in the grimness and terribleness of it ; he shall feel it in all the extremity that the wrath of God can inflict upon the children of disobedience.

Thirdly, I have to command and require you, in the name of the Lord Jesus Christ, that you apply yourselves to a thing tending so much to the honour of him and to the commodity and comfort of your own souls.

I have showed you that Jesus Christ hath revealed a way how you should escape the danger of death eternal, and the hurt of death natural. I beseech you now fall a-doing at once, as you have now been busied in hearing. To what purpose is it that you flock to hear sermons and throng to receive the word, except you lay it up in your hearts, and apply yourselves to practise? If thou hast not begun before, now begin : if thou hast begun before, now resolve to proceed with more life and courage. Either begin or persist in the practice of the doctrine of the Gospel.

If thou hast not yet repented, I require thee, in the name of the living God, to make this hour the first beginning of thy repentance; and apply thyself to lay the foundation of that work before thou lay thy head to sleep. Go and call to mind thy sins, and make thy cheeks wet, at least thy heart heavy, for the multitude of thy great offences: down on thy knees in thy closet; make thy confession of them to God; sigh for them; mourn for them; labour to weep for them; afflict thy soul with great sorrow and remorse: then cry for pardon and remission. As the thief begs at the bar for mercy, so do thou for the forgiveness of thy sins through Christ Jesus; and put upon thyself a firm resolution and steadfast purpose to go on no more in the ways of wickedness, to practise gross sins no more, nor no more to allow any sin that thou knowest to be a sin, though it seem never so small.

Do thus, my brethren, and then you may and will (it will follow almost of itself) rest on Christ for salvation. He that so seeth his own sins as unfeignedly to lament for them and to judge himself before God, if he apprehend the truth of the doctrine of the Gospel, he cannot, for his life, but come on amain and throw himself down before Christ, to embrace and receive and entertain him, and lie in his bosom.

And that man cannot for his life, when he seeth the sweetness of the grace of God in Christ, but resolve to obey him, and determine to walk in the ways of holiness, and take pains, and use industry, for the overcoming of all sin. And by the virtue of Christ, he shall prosper in this.

I beseech you therefore, set yourselves a-work about this great business, to get *repentance* and *faith* and *new obedience:* it is much more needful than sleep, than meat, than attire: there is nothing in the world so requisite for thy welfare as these things.

Scrape thou riches together, in the same quantity that Solomon did, and ten thousand times more—yet death shall take them all from thee, within an hundred or half an hundred years. Get wisdom—yet thou shalt see death after a few years. Take pleasure with as much greediness as Solomon did once, when he forgat himself for a space—yet soon thou shalt see death. These things that the foolish world hunts after with so much earnestness of desire, will not secure thee from the sight of the King of fears. But if thou once get faith and repentance and new obedience, then thou hast obtained that that all the riches and honour and pleasures and learning, or whatsoever seemeth desirable in the world, will not help their possessors to.

What will you do, brethren; grovel still on the earth, and still be mad after things that perish with the using? or will you now begin to think—I must die; I must shake hands with that dismal enemy, pale-faced death, that is able to strike terror into the strongest heart and amazement into the stoutest soul that is not well confirmed: and if this death find me destitute of true repentance and faith and new obedience, it will seize upon me and drag me before the judgment-seat of God, where I shall be henced away with a malediction and a curse, and be forced to take my place with the devil and his angels in unquenchable flames? Oh what shall I do then to secure myself from the great, from the strong arm of death? I will repent; I will begin now: Lord, draw me, help me that I may do it. I will believe now: Lord, do thou work faith in me, thou that requirest it. I will obey: Lord, enable me to perform such needful duties as thou commandest me. Shall this be your practice when you come home? Will you thus study to practise repentance, and faith, and obedience? and study to cry and call for it, and use all your endeavour? or what will you do? Will you be as idle and careless, as negligent and slothful in making after these graces, as before? Will you be as greedy of the transitory vanities of this life as in former times? Oh, abuse not the word of God: if thou go out of the church without a full purpose to apply thyself, from henceforward, either to begin or to proceed in the practice of the saying of Christ, then—cursed art thou in thy hearing; cursed is this hour that thou hast spent and thy misbestowed labour, thou dissembling hypocrite.

But if thou labour to practise this of Christ, namely, to keep his sayings, to repent, to believe, and to obey, then blessed art thou in thy hearing, and in thy doing, and in thy obedience:

happy is the time and the place and all things that concur to draw thee to so needful a work.

I pray, brethren, set not your labour upon gold and silver and money and trash: not upon the pleasure and delights and contentments of the world, nor on any other earthly thing: but mainly and principally, above all things, let your chief care be for faith and repentance and obedience. If you strive for these things earnestly and heartily and constantly, as sure as the Lord is in heaven he will bestow them upon you, and with them the benefit of benefits, freedom from death.

And now, *lastly*, I shall speak comfort to those few that are in the world, that keep these sayings of Christ. Let them be of good comfort: if their capital enemy, the King of fears and the King of afflictions, be held from a possibility of doing them harm, nothing can harm them. Him that death cannot hurt, pain cannot hurt, poverty and disgrace cannot hurt, nothing can hurt him. You know, if the king of an army be reconciled to a place he will keep his soldiers from spoiling and burning and destroying that place. If death be put out of power to do thee hurt, and God be reconciled in Christ because thou keepest the saying of Christ, nothing can hurt thee; thou art the happiest man under the sun.

Why should the poor, sad, afflicted, grieved, mourning, lamenting, saints of God, envy them that are rich and jolly and merry worldlings any of their pleasures and profits, any of those things wherewith they, like idiots, make themselves laughed at? What! hath not God given thee better things than these, that thou shouldest murmur and whine and weep for want of them?

Remember what St. James saith: *Let the brother of low degree* (that is abased and despised in the world) *rejoice in that he is exalted.* This is the exaltation of the saints; Christ, writing his Spirit in their hearts and inclining them through the operation of his Spirit and the powerful work of his word, to repent and believe, hath freed them from the danger of death and made them heirs of eternal happiness and of that bliss that no tongue can express nor no heart conceive. This is thy happiness. It is not to be rich, nor to be great; for these cannot deliver the owner from the hurt of death natural, nor from the danger of death eternal: but to have faith and repentance and obedience; this is riches and exaltation: for he that hath them shall not alone escape the dungeon of eternal darkness, but be advanced to the palace of everlasting felicity. The saint is the happy man; the penitent believer and true practiser of Christian obedience, he is the sole and only happy man under the sun: for whatsoever storm he suffereth in this present world, he shall certainly escape death and obtain glory.

Bless God and bless thyself in God; magnify him, rejoice in him, take comfort in thy lot and portion. Death, that devoureth kings, that destroyeth emperors, that conquers captains and men of valour, shall not be able to approach thee for thy hurt; for thou keepest the saying of the Lord Jesus Christ. Rejoice, I say, in this; magnify him that is the author of it; and account thyself happy that thou hast received from him so excellent a gift, as to be in some measure enabled to *keep his saying*.

Yea, if it were so, may some Christian heart object, then I should esteem myself the happiest man alive: but alas, where is this repentance you describe? where is this new obedience in me, that still, still find myself captive and thrall to this and that and the other lust and passion and corruption? Where is, I say, that repentance, when I find so much sin? where is that faith, when I find so much wavering and quaking, so much aptness to distrust and almost to despair?

Where is it? It may be in thy heart, for all thy complaining: tell me, when thou findest those corruptions whereof thou speakest, and for which thou exclaimest thus against thyself, dost thou allow them or not? dost thou confess them and lament them, or not? Art thou sorry for them? Is it such a sorrow as draws thee to God and drives thee out of thyself? such as makes thee to fall before him and judge thyself worthy to be damned, and to submit to his justice? Is it such a sorrow as makes thee confess, and then purpose amendment? such as makes thee cry to him for power and strength? such as makes thee rest on him for ability? Dost thou determine still, still to amend that which still troubleth thee? Dost thou continue to fight with the lusts of thy flesh by the spiritual weapons that God hath ordained for thee? Then I say to thee thy repentance, thy faith, thy new obedience, may be true, though they be weak. When a man hath a shaking, palsied hand, yet it is a hand. A sick, weak man that lies crying and groaning, and can scarce turn himself between the sheets, is yet a man, a living man. A poor child that is new-born and hath nothing almost that discovereth reason, but the shape of a man, that poor child is a reasonable creature. Faith beginneth with weak apprehensions and faint leanings on Christ. Deep godly sorrow and other parts of repentance may bring small fruits at first, and amendment of life may proceed but gradually; but if it be true and sincere, and constant,—if thou go on and continue, daily renewing thy repentance and obedience and faith, and striving by God's help to get the increase of these graces and to be upright and sincere in them, then thou art blessed notwithstanding thy weakness: take comfort in a little, and be thankful for it: God will give more; and the only way to get more is to take comfort in a good measure in that thou hast; and the way to take comfort is to labour to increase these graces. Let not the weak, trembling, feeble Christian be troubled in mind as if he had no grace, because he hath but a little; as if he did not at all keep Christ's sayings, because he keepeth them but a little. He is a scholar in the school, that is but just entered: he is a student in the college, that beginneth but in a low book with the first rudiments of logic; and he is a member of a family, that began to be an apprentice but yesterday, and comes not yet to a deep knowledge of his art and mystery, but is glad to do sorry work.

Believe it, brethren, there may be great conceits of repentance and believing and obeying, that may make a man good in his own eyes, and yet be altogether false. There may be a small measure of repentance; but if one be humbled in the smallness of that measure, and labour and desire and pray and beg for the increase of that measure, and take pains to edify himself in it by the means of God, then it is true and upright, and shall save him.

It is not with the covenant of grace as it was with that of works. The covenant of works, the law, required perfection of obedience to all the things prescribed: a man must not only love God, but love God perfectly. But the Gospel satisfieth itself with accepting earnest endeavour to the thing required. If there be repentance, though it be not in full perfection; if thou believe, though not with the fullest measure of believing; if thou obey, though not in the highest degree of obedience; this Gospel, this sweet, this favourable, gracious doctrine, giveth thee consolation enough. Go home therefore, comforted in the beginning, and resolve to proceed, and know that thou shalt enjoy that which Christ hath promised — freedom from condemnation; *Thou shalt never see death.*

SERMON VII.

THE PLATFORM OF CHARITY;

OR,

THE LIBERAL MAN'S GUIDE.

GALATIANS, VI. 10.

"AS WE HAVE THEREFORE OPPORTUNITY, LET US DO GOOD UNTO ALL MEN, ESPECIALLY UNTO THEM WHO ARE OF THE HOUSEHOLD OF FAITH."

IN the sixth verse of this chapter the Apostle begins to persuade the Galatians to beneficence, and in the ninth verse he giveth them great encouragement in this course: *Let us not be weary,* saith he, *in well doing: for in due season we shall reap, if we faint not.* The words I have now read to you are an inference upon that which went before. Seeing that, if we hold out, we shall in due time reap the harvest of our labour, therefore *as we have opportunity, let us do good unto all, &c.*

As we have opportunity. The old translation reads it, as we have *time;* but the word signifieth more: there is a *chronos* and a *kairos*; a time, and an opportunity of time: there is a time, taken in the largest sense; and there is an opportunity of time, that a man may make to himself for the performing of any duty that God requires of him. This must be understood with reference to what was spoken of before,—*We shall reap, if we faint not.* There is a time for all things: a time to sow, and a time to reap. Now is the sowing time: let us, while it lasts, embrace the opportunity of doing good.

Do good. This precept is of large extent; of as large an extent as the law. All is good that is agreeable to God's will revealed. But in this place it is limited to some particular acts of beneficence towards men, towards the servants of God, which are then said to be good deeds, when both the action and the affection are according to the rule.

First, there must be deeds. It is not enough to speak good or to mean good; we must *do* good. Solomon compares such charity as goes no further than outward expression to clouds and winds without rain.

And *secondly*, these actions must have a good rise: they must proceed from a good affection, or else they deserve not the name of good actions. Make the tree good, and the fruit shall be good; the actions are not good if the affections be nought. And therefore the same God that requires beneficence, commands benevolence also; a good will as well as a good work: he would have men become tender-hearted, and put on bowels of compassion; that they should sympathise with others, and be like affectioned to them; to mourn with those that mourn, and to be with those that are bound as being bound with them. This our Saviour called being merciful: *Be ye therefore merciful, as your Father also is merciful:* he saith not only—do works of mercy; but, be merciful: do such works from a merciful heart, from bowels of compassion that yearn towards those that are in necessity. That is the second thing.

But then, *thirdly,* these actions and these affections whence they rise, must both hold conformity with the law. There is no good but what is conformable to the rule of goodness, that is the written word of God; and therefore all those will-worships and almsdeeds which are done to be seen of men, are not good works, because they want that good rule that should uphold and make them so. Good deeds, then, are such actions as rise from a sanctified affection and receive ground and warrant from God's will, revealed in his holy word.

There is yet a third term.—Do good *to all men.*

What, doth the Apostle mean that every man should receive the fruits of our beneficence? There are some men notoriously idle and wicked, and rather to be punished than relieved. The Apostle means not such, for he giveth a caution: *If any man work not, neither shall he eat.* Relieve not him that hath ability to get and will live idly and unprofitably, but do good to all men, that is, to all men so far as you see them in extreme want, and unable to help themselves. If their lawful necessities call upon your charity, then all men must be looked to; but especially the household of faith.

By household of faith is here meant the multitude of true believers; and not only those that dwell near us and about us, but those that are dispersed throughout the whole earth,—all members of the church of God. All the saints of God, in what difference or distance soever one from another, yet they are of the same household together, of the same Church of God. So the Church is called *the House of God.* Christ so speaketh of the church triumphant,—*In my Father's house are many mansions:* and St. Paul exhorts Timothy how he should carry himself in the *House* of God—that is, in the church militant. As for the saints that be above us, they need not our good works and actions, therefore the household here intended is the church militant, and that is called God's household, because there is such a communion among believers as among those that abide in the same house, that live under the same government, that eat at the same table.

So then you have the meaning of all the parts of the text, which is no more than this: Take those opportunities which you can obtain to do such actions of mercy as tend to the relief of those that want them. *Whatsoever thy hand findeth to do, do it with thy might,* or the occasion may slip by unprofitably. If there be extreme necessity, do good to all, but if you may make choice of persons to whom you shall do good, then choose the household of faith.

Thus you have the substance and the meaning of the words, and in them you may observe these three parts :—

The FIRST is a determination or limitation of time, to which the saints are tied in the performance of the duties that are enjoined them,—*As you have opportunity*, and while you have time.

SECONDLY, there is a declaration of duty,—*do good.*

THIRDLY, there is a description of the persons to whom this good must be done—first, more generally, *do good to all;* and then more particularly, *especially to the household of faith.*

First then, embrace the times and opportunities of doing good. You shall not always have life to do good; and it may be, if you have life, you shall not always enjoy means and ability to do good. While you have life therefore, while you enjoy means, embrace these opportunities: do good.

Do good while you have life; let your good works go before you. Do things while you live, and defer not the performance of them till your death. *Make to yourselves friends of the mammon of unrighteousness, that when ye fail, they may receive you into everlasting habitations.* Not only that which is unlawfully *gotten* is called unrighteous mammon, but that which is unlawfully kept is unrighteous to you; and if you would dispose of it rightly, do so now, that when your time and your worldly possessions come to an end, you may be received into everlasting habitations. It was the folly of the five virgins that they took not the opportunity of life (while the Bridegroom tarried): they left all to the last, and hoped to effect that in a trice which would have given them employment through all the days of their lives; and therefore they came short of heaven: the gates were shut against them, as you see, when the Bridegroom came.

If any man imagine, because it is said, *Blessed are the dead that die in the Lord, for they rest from their labours, and their works do follow them,* that therefore it matters not so long as a man doth good at his death, though he may have neglected the ways of goodness all his life; let him know that in this text is not meant the actions of men, but the fruits of their actions. *Their works follow them,* not the works they have deferred until death, but the fruit of those works they did while they were living, and of which they received not the benefit before. It is more good and pleasant by far to have the actions go before and the fruits and comfortable effects to succeed and follow after.

But if any man yet suppose that he may make that up in his will, which he hath neglected all his life long, and though he have lived miserably, covetously, and unprofitably, may hope by charitable bequests to make at the last fit compensation and satisfaction for neglect of former duties, this is a pitiful delusion; for this is a sign of infidelity,—that a man will not trust God, for fear he should want in his life-time: what is the reason else that he defers doing good in health, unless it be for fear of wanting himself? such distrust hath he in the providence of God. Besides, the same God which bids thee do good when thou hast opportunity, and while thou enjoyest the advantage of life, he expects it now; and it were no good deed, no gift at all, to resign that which thou canst keep no longer: this were no sacrifice acceptable to God, that costs thee nothing. It may be truly said of many that neglect the times of doing good while they live, and would supply the defect when they die by the large benevolence of their wills, their *will* is good but their deed is nought.

But thou must not only take the time of thy life,—thou must use also the opportunity of thy means and of thy estate, while there is yet a price in thine hand. The time may come when you may desire to do good but cannot, wanting an estate and opportunities whereby to do it. It is the vanity of men that they still forbear and stay while their estates increase, pretending that they shall be better able to do good, and to extend themselves more largely by and by: but why wilt thou trust in a thing of nought? Riches make themselves wings as an eagle, and fly away; thou hast them now in thy possession and retainest them fast in hold, but presently they are departed. Solomon, when he exhorteth men to cast their bread upon the waters, he gives them this reason,—*Thou knowest not what evils God will bring upon the earth.* Thou knowest not what judgments and calamities God intends to bring upon that nation where thou livest, upon the city, upon the family wherein thou dwellest, upon thy person or estate.

Observe the case of Job: he discourseth of this very point. He was now a man stripped of all he had,—but the other day the richest man in the East. In a moment all his goods, his cattle, his children, were taken away. Yet there was one thing that ministered comfort in the day of his affliction, and it was this: saith he,—*If I have caused the eyes of the widow to fail, or have eaten my morsel alone, and the fatherless hath not eaten thereof*, &c.: if I have not done thus and thus, then let the Lord's fiercest judgment fall upon me: but herein consists my comfort—my conscience bears me witness, that when I had wealth and estate, and enjoyed the goods of this life, I did good; I was *a father to the poor, feet to the lame, and eyes to the blind.* I did all the good that lay within the compass of my power when I had the means to do it.

Little dost thou know, whosoever thou art, how soon God may turn his hand upon thee, when thou mayest be as Job was on the dunghill, deprived of all comforts. What should be thy consolation then? that *when thou hadst* wealth thou didst good with it. It will but add to thy affliction, if having had great possessions, thou didst neither glorify God thereby nor do good to men.

Now this point serveth to the reproof of many

to whom God hath given the price into their hands, but they want hearts to embrace the opportunities of doing good. Remember what Solomon saith: *Say not unto thy neighbour, Go, and come again, and to-morrow I will give; when thou hast it by thee.* The Lord will not only have a man not *deny* to do good, but he would have him not *delay* to do it; and how often does it arrive that men delay their purposes until they lose them altogether?

Nothing is more ordinary, than in cases of distress and sickness for men both to purpose truly and to promise heartily, that if God will deliver them from such and such fears and dangers they will perform these and these acts of mercy. But how many of these promises and purposes come to nothing! They flattered the Lord with their lips; they vowed, but they have not paid. Is it not so with many of us? Have we not promised many things,—one to become more liberal and bountiful; another, to make restitution of unjust gain; another to be more gentle and courteous towards his weaker brethren; and the Lord hath waited, week after week, month after month, year after year, and yet you are the same men, as far as ever from accomplishing your promise to God, or rendering him his due.

Again, let this stir up every one of us not only to *take* opportunities of doing good, but also to *seek* them. In Judges, xix. we see a good old man, as he observes a stranger passing in the streets, taking occasion to question his wants, not waiting till the man complain. We see also David inquiring if there were any of the house of Saul to whom he might show kindness, for Jonathan's sake. So should we do. Is there any of the household of faith unto whom I may show kindness, for the Lord's sake? He hath been better to us than Jonathan was to David, and yet we are much more backward in thankfulness than David was to Jonathan. We ought always to inquire after men's needs, that we lose no opportunity of doing good.

So much for the opportunity. I come now to the SECOND point of the doctrine:—*Let us do good.*

I told you what this goodness is that the Apostle here intendeth: it is a relieving of those that are in necessity,—and it is the especial duty of God's servants to employ themselves in this wise.

Men are apt to think they do well whenever they spare any little trifle out of their abundance for the relief of their fellows, and not very ill in omitting such deeds of mercy. They conceive charity to be a thing of choice, and not a duty of necessity. They agree that it is a duty to lay up wealth, but they forget that is a still greater duty to lay it out as stewards for God. And here is the reason why there are such lavish expenses bestowed upon every vanity, that the portion which by virtue of God's commandment belongeth to the poor is swallowed up. It is spent by some in excessive apparel—by others in superfluity of diet—by others in hawks and hounds and dogs; and thus is the portion of the poor consumed, and themselves, for want of the same, exposed to all the misery that the world can inflict. What is the reason of it, but that there is naturally, in the heart of every man, rebellion against God, so that they will employ their estates in any way rather than to that purpose for which they are given by God? Oh what account shall such be able to make at the day of judgment, when the books shall be opened, and they shall find that the money they have wasted is all set down by God, though *they* have never troubled themselves to keep account thereof? What shall they answer when the diaries and passages of their life shall be examined? *Item,* so much for a feast. *Item,* on such a day, for such another feast; and many a hundred *items* for as many hundred feasts, while thousands of the servants of God have endured extreme want, because thou couldest find nothing for one of them in a corner of thy purse! What, nothing for the servants of God? Are they so empty while your houses appear so full? live they so poorly while you are richly clad? can you spare nothing for Christ and the suffering members of his household all this time? Oh my beloved, remember what St. James saith: *Go to now, ye rich men, weep and howl, for your garments are moth-eaten* whereon you have bestowed so much cost; *and your gold and silver is cankered; and the rust of them shall be a witness against you and shall eat your flesh, as it were fire.*

But how shall a man, in his actions of mercy

and bounty and liberality, make it appear that he doth good? for this is the main point to be endeavoured after. Take, briefly, some helps in this.

And *first,* he must do what he doth *justly;* he must not, out of mercy to one, injure another; he must not do evil that good may follow; he must level his charity by his own ability.

You see how Zaccheus gives: *If I have wronged any man, I restore it fourfold; and half of my goods I give to the poor:* that is, I will first make full restoration of what I have unjustly gotten, and then, of the remainder I will give half to the poor.

Secondly, he must give wisely; for this is the mark of a man fearing God,—*A good man showeth favour, and lendeth, he will guide his affairs with discretion.* So must thou order thine affairs, or perchance, thou mayest give that which is not thine own, so that another man may lose by thy liberality. Also, thou must consider wisely of those to whom thou wilt afford relief. There are some persons, as I told you before, who ought not to be relieved, except in extreme necessity. Extend thy benevolence to those of the household of faith. Give unto Christ, and to the naked and hungry members that belong unto him, and thou shalt not want a sweet and comfortable return of thy charity.

Again, as it must be done justly and wisely, so, if we desire to do good in relieving, we must do it simply, in the simplicity and plainness of our hearts: *Let him that distributeth, do it in simplicity*, saith the Apostle. What is this simplicity? When a man looks up to God, and respects God only in his actions of charity, and makes no other reckoning of any outward object, then he looks with a single eye: for the eye may be said to be single when it views but one object at a time. A double-minded man, he looks up to God, and yet carries some respect to the outward honour which he expects of the world, and more, oftentimes, to the world than to God. But he that desires to bestow his benevolence with a purpose to receive recompense from above, let him do it for his sake that commands it, and reflect upon God in all things. *This is the testimony of our conscience*, saith the Apostle, *that in simplicity and godly sincerity we have had our conversation in the world;* not affecting the praise of men, but aiming to approve ourselves to God in that we do. This is that that Christ advised his disciples: *Let not thy right hand know what thy left hand doeth.*

Lastly, as it must be done simply, so it must be done cheerfully. *God loveth a cheerful giver:* and this is a perfect sign of cheerfulness, when a man doth not only give without grudging upon all occasions, but will also be careful to seek opportunity, as I said before. So much for the second point—the duty itself.

Now I proceed to the last thing—that is, the description of the persons to whom this must be done. First, generally, *all men;* and then, particularly, *the household of faith.* It is, as I have told you, to all that endure such wants and necessities, as that it may be a work of mercy, and no transgression of the rule, to relieve them. Though they live wickedly and unprofitably, yet if they be in extreme necessity, relieve them. *Have we not all one Father?* saith the Prophet; *hath not one God created us?* So then we are children and brethren by creation, though not, it may be, by adoption and especial grace,—and as they are the creatures of God and bear the image of their Maker, there ought on this account to be some consideration extended towards them in their extreme necessity.

But some man may reply in this fashion,—My will is to do good, but I have nothing to do with such and such a man; he is a stranger to me, and one with whom I had never any acquaintance. What is this but the churlish reply of Nabal to the servants of David? *Who is David? and who is the son of Jesse? Shall I take my bread and my flesh and my water that I have provided for my shearers, and give it unto men whom I know not whence they be? Nabal was his name, and folly was with him.* Abigail did truly interpret his nature to be answerable to his name, which signifieth a man of folly; for if he had been otherwise he would not have sent the messengers empty to their master, knowing their absolute necessity, which ought to have been relieved though they were strangers.

Another may object,—Such an one is not a

stranger, I confess; but he is an enemy: when it lay in his power he procured me all the mischief he could, and should I relieve him now?

Mark the rule of the Apostle: *If thine enemy hunger, feed him; if he be naked, clothe him; if he thirst, give him drink.*

But some man will say,—There remains so much unthankfulness in the world, that one is soon discouraged by people's ingratitude from doing good.

But what saith the Lord,—*Cast thy bread upon the waters, for after many days thou shalt find it.* Though it may seem to thee but as a stone sunk down into the deep, or as a morsel of bread in the water that floats from the sight of him that cast it in, yet cease not to cast it there; for after many days thou shalt find it.

But some man replies,—I do good to some already; I give something to the education of a poor scholar; somewhat I do for binding a poor orphan child to an apprenticeship; I contribute to these and these good works: is there to be no end of doing good?

Mark again the advice of Solomon for that: *Give a portion to seven, and to eight.* If thou have done good to one, extend it to a second, to a third, to a fourth; nay, cease not while there remains any object of mercy, and power in thine hands to do good.

Some may argue, that by this course, if all bestow their benevolence so largely, none could become rich; and God appoints some rich men in this world as well as poor.

Solomon answereth this objection also,—*If the clouds be full, they pour down rain.* God hath bestowed riches on men, as he hath given rain to the clouds; he gave them that superfluity of waters to pour down on the earth for the benefit of the same, and not that they should detain it to no purpose at all. So God hath given riches to men, that when they arrive at a fulness of estate, they should then pour down and distil the fruits of that blessing on them that live in necessity, as the rain descends upon dry clods of earth.

But some may answer again,—I have continued a great while in the exercise of doing good; I am now old, and have continued thus long at my trade; or thus long I have had an estate, and all this time I have busily employed myself in the performance of good offices for others. Is it not yet time to cease? No, saith Solomon, *In the morning sow thy seed, and in the evening withhold not thine hand.* Give in the morning of thy life, when thy condition begins to improve; and then in the evening of thy life, when thou hast left off gaining, cease not to persist in giving.

Saith another man,—You must not lop the twig too soon that is but beginning to grow. I am now in the way to thrive, and when I am further advanced in that course I will not fail to extend my goodness to others.

Fear not that you will lose by deeds of charity and mercy. *He that giveth to the poor, lendeth to the Lord; and look, what he layeth out it shall be paid him again.* God is able to pay thee back with interest, and if thou wouldest prosper, make him thy friend. *If thou hast little, do thy diligence gladly to give of that little.* Sow thy seed in the morning of thy life.

But, saith another man,—I have done that already; and now it ceaseth to be with me as before, by reason I follow not my trade, and have no more possibility of getting.

But let not thy hand cease in the evening, saith God. When thy shop windows are shut up, thy compassion must still continue open. When thou hast bid adieu to gain, still, if there remain ability in thy hands to do good, thou must not cease from bestowing, though it be evening with thee.

Thus, we see, there is no time excepted, nor any person to be refused, if necessity require; but a man must do good to all men, at all times. So much for that.

It remaineth only to point out those to whom we are to have especial regard in our charity,—*especially to them that are of the household of faith.*

This tells us, *first,* that God hath in the household of faith some that stand in need of relief; and *secondly,* that all who are better off in the household should especially look unto them.

There are many true believers who suffer want in this world. Christ speaks as it were for himself, when he speaks of them: I was hungry, and you did not feed me; naked, and ye clothed me not. Those that Christ owns as his, and accounts as a part of himself, even those are hungry and naked. And so likewise *God hath chosen the poor of this world, rich in faith.* They be rich in faith, and so of God's household, yet poor, nevertheless, in the world. You may find many examples of this. One shall suffice. We see a poor man, and yet an heir of heaven, lying full of sores and in want at the gate of that Dives who was afterwards thrown into hell. An heir of heaven, and yet on earth a beggar.

You see then, beloved, this point is true: now we will descend, and see how it appears to be so, and wherefore it comes to pass, by God's providence.

First, it becomes so that there may be a conformity between the head and the members: for Christ, that was rich, yet for our sakes he became poor; so poor that the foxes had holes and the birds of the air had nests, yet our Redeemer had no shelter, no not so much room as to lay his head. Now if the root be poor, the branches will be poor also; if the head be afflicted, all the other members suffer with it.

Again, if you observe the condition of God's saints on earth, you shall find small occasion to wonder at their simple estates, since they are but a company of travellers and pilgrims in this world. *I beseech you, as strangers and pilgrims,* &c. Here they have no abiding place: they are travelling from one place to another, and the proverb is true, that a rolling stone gathers nothing. They are pilgrims, and desire nothing further in this life than a staff and a scrip.

There is another reason for their poverty, and that proceeds from the opposition they find in the world against their course. The world hateth them, and striveth against them. You shall find that our Saviour, intending to go to Jerusalem, made his way through Samaria, and despatched some before to provide him lodging. But the Samaritans, suspecting that he was going thither, refused to entertain him. They would not receive him, saith the text: Why? because he was going to Jerusalem. Beloved, thus deals the world with the members of Christ. The world, which persecuted him, persecuteth his disciples also: if they would rely on the world and make that their end, then riches should flow in in abundance and all would go prosperously for a little time; but if their minds be resolved for Jerusalem and their eyes turned that way, let them seek their own entertainment, for the world will give them none.

Lastly, God disposeth it so, by his wondrous providence, that his glory may be so much the more conspicuous and open. He provideth that they of the household of faith should endure the scourge of poverty on earth, that so the work of his grace may appear the more in them: for when doth grace make itself more manifest in the heart than in the midst of such extremities? The stars make the brightest reflexion in the obscurest night, and grace appears most glorious in the deepest distress. *Ye have heard of the patience of Job:* but had not Job endured much sorrow and been exercised in many afflictions, the world had been ignorant of his virtues. You have heard of the faith of those which wandered in sheepskins and goatskins, but how could you have been acquainted with their faith if you had not heard of their clothing?

Is it so then that God's servants are thus? Then let the world wonder their fill at it; but let not us account it a strange matter, when we see those of the household of faith in poverty, that God bestows not riches in this world to one that is rich in grace. You see a multitude of believers stripped of all they had, and yet they were holy and good: and you see that God had wise and merciful reasons for dealing so with them.

Seeing then there be many poor who are of the household of faith, it is our duty to look *especially* unto them. David saith, *My goodness extendeth not to thee, but to the saints that are in the earth;* and the Apostle witnesseth of Philemon, that he had *refreshed the bowels of the saints.* This is the duty.

And the reason of it is that God hath, for this intent, given riches unto some that have grace, that they might especially administer the comfort that wealth brings with it unto those that are poor, of the same household and profession of grace. *Let the brother of low degree rejoice in that he is exalted, but the rich in that he is made low.* What is the low bringing of the rich brother, but that he becomes servant to him of low degree? his wealth and revenues, nay, all that he hath, he confesseth to be for the service of the poorest Christian. Also the near union and relation between one member and another should be a strong obligation upon those that are rich to extend their care to those of low degree, and not to please only themselves. For they are brethren: they have all the same Father, being begotten by the same word of truth; and they enjoy the same mother, the church: *Jerusalem that is above is free, and is the mother of us all.* Therefore let us see and acknowledge this, that whatsoever difference there may be of nation, yet all that believe are of the same household in this respect: they are brethren together of the same family. The Jews, notwithstanding they were distinguished by tribes, yet they are denominated together—the house of Israel: so all the people of God are called—his family upon earth. Beloved, let us look to this point: whatever differences there may be in respect of wealth, of natural birth, of descent, or outward ornament, we are all brethren and all of the same house.

Is it not a shame, when one brother is full, to suffer another to die with famine and hunger in the same house? or to let him sink under reproach and disgrace, not offering a hand to help him, and to prevent his extremity? It is therefore the duty of Christians to look especially to the wants of their brethren, and to let the respect they bear to the people of God be advanced above all the affection they bear to others.

And the more to incite you to this duty, know that Christ calls for it, and doth continually expect it. Neither doth he demand anything that is not his own: as David confesseth, in his provision for the temple—*of thine own have we given thee*—so you may account of whatever Christ calls for: if you possess it, it came from him; he entrusted it to you to be used according to his command. If you confer any gift on your children, you think you may reserve to yourselves the power to take it again at your pleasure; and shall not God be allowed that privilege—he that confers so many liberal blessings on thee? Sure thou art much in his debt, and it argues too foul an ingratitude if he lend thee a million and thou refuse to pay him a mite.

Again, if he call for it thou shalt not lose thereby, but he will give thee better riches. *Ask of him, and he will give you the Holy Ghost*, nay the *kingdom of heaven*, and these are riches far above the value of any substance thou enjoyest. Ask of him, and he will forgive thy sins—ten thousand talents; whereas he demands but one penny of thee. If you do his will you may ask for these great mercies, and you will receive: but if you refuse to obey his commands then he will not hearken to your prayers: he will answer only, *Why call ye me Lord, Lord, and do not the things that I say?* I dare say he doth greater things for thee already than he desires at thy hands for others.

And mark who it is that asks this from thee: even he whose favour thou must one day seek, for whose countenance thou wouldest then give all the world. It is he, before whose judgment-seat thou must appear, poor and blind and naked, except he make thee rich in the merits of Christ, and clothe thee with his righteousness. No man, desiring the favour of a prince or judge in some business of importance, but would gladly embrace an occasion of doing him a pleasure before the trial of his cause, that so the judge may take notice of his good will, and deal with him kindly. Beloved, we have special need of the favour of Christ, and we have opportunity sufficient to do him pleasure by relieving his poor members: for inasmuch as ye do good unto one of the least of his people, ye do it unto him; and what ye deny unto them, he takes it as an injury to himself. Therefore look, how you extend mercy here, to enjoy it hereafter; and as you desire the favour of the judge, make way for his kindness by the performance of his will. He that useth not mercy here, shall find none hereafter; and judgment shall be merciless, saith the Apostle, to them that show not mercy. Wouldest thou reap liberally in the last day? then sow liberally whilst thou hast opportunity. Do according to your several abilities; seek occasion to do good; take it cheerfully, and make use of it willingly. Look to it, for Christ looks for it. It will much commend thy love to religion, and greatly improve thine own good in the end.

SERMON VIII.

THE PERFECTION OF PATIENCE;

OR,

THE COMPLETE CHRISTIAN.

JAMES, I. 4.

"LET PATIENCE HAVE HER PERFECT WORK, THAT YE MAY BE PERFECT AND ENTIRE, WANTING NOTHING."

IN the second verse of this chapter, the Apostle persuadeth the distressed servants of God to bear their afflictions cheerfully: *My brethren,* saith he, *count it all joy when ye fall into divers temptations.* This exhortation he presseth, in the third verse, by showing the gracious effects of temptations when God sanctifieth them; *knowing this, that the trying of your faith worketh patience.* Yea, but if this be all the fruit of our afflictions and temptations, that we shall be made patient—what great matter is that? what great advantage cometh by patience? it is but a dull grace, it is merely passive. The Apostle answereth this objection in the text, and telleth them that it is, notwithstanding, such a grace as is necessary to the being and perfection of a Christian. *Let patience have her perfect work, that ye may be perfect and entire, wanting nothing.*

I shall speak something for the explication of the terms and phrases used here, and then come to elect such points as shall offer themselves to us from them.

First: I will show you what is meant by *patience.*

Secondly: What is meant by letting *patience have her perfect work.*

Thirdly: What is meant by this, that, doing of this, ye *shall be perfect and entire, wanting nothing.*

Patience, in a word, it is a grace or fruit of God's Spirit, whereby the heart of a believer willingly submitteth itself to the will of God in all afflictions and changes in this life.

I say it is a work, or fruit, of God's Spirit. He is called the God of patience; and long-suffering, which is the same thing with patience, is said to be a fruit of the Spirit.

And the effect of this patience is to make a man submit himself willingly to God in afflictions. I say willingly, for there is a submission which is by force—when God subjects a man to himself, not by a gracious and sweet inclining of the will, but by a powerful subduing of the person.

Now when I say there is such a willing submission to God in afflictions, the meaning is thus—that there may be in a believer, in a child of God, an inclination of the will, a natural desire to be freed from afflictions; yet, nevertheless, there is in him that willingness to suffer that is able to subdue every other longing.

In every renewed soul there is a principle of nature and a principle of grace: there is a desire that ariseth from nature, and that tendeth to the conservation of a man's being, and to the conservation of a man in all the comforts and contentments of his being. This is, and may be, in a child of God; but then it is overswayed by grace, which makes a man now resign up this will of his to God's hand—to be content against his own natural desires to be disposed of according to God's will. This we may see in our Lord and Saviour; *Father*, saith he, *if it be possible, let this cup pass from me.* Here is a desire to continue, not only in his natural being, but to continue in the comfort of nature and life; and this is a lawful and good desire, for these affections are the works of God upon the soul of man. The will of man moveth naturally by these affections: these desires, they are the fruits of nature, and so the works of God in nature, and therefore in themselves not to be blamed. But now that which keepeth them within compass is an over-ruling work of grace, whereby the creature is made to acknowledge his distance from the Creator, and that subjection he oweth to God as the Sovereign Lord of nature and of all creatures. And in this sense our Saviour, Christ, doth check his natural desires: *If it be possible, let this cup pass from me; nevertheless, not as I will, but as thou wilt,* saith he. So here is a work of grace ordering and over-ruling nature. And this is the kind of willingness we mean,—such a willingness as, in the issue and close, resteth in God's will.

The object of this patience is—affliction and the changes of this life. Affliction is, properly, anything that is grievous to a man's sense, anything that crosseth a man's will. There are some things that are indeed afflictions, but not to this or that person, because he is not sensible of them, or because he is not carried away by any desires against them. But when a man is crossed in his will, that is an affliction to him, and that is an object for patience. When a man that hath tasted the sweetness of prosperity is suddenly cast down into the depths of poverty and distress, as was Job's case, this is especially an object for patience. *Ye have heard of the patience of Job.*

But how did Job's patience appear in the afflictions and changes of his life? In this: that notwithstanding he had felt the sweetness of a prosperous estate and the comfort of friends, yea and the comfort of God's favour shining upon his heart, and many other particular mercies, yet when God turned his hand and took away the comforts of his life, the society of his friends, the comfortable expressions of his own love to his soul, and threatened the taking away even of life itself, Job could now, in this case, resolve to rest in the determination and appointment and will of God. Here now is patience.

Thus briefly you have heard what the duty is

to which the Apostle exhorteth. It is patience: that is, a willing resignation of ourselves to God's appointment in the changes of our life.

But now that is not enough. The Apostle contents not himself to say, *Have patience*, but *Let patience have her perfect work.* He would have them grow in patience; to grow from one degree to another; to abound in patience (as the Apostle speaks of hope and joy); that they might not only have patience, but have it brought to perfection, which is called *all long suffering;* that there might not be the least defect, that they might have a measure of patience proportionable to the measure of trials,—that as God suffered the measure of their trials to increase upon them, so they might have more and more patience to answer those trials, and to support the heart when the greatest weight should be laid upon the soul to press it down. And the word here translated patience, signifieth to bear up a man, to support him under a burthen, that he be not pressed down by it. So he would have them have such a measure of patience as might bear up the soul in the greatest pressures, that though they were afflicted, they might not be broken in their afflictions. Thus you have the duty opened. *Let patience have her perfect work.*

The reason is, *that ye may be perfect and entire, wanting nothing.* That you may be entire. Some understand it thus, that you may be entire in respect of every grace, in respect of all gracious habits; that you may have one grace as well as another; that as you have knowledge and faith, so you may have patience too, which is a necessary grace for a Christian, as well as for any other.

Others by entireness, and wanting nothing, think that the Apostle meant this; that they might have that which could supply comfort to their souls in all their wants. A man is then said to want nothing when he is content and satisfied with that estate wherein he is, as if he had all things. So David, when Ziklag was burnt, his wives carried away captive, his soldiers beginning to mutiny and to threaten him, yet he seemed in these troubles to want nothing, when he could comfort himself in the Lord his God. *Godliness is great gain;* but how? *with contentment:* that is, there is such a sufficiency, with contentment of heart, as if a man had all the things he wants. So then, here is the point, that you may be entire in respect of all gracious habits necessary to the being of a Christian: that you may have that inward store and supply of comfort that may support your hearts in all outward wants. Thus you have the meaning of the words.

The parts of the text are two: an exhortation to duty, and an argument to enforce that exhortation. The duty whereto we are exhorted is that we should be perfect in patience. *Let patience have her perfect work.* The argument whereby we are persuaded to this duty is that we may be *perfect and entire, wanting nothing:* that we may have all that is necessary to a Christian.

We may observe two conclusions hence, which we will follow at this time. The first is this: that patience is necessary to the perfection of a Christian; or a Christian is not perfect without patience. The second is this: that every Christian should strive for the perfection of patience; he must labour to attain the highest degree and perfection in patience. These two conclusions we will handle separately in the explication and proof, and join them together in the application and use.

For the first then, that a Christian is not perfect without patience. Our Saviour, exhorting his disciples to patience because they should meet with many enemies and injuries in the world, concludeth thus,—*Be ye therefore perfect, even as your Father which is in heaven is perfect.* What perfection speaks he of here? Such a perfection, such a work of grace, as might enable them to carry themselves as became them in the midst of those many enemies and oppositions they should meet withal.

There is a twofold perfection of a Christian: there is a perfection of parts, and a perfection of degrees. A child is a perfect man in respect of parts, but not in respect of degrees; because it is not yet come to that measure of strength and stature which a man hath.

Now there is a necessity that there should be a perfection of parts, for this is but the making up of all those graces which are necessary to a Christian, and without which he cannot obey

God, nor walk according to the rule. And patience is one of those parts—one of those habits of grace with which every renewed soul is endowed, and without which a man is not truly sanctified. St. Peter saith, *Add to your faith, virtue; and to virtue, knowledge; and to knowledge, temperance; and to temperance, patience; and to patience, godliness; and to godliness, brotherly kindness; and to brotherly kindness, charity.* Thus, patience is one of those necessary graces which make a man to be *neither barren nor unfruitful in the knowledge of our Lord Jesus Christ.*

But it is more than this. It is a means for preserving and keeping alive other graces in the soul: this is *its perfect work.* Patience is as the wall of the soul, whereby those riches and treasures of grace that it possesses are defended from a battery of temptations, and from the fiery darts of the enemy. *In your patience possess ye your souls.* The soul, which is the seat and subject of grace, cannot itself be kept without patience.

For once let impatience into the soul, and you let in all sin with it. Impatience is a destroying of all grace, a pulling down of the wall. Nay, what is all sin but a species of impatience? What is pride but the impatience of humility? What is uncleanness but the impatience of chastity? What is covetousness but the impatience of abstinence? Every sin beginneth in impatience; so you see that, for the very preserving of the soul—the subject of grace, and of grace—the treasure of the soul, it is necessary we should have patience.

Again, it will plainly appear that a Christian cannot be perfect without patience, because he cannot do his work without it. He cannot do the works of religion, the task that God lays on him, without patience. Look, in what measure patience is defective, in that same measure he halteth in his duty, and in the very acts of religion he goeth about.

Take any one duty of religion that you can name, and see whether a man can do it without patience. Suppose it be prayer. How can a man go on in the duty of prayer without patience? Sometimes God delayeth the grant of a man's petition: now will he sink and give over in discouragement if he have not patience to support the soul.

The Canaanitish woman, when she came to Christ and spake unto him and he did not answer a word, she had so much patience as to speak the second time to him, and then he answered her, yet not favourably: but her patience held her to the third trial, and at the last she received her desire. Had she not been patient to go on with her request and to repeat her prayer, she had lost her petition. The Apostle Paul saith, *For this thing I besought the Lord thrice.* He would have given over at the first seeking of the Lord, if he had not had patience to uphold him to the second and third petition—to the renewing of his suit twice, yea thrice.

Come from praying to hearing the word preached. How can a man hear the word profitably without patience? Therefore, those who are like the good ground are said to hear the word, and to bring fruit *with patience:* and it is the commendation of the church at Philadelphia, *Thou hast kept the word of my patience.* There is need of patience if we would profit by the word.

For first, if a man will obey the word, he shall be sure to have many set against him in the world. He had need of patience then, or else he will leave the rule of the word because of the reproaches of the world. Again, there are many secret corruptions in his own heart that will be shown him in the preaching of the word, which a man cannot abide to hear of; but he will be vexing and fretting and discontented at it (as we see in Ahab and divers others), unless he have patience to keep him from raging against the preacher and the word preached to him. You have need of patience, that you may bear the reproofs and exhortations of the word. Therefore saith the Apostle James,—*Receive with meekness the engrafted word, which is able to save your souls.* There is no engrafting the word in the heart, except those forms of impatience, those hindrances of the growth of the word, be taken away.

But, further, the whole life of a Christian is a continual exercise of patience; and a man, though he begin in the spirit, yet he will without doubt end in the flesh, if he have not patience to persevere in well-doing. Therefore, saith the Apostle, *ye have need of patience, that after ye have done the will of God, ye might receive the promise.* You have need of patience, because, between the time of the making of the promise and the time of its accomplishment to the soul, there is often a great distance; and you must wait after you have obeyed the word, and not expect the promise to follow immediately. You must run with patience the race set before you; looking to Jesus, the author and finisher of your faith. Our Lord himself had not perfected the work of our redemption if he had wanted patience; neither can we finish our course of Christianity, wherein we must follow Christ, except we have patience added to other graces. You see then, a Christian cannot be perfect without patience. This is the first point.

The second point is, that it is the duty of a Christian to strive to bring patience to the uttermost perfection; to make this the effort of his life, that patience may have her perfect work—that there may be no defect in it. The Apostle prayeth for the Colossians, *that they may be strengthened with all might unto all patience and long-suffering.* And our Saviour speaketh expressly concerning patience, in that place where he telleth his disciples, *Be ye perfect, even as your Father which is in heaven is perfect.* This then is the duty of a Christian to aim at perfection, as in other graces, so especially in this grace of patience.

Why so?

First, because a Christian is to follow the best pattern. The best patterns are propounded in the Scripture, and God doth not propound patterns and examples in vain: but as he gives us rules and precepts to tell us what we should do, so he giveth us patterns and examples to direct us in the degree and manner of doing. Therefore we have God set as a pattern of patience,—*Be ye followers of God as dear children.* Wherein? In all those examples wherein you have a rule; for the examples of God and Christ and the saints bind men no further than there is a rule in the word. There are many things in which we cannot follow God, but the patience of God is expressly set forth as a pattern for us. In that glorious proclamation of him in Exodus, among other of his attributes he is set out to be a God *long-suffering and patient:* and saith St. Peter, *God, that he might show his long-suffering and patience, bore with the world.* God hath borne with this ungodly world many ages, many thousand years already; and yet beareth still with the world. The most holy God, that perfectly hateth wickedness, yet showeth his patience in bearing with the ungodly; the mighty God, that is able to destroy the earth and the heaven with the breath of his mouth, even as by a word he made them, this mighty God beareth with weak rebellious men; he suffereth all their sin and hardness of heart and contemptuous boldness, that his patience and forbearance may appear. So then you have God for an example.

And Christ for an example too; and for this very end are you predestinated, that you may be *conformed to the image of his Son.* Wherein? In all imitable and necessary graces; and this his patience among the rest. See the patience of Christ—in his carriage towards his Father, how he bore the displeasure of God with submission; —and in his carriage toward men, when he might have commanded fire from heaven upon his enemies, how he bore with them and rebuked his disciples,—*Ye know not what manner of spirit ye are of. He was led as a lamb to the slaughter; and as a sheep before her shearers is dumb, so he opened not his mouth.*

Again you have the example of the servants of God. *Take, my brethren,* saith St. James, *the prophets, who have spoken in the name of the Lord, for an example of suffering affliction and of patience.* The prophets suffered long, and endured the frowns of the world and the rage of princes: they endured a thousand miseries, and all to discharge their duty. Again, *you have heard of the patience of Job,* and what end the Lord made with him; and this was written for our example, to teach us to be as patient as he was.

Again, as it is necessary for a Christian to strive for the perfection of patience in the degrees of it, because of the conformity that should be between him and those examples of God, of Christ, and of the saints; between God the Father, and believers his children; between

Christ the head, and believers his members ;—so also it is necessary in respect of the trials whereunto a Christian may be put; you had need to strive that you may be perfect in patience, because you know not what trials ye shall be put to, what times ye are reserved to. Every man must expect troubles and afflictions, which are called tribulations; and you know what *tribulum* was,—an iron ball that was full of spikes round about, so that wheresoever it was cast it did stick: an instrument used in war. Tribulations are unavoidable: they will fall and stick; ye cannot escape them on any side, by any turning to the right hand or to the left. It is the will of God that through many tribulations we should enter into the kingdom of heaven, and whosoever will live godly in Christ Jesus must suffer persecution.

Now, beloved, is this so, that this is a statute in heaven, decreed and ordained by God, and one that, like the laws of the Medes and Persians, will not be reversed, that every man must pass to heaven through much tribulation and affliction upon earth? Then it concerns every one to be armed and prepared with such a measure of patience as may support him in such afflictions. Ye know not what afflictions ye may have, what particular trials God may put you to. How miserable is the case of that man who, when he is in the midst of the pikes, hath to seek for his armour: yet he is no worse than the man who when he is in the midst of trials, disturbed and distracted with vexation of spirit, hath then to seek for patience. What foolish, disorderly speeches proceed from men in the time of affliction! We may see it in David: *So foolish was I, and ignorant,* saith he, *I was even as a beast before thee.* What foolish, senseless, brutish speeches, unreasonable absurd passages, proceed from men in these times of trouble, if they have not got to themselves beforehand this grace, and are not fitted in time to a Christian carriage by patience.

Thus ye see the necessity of patience for the perfection of a Christian, and of the perfection of patience for the ornament of a Christian. We come now to make use of both these together.

First, it serveth for the just reproof of Christians that are careful for other parts and acts of religion, and are not so seriously mindful of this duty of patience as they should be, but are so far from striving for patience that they seem rather to strive for impatience, that makes their crosses more heavy and their afflictions more bitter than they would be. Indeed we make God's cup (that of itself is grievous enough to nature and to sense) far more bitter that else it would be, by putting into it our own ingredients, that are inbred in our own earthly minds, in our own passions and pride and self-will.

Far from perfecting patience in themselves, men take divers ways whereby they wholly destroy patience. I will enumerate some of them, that you may be warned against them.

The first is, by aggravating of their afflictions, exaggerating them by all the several circumstances they can possibly invent. All their eloquence is used in expressing the grievousness of that cross and affliction that is upon them. They that in the times of mercy would scarcely even drop a word of thankfulness and acknowledgment of God's goodness to them, now they can pour out floods of sentences in expression of God's bitter and heavy dealing with them in such afflictions and crosses and distresses that befall them. As the Church speaks in Lamentations : *Is it nothing to you, all ye that pass by? Behold and see if there be any sorrow like my sorrow, wherewith the Lord hath afflicted me?* The like is, ordinarily, in the mouths of those that are in trouble. Is there any affliction like mine? Who is so wronged in name and credit as I am? Who suffereth such pain of body or such heaviness of heart as I do? Never any man hath endured so many injuries, by friends, and enemies, and all sorts of people, as I have. As if all the afflictions in the world, the waves and billows of trouble, were met together upon one person. This is the language whereby men aggravate their afflictions and increase impatience in themselves.

Another way whereby they do this is, by giving free vent to their passions. Passions are like a wild horse; if they have not reins put upon them, if they be not pulled in, they will fly out to all excess. If once we give our passions vent, there is no stopping of them. David, we see, checks himself—he hath a curb to bridle his passions. *Why art thou cast down, oh my soul?* But otherwise, when men give the reins to their passion and do not stop their course, but think they have reason for it, they break out into all exorbitancy. Jonah, when the Lord challenged him for his anger: *Doest thou well to be angry?—Aye,* saith he, *I do well to be angry.* So David, though as we have seen, able to check himself sometimes, yet breaks out for the loss of his son: *Oh Absalom, my son! would God I had died for thee, oh Absalom, my son, my son!* What hurt was done to David? What wrong had he that he should take on thus? His son was taken from him, but it was that son Absalom, who if he had lived, would have killed his father: and yet he takes on as if the father could not live because the son that sought his death was taken from him. Such unreasonable passions, such causeless distempers ofttimes are in the souls of men, that they mistake God's ways; and that very way in which he intendeth and doeth them good, they complain of it as if it were their utter undoing.

Again, another way whereby men increase their impatience and distemper is, when they will not give way to consolation, refusing to be comforted: they will not only be exceeding vehement and intent upon their passions, but besides, stop all passages and inlets against comfort. This was Jacob's fault concerning the death of Joseph; when he hears that Joseph is dead, not only his heart sinks within him but he rends his garment and covers himself with sackcloth, and takes on so, that when his sons and children rise up to comfort him he will not be comforted: why?—because Joseph is not, and I will go to the grave to Joseph. Nothing would comfort Jacob, but he would go down to the grave to Joseph by all means: what an extravagance was this! He only heard that Joseph was missing, he heard but a present sound of fear, and he was carried away with that. Joseph was yet alive, and if Jacob had gone down to the grave to seek him, he had not found him there. So it is with us; the very apprehension and fear that we entertain are as bad, or worse to us, than the things themselves could be. The more we think on them the more we multiply our fears and evils, because we will not receive counsel nor comfort.

Again, a fourth thing whereby men increase impatience in themselves and aggravate their sorrows is this: they are apt to look only upon their present afflictions and not upon the mercies they enjoy, as if they had but one eye to behold all objects with; and so could only look upon one thing at a time. There should be a looking upon the affliction, and a looking upon the mercy too. This was Haman's case: when he was vexed that Mordecai did not do him reverence, all his wealth and his honours could do him little good. He had much wealth, and the glory of his house was increased; he had the favour of the king, and every worldly advantage he could desire; yet *all this availeth me nothing*, saith he, *so long as I see Mordecai the Jew sitting at the king's gate.* He looks only on this particular that vexed and grieved him, and not upon the rest. So it is with us. If there be but one particular affliction upon us, we fix our eyes upon that. Like a fly that flieth about the glass, and can stick nowhere till she come to some crack; or as a gnat, that cometh about the body of a beast, that will be sure to rest on the galled part, or on some sore or other: so it is with these disquieted thoughts of men, that are of no other use but to further Satan's ends to weaken their faith and discourage their own hearts; men stick on the gall, on the sore, of any affliction; and there they will rest. It is true, they argue, God hath offered us such and such opportunities; but what is this? This and that particular affliction is upon me, and I can think of nothing else. This it is that increaseth impatience, when a man will not look on the mercies he receiveth, but only on that that he wanteth.

Again, a fifth course that men take to aggravate their sorrows and increase impatience in themselves is this: they look upon the instrument of their sorrows and afflictions, but never look up to God that ruleth and over-ruleth these things. Men look upon such a person, such an event, that bringeth them into trouble, and no more. Ye see how David was disquieted at this: if it had been an enemy that had reproached him, then he could have borne it; *but it was thou, a man, mine equal, my guide and mine acquaintance:*

we took sweet counsel together, and walked unto the house of God in company. This troubled him; by this he multiplied his sorrows, looking on the instrument: but when he looked to God he found quiet and resignation: then, saith he, *I was dumb, I opened not my mouth, because thou didst it.* There is no quiet in the heart when a man looks upon *man;* nor till he looks to God, that ordereth all things by his wisdom and counsel.

Lastly, men aggravate their sorrows and increase their impatience by another course they take: that is, when they look on their sorrows and afflictions only, and not upon the benefit of affliction: they look only upon that that flesh would avoid, and not upon that which, if they were spiritual and wise, they would desire. *No chastening,* saith the Apostle, *for the present, seemeth to be joyous, but grievous; nevertheless, afterward it yieldeth the peaceable fruit of righteousness unto them which are exercised thereby.* Now men look upon that only which is grievous in affliction; upon the smart of it, but not upon the profit, the quiet fruit of righteousness that cometh thereby. As if a man, when he hath a corroding plaister put to a sore, should cry and complain of the smart it causeth him, and take no notice of the healing that cometh by it and the cure that followeth. Men complain thus of God, as if he grudged them the comfort of their lives; as if he intended to rob them of all conveniences, and to make them utterly miserable, to begin a hell with them on earth; because they never look how God, by this means, fitteth them for heaven, purging out corruption and strengthening grace in them: *We are chastened of the Lord, that we should not be condemned with the world.* Men look too often upon the affliction, not upon their freedom from condemnation, to which God intends to lead them by that means.

So much for that. I come now to a *second* use. Let the doctrine and admonition contained in the text stir us up, every one, in the presence of God, to set ourselves upon this task of Christianity; to labour for patience, that we may be perfect Christians. *Let patience have her perfect work.*

But all the question is, how a man may get it. As there are two sorts of afflictions in a man's life, so patience hath two offices.

One affliction is, those present evils that a man undergoeth and suffereth. Patience is to support him in the miseries and calamities of this present life.

Another sort of trial is, when the good that a man expects is delayed and is not presently granted. Patience is necessary in this case also.

I will show you how a man may set patience a-work in both these cases, and so conclude.

First, for the present calamities of a man's life, whether it be sickness of body, or sorrow and distress of mind; whether it arise from the loss of friends, leaving a man destitute of all joys and helps, *like a pelican in the wilderness;* or from inward dejection, spiritual desertion, when he seemeth to be as in a cloud, under the frowns of God;—the way to get patience under all such afflictions is this: to consider that there is no change in thy life, no condition whatsoever that thou art called unto, but it is ordered by God. Set thy soul a-work now, to give God his glory in that particular change of thy life.

Give God the glory of his absolute sovereignty. Acknowledge him an absolute, independent Lord, that doth what he will among his creatures. His will is the rule of all his actions upon the creatures here below, and uncontrolled, unquestionable. It is high arrogancy and presumption and pride of spirit, for the creature to contest with his Creator concerning his actions on earth. I must give God the glory of his sovereignty, and acknowledge that he hath power and right to rule all the families of the earth: and why not *mine* as well as another? Why not *my* person as well as another's? Why not to order all the change of *my* life as well as another man's? That which Benhadad spake proudly to Ahab, *Thy silver and thy gold, thy wives and thy children, and thy house and thy city, are mine:* that may God say truly, and by right, to thee. All that thou hast and all that thou art is his; therefore give him that glory that Job did, in the change of his life: *The Lord gave, and the Lord hath taken away; blessed be the name of the Lord.* The Lord that gave hath a right to take what he will. There is nothing that will keep the creature in his due place but the consideration of

God's absolute sovereignty. It was this that meekened the spirit of Eli, when that heavy message was brought to him that there should come such misery upon his house that whosoever heard it *both his ears should tingle.* Well, said he, *It is the Lord; let him do what seemeth him good.* It is the Lord; and it becometh not servants to stand and contend with their lord. So David, when the priests offered him their service to go along with him to the field from Absalom, saith he, *If I shall find favour in the eyes of the Lord he will bring me again, and show me both it and his habitation: but if he thus say, I have no delight in thee, behold, here I am; let him do to me as seemeth good unto him.* David considered that he was under the hands of an absolute Lord, and this it was that humbled him and armed him beforehand with patience and submission. *Let him do to me as seemeth good unto him.*

And as thou must give God the glory of his sovereignty, so also of his wisdom. Know that God ordereth all his ways with wisdom and counsel: he knoweth what is good for his children. Ye are content, when ye are sick, that the physician should diet you, because ye account him wise, and one that hath skill in that course. If God diet thee for the purging out of some corruption and for the curing of some spiritual disease in thy soul, submit to God in this case; be willing to resign thyself up to be ordered by him. A man that hath a gangrene or such other dangerous disease in his body, submitteth to the surgeon in his course: though it be the cutting and sawing off of a limb, though it be never so painful and the loss never so great, yet he is, for the saving of his life, willing to have that taken away. God is a wise God, that knoweth what estate is best for thee, not only when trials are better than comforts, but when one kind of trial is better than another. It may be it is better to exercise one with poverty, another with disgrace, another with spiritual trouble, another with restraint of liberty. God knoweth which particular trial is necessary to cure that disease, and which this, that is in thy soul. The Heavenly Physician will bring that upon thee as a spiritual prescription, and a heavenly course that he takes, in infinite wisdom, to cure thee.

And in all this give him, moreover, the glory of his mercy. Believe that mercy is still the motive and intention of God, even in those changes of thy life that seem most grievous to thee. What hast thou lost but thou mightest have lost a great deal more? What dost thou suffer but thou mightest suffer a great deal more? As Alcibiades, when he was told that one had stolen half his plate; *I have cause*, saith he, *rather to be thankful that he took no more, than troubled that he took so much.* I am sure it is true of God in this case. What hath God taken from thee? Some part of thy estate, some friend, some comfort of thy life, some one or other particular comfort. Could he not have done more? Hath he afflicted thee in thy body?

He might have afflicted thee in thy soul; and *a wounded spirit who can bear!* Hath he afflicted thee in some one member of thy body? He might have cast both body and soul into hell. There is not a trial upon thee but God could have made it heavier: let that make thee submit, therefore, with a more meek heart and willing spirit to God, as a merciful God.

The Church appears as an example of this, in the second chapter of Lamentations: *It is of the Lord's mercy that we are not consumed.* The Jews were in great affliction when the Babylonians came upon them, and they were driven from the house of God, and from their own houses: but yet, it was of God's mercy that they were not destroyed wholly. So the prophet Jeremiah telleth Baruch, in the Captivity: *Seekest thou great things for thyself? Thy life will I give unto thee for a prey.* Baruch was wondrously disquieted. He complained that the Lord had added grief to his sorrow. What grief was that? —that he must go to Egypt, and after to Babylon. Well, saith the prophet, thy case is not so heavy as thou seemest to make it. Thou shalt have thy life for a prey in all places wheresoever thou goest. God might have taken away life and all, but thy life shalt thou have; therefore be content with so much. So I say to thee, When great afflictions come upon thee,—they might have been greater; therefore give God the glory of his mercy in all things.

Remember, moreover, that the cause of all

thy sorrows is in thyself. It is sin that deservedly draweth on all the afflictions of this life. Consider, thou hast fallen by thine own sin under God's displeasure; therefore, whatsoever affliction befalleth thee, thy sin hath deserved that at the hands of God. The Lord now dealeth with thee as a just God, and though not in the extremity of rigour, yet doubtless there is a righteous proceeding in it; as the Church confesseth, *Righteousness belongeth to thee, O Lord.* Though the Church was then in great affliction, yet *she confessed* there was righteousness in her visitation.

It is profitable to consider this, and not only to say, with the thief on the cross, *We receive the due reward of our deeds,* but to confess that we suffer not so much as our sins deserve. Our sins deserve far greater punishment at the hands of God than he, in this life, inflicteth on us. We see that a change of punishment, a less for a greater, is ever esteemed a mercy. When a malefactor deserveth to be put to death, he is not only content to be burnt in the hand, but esteemeth it a mercy to be so dismissed. So it is with us: whatsoever affliction God layeth upon thee thou mayest conclude, I have deserved greater. Saith the Church, *Wherefore doth a living man complain; a man for the punishment of his sins? Let us search and try our ways and turn again to the Lord.* So let this be the main business of thy life in this case. Rather bethink thyself how to get the favour of God, than to be eased of such a trouble. Let a man look to sin in all this.

Lastly, consider the gracious and comfortable fruit of affliction that is borne with patience. Patience lesseneth the judgment which impatience would but increase. A struggling child is the more punished. A man in a fever, the more he struggleth and striveth, the more he increaseth his pain; and the more patiently a man yieldeth himself in the hands of God, the more, by God's mercy, he findeth ease and mitigation of the affliction. God will take off the affliction when once he hath perfected patience by it; for this is God's aim, in all the trials he layeth on men, to perfect patience in them: therefore the issue will be good: there will be, for the present, the more ease to the heart, and afterwards a gracious issue and deliverance from trouble when thou art exercised by patience.

But beside those afflictions of our life, in which there seemeth to be something of positive evil, grievous to nature and sense, there is a suffering which ariseth from mercies delayed, and from that hope deferred which maketh the heart sick. It is an affliction to a man to be kept and delayed in the expectation of that good he hath not, and which, if he seem to catch at it, is drawn from him further and further. Many men have sent up their prayers earnestly to God, yet the thing they ask is not granted to this day. Many a man hath waited long and sought the Lord, yet he hath not obtained that which his soul desired.

P

How shall a man come to exercise patience in such a case as this?

In such cases, when God delayeth, know that God's delays are not denials. Though God defer the thing, he may and will certainly grant it at length, if it be for thy good. What doth he expect of thee? To wait with patience. This is an act of faith. *He that believeth shall not make haste.* Whatsoever God has promised in the word, and thou hast a warrant to believe,—wait for it.

And God's delays are not only not denials, but they are a mean which he useth for improving his favours. God increaseth and commendeth the excellencies of his mercies by delay: he recompenseth our expectation and waiting for his favours, by putting greater sweetness into them when they come. God increaseth the comfort according to the delay, as in Isaiah lxi., where, comforting the distressed church in the time of calamity, he promiseth, *for your shame ye shall have double.* Double what? Double comfort after their trials. *Our light affliction* (saith the Apostle), *which is but for a moment, worketh for us a far more exceeding and eternal weight of glory.* This is the issue: a weight of glory, for light afflictions; an eternal weight of glory, for momentary, passing troubles. As the sufferings of Christ abound in us, so our consolation also aboundeth by Christ. This is the course of God, if we will only yield ourselves with patience to his will.

Remember also that God's delays are never long. At the longest they are but for a short time. What if he delay a year! what if twenty, thirty, forty years! What if the whole life of a man! This is no great delay. Compare this time of thy waiting for mercy (I mean for any special mercy, as relief from poverty, or pain of body, or distress of mind,—for, even at the worst, we are still surrounded in this world with mercies innumerable)—compare this time of thy waiting for mercy with the time to come, in which thou shalt enjoy the perfection of this and every other bounty. Compare the time of thy suffering with eternity. What proportion is there between them? A moment to eternity! If the life of a man should extend to an hundred, a thousand years, yet that is but a moment, yea even as a point *that hath no parts,* compared with eternity: a thousand years past, a thousand years to come, they are but as yesterday with God. Take the eternity past and the eternity to come, and put the life of a man between these two, and it will be but as a point too small to be accounted of.

Stretch out the duty of patience, then. Hast thou waited a week? wait a month, a year, seven years, seventy years, nay, seventy ages, all the ages of the world, if that were possible. All these are but a moment to eternity.

And where is the man that hath waited so long, but God, that his servants may not faint in their expectation, either supports them with other comforts, or else giveth them that which they desire before their hearts faint? Know therefore, that it is no such great matter for a man to wait upon God, for it is but for a short time; and reflect, in the time of thy waiting upon this, that when thou art fittest for mercy it shall come; and when it cometh it shall come with an abundant weight and sweetness, such as shall countervail all thy expectation and longing.

Patience must be exercised by faith, it must be strengthened by hope, and at length perfected by self-denial. We have need of patience; we cannot be perfect or acceptable to God without it; we cannot wait for his promises, nor receive them at the last without it: it is the offspring of faith and hope, which are but barren trees except they bear this fruit. Then, brethren, in all conditions and circumstances of your life, get patience, exercise patience, *perfect* patience. *Let patience have her perfect work, that ye may be perfect and entire, wanting nothing.*

SERMON IX.

SIN'S STIPEND AND GOD'S MUNIFICENCE.

ROM. VI. 23.

"THE WAGES OF SIN IS DEATH; BUT THE GIFT OF GOD IS ETERNAL LIFE, THROUGH JESUS CHRIST OUR LORD."

THE latter part of this chapter, from the 12th verse to the end, is spent in a grave and powerful dehortation of the faithful from security in sin, against which the Apostle useth sundry arguments. That which he presseth most is drawn from the several ends to which sin and righteousness do lead men. The end of sin is death; therefore that is not to be served: the end of righteousness is life everlasting; therefore that is to be embraced. And because there is a great difference in the manner of these two consequences — death coming from sin as the meritorious cause, but life from righteousness as a free gift, therefore the Apostle adds this epilogue and conclusion in the last verse,—*The wages of sin is death; but the gift of God is eternal life, through Jesus Christ our Lord.*

In which words we have a description of a twofold service;—of sin in the former clause; and of God, or righteousness, in the latter; and how both these are rewarded;—the one with death; it pays us justly: and the other with life, which is bestowed by the free gift of God, through Christ. These are the two parts, the two general points that we are to consider.

The wages of sin is death, saith the Apostle. By death is here signified both temporal and eternal death, but especially eternal death; for in the next clause of the sentence it is opposed to eternal life: therefore it is *eternal* death that is intended. And by sin is meant—the corruption and depravation of our nature, which is the mother of all sin; and so it includeth every evil word or thought or deed that we commit, touching which it is said in another place, *Sin, when it is finished, bringeth forth death.* This for the exposition of the terms.

The point to be observed from this first part of the text is this, that death is due to sin, as wages to one that earns them.

To him that sinneth, wages are due in strict justice. If a man have a hired servant he may bestow a free gift on him, if he will; if he will not, he may please himself; but his stipend, or his wages, he must pay him, unless he will be unjust: for it is the price of his work, and so is fairly due to him. After such a manner is death due to sin: the very demerit of the work of sin requires it, as being earned. God is as just in inflicting death upon sinners for their sins, as any man in paying his labourer or hired servant his wages.

God appointed it so in the beginning, when he told Adam concerning the forbidden fruit, *In the day that thou eatest thereof thou shalt surely die:* and the same is repeated by Ezekiel, *The soul that sinneth, it shall die:* plainly declaring that death is the recompense of sin, and that if sin have its due, then death must follow. So the Apostle Paul had showed before in his epistle, that *by one man sin entered into the world, and death by sin; and so death passed upon all men, for that all have sinned.* All had sinned, therefore all were paid with death. These places are evidences that death, by God's ordinance and appointment, is the due recompense of sin; as due to it as wages to a hired servant, or to one who hath diligently earned them.

What death is it that is due to sin? Both temporal and eternal death: I say both deaths, concerning both which the truth is to be cleared from some doubts. It was the Pelagians' error to think that man should have died a natural death though he had never sinned: so they thought that the natural, temporal, bodily death, was not the wages of sin; contrary to the Apostle, who makes that death that *passed upon all men*, and which must needs be natural death, to enter by sin: death entered by sin—no sin, no death at all.

But it may be objected, when God told Adam

that in the day when he should eat the forbidden fruit he should surely die, he meant not temporal death, as the event showed; for no such death was inflicted upon Adam in the day that he sinned, since he continued living naturally in the world many years.

I answer, notwithstanding all this, Adam may be said to have died a natural death as soon as he sinned, because by the guilt of his sin he then presently became subject to it, and God straightway denounced upon him the sentence of death: therefore it may be said, he straightway died: as a condemned person is called a dead man, though he be respited for a time. Besides, the messengers and sergeants of Death presently took hold of him and arrested him for sin, as hunger and thirst and cold and diseases, daily wasting of the natural moisture, to the quenching of life. Indeed God spared him for a little time that he might give him the means of salvation, the promise of Christ being after made, and he called to repentance, and by that means to attain a better life by Christ than he had lost by sin.

If it is objected, again, Christ redeemed us from all sin and from all the punishment of sin, but he did not redeem us from temporal, bodily death; for the faithful, we see, die still, even as others do: therefore temporal death is not the wages of sin, for then, when we are free from sin by Christ, we should be free also from that;— our answer to this is, that Christ hath freed all his elect, not only from eternal but even from temporal death, though not from both in the same manner.

First, from temporal death; in hope of which deliverance the Apostle saith, *The last enemy that shall be destroyed is death;* and *this mortal shall put on immortality:* and in the mean time, it is destroyed in hope, though it remain indeed and must be undergone, even of the faithful, in this life.

Howbeit to them God hath changed the nature of it, and now they no longer undergo it as the wages of sin, but for other causes.

First, for the exercise of their graces, their faith and hope and patience, and the rest: all these are exercised, as in other afflictions, so also in the death of God's children.

Secondly, for the total removal and riddance of the reliques of sin, from which they are not freed in this life: but when they die, then all sin is taken away; for as, at the first, sin brought death into the world, so to the faithful now, death carries it out again.

Thirdly, for their entrance into heaven and to be at home with the Lord, from whom they are absent as long as they are at home in these bodies. Death is but the passage from this life to life eternal.

Fourthly, to prepare their bodies for renewing at the last day. As a decayed image or statue must first be broken that it may be new cast, so these bodies of ours must be broken by death that they may be cast into a new mould of immortality at the general resurrection; and this is the work of Christ.

Thus even temporal death is left to the children of God to be undergone before they come to heaven; for as sin remains here, so death remains: and though they be in Christ, yet they are still in that estate wherein *it is appointed unto all men once to die.* It is left to them, I say, and that justly, in respect to the remnants of sin; yet they undergo it in no other way than for their own good and benefit. Nevertheless, to an unbeliever, temporal death is in its own nature the wages of sin.

And as temporal, so, in the SECOND place, eternal. For when God told man that in the day he sinned he should die the death, he meant not only temporal but eternal death; and the latter more particularly (as I showed before, in that the Apostle opposeth it to eternal life, in the next clause of the sentence). Now Christ hath freed all believers actually from eternal death.

But how eternal death should be the wages of sin may be doubted, because, between the work and the wages there must be some proportion, that seems not to be between sin and eternal death: for sin is a finite and temporal thing, committed in a short time, and that death is eternal, and to visit a temporal fault with an eternal punishment would seem to be against justice.

But for an answer to this doubt, we must know that, however sin considered in the act and as a transient action may be finite, yet in other respects it is infinite, and that in a threefold consideration.

First, in respect of the object against whom it is committed: for, being an offence against infinite Majesty it deserves an infinite punishment; for we know that offences are reckoned of for their greatness, according as the greatness of the person offended. If he that clips the king's coin, or defaces the king's arms, or counterfeits the broad seal of England or the prince's privy seal, ought to die as a traitor, because this offence is against the person of the prince, much more ought he that violates the law of God to die both the first and the second death too, because this tends to the defacing of the image and the disgracing of the person of God himself, who is thereby contemned and dishonoured.

Secondly, sin is infinite in respect of the subject wherein it is—the soul of man. Seeing the soul is immortal and of an everlasting substance, and that the guilt of sin doth stain the soul as a crimson and scarlet die upon wool, and can no more be severed from the soul than the spots from the leopard, it remains, as the soul is eternal and everlasting, so sin must be infinite in durance, and deserve an infinite wages and punishment, which is eternal death.

Thirdly, it is infinite also, in respect of the desire and endeavour of an impenitent sinner; for his desire is to walk on still in sin, and, except God cut off the line of life, never to give over sinning; but he would run on infinitely, committing all manner of sin *with greediness*. And it is reason that, as God accepts the will for the deed in godliness, so he should punish the will for the deed in wickedness. If we sin according to our eternity, in our will and purpose, God will punish us according to his eternity: it is just that they that would never be without sin, if they might have their own will, should never be without punishment.

Thus we see eternal death is the wages of sin, and though sin be committed in a moment, though it be a transient action in itself, yet it is just with God to give it the wages of eternal death.

Therefore death, both temporal and eternal, is the wages of sin.

The point being thus declared, we come to make some use of it by application.

First, it teacheth us, contrary to the doctrine of the Church of Rome, that original lust and concupiscence, in the regenerate, is a sin: for how else could God be just in inflicting temporal death upon infants that are regenerate? Actual sins they have none; and if they have no original sin neither, then the wages of sin were inflicted where it had never been deserved, which cannot be, because there is no unrighteousness with God. Therefore certain it is that, after regeneration, this original lust, though the guilt of it be taken away, yet, as sin, it remains; that is, the substance of it still remains, and will remain as long as we live in this world. For it is in us as the ivy is in the wall, which having taken root, so twines and incorporates itself that, though it die, yet it can never be quite rooted out till the wall be taken down. So, till body and soul be taken asunder by death, there will be no total riddance of the original corruption and depravation of our nature; it is still in us, as appears by the temporal death even of the best saints, of those who are most sanctified in this life: for if there were no remainders of corruption in them, they would not receive the wages of sin: there would be no death for them if there were no sin in them.

Another use of this point is to take away a fond popish distinction of mortal and venial sin. The Church of Rome teacheth some sins to be venial, that is, not in their own nature deserving of death; whereas the Apostle here, speaking of all sin in general, saith, *the wages of sin is death.* And how can it be otherwise when all sin is the transgression of the law, and all transgression of the law deserves and is worthy of the curse, which is both the first and second death? for *Cursed is every one that continueth not in all things that are written in the book of the law to do them.* There is no sin, therefore, but it is worthy of death; and therefore there is no such venial sin as they dream of.

We deny not that some sins are venial and some mortal, in another sense; not in respect of the nature of the sin, but of the estate of the person in whom the sins are. So we say, all the sins of the elect are venial, because though they be greater in themselves, being committed against light and knowledge, yet, through God's mercy, they shall be pardoned: and all the sins of reprobate persons are mortal, because they shall never be pardoned. It is the mercy of God, and not the nature of the sins, that makes them venial; for, otherwise, every sin in itself considered, be it never so small, is mortal: for if it work according to its own nature, it works death both of body and soul.

It is a foolish exception that they bring against it, that thus we make all sins equal; and that we bring in, with the Stoics, a parity of sin, because we say all are mortal: for it is as if one should argue, because the mouse and the elephant are both mortal creatures that therefore they are of equal bigness. Though all sins be mortal, they are not all equal; some are greater and some are lesser, according as they are extended and aggravated by time, and place, and person, and sundry other circumstances.

Suppose one should be drowned in the midst of the sea, and another in a shallow pond: in respect of death all were one—both are drowned; but yet there is great difference in respect of the place, for depth and danger. So there is great difference in sin; yet the least sin is in its own nature mortal, and as the Apostle here saith, the wages of it is death.

Again, seeing the wages of sin is death, this

should teach us what use to make of death whenever it is presented to our minds or before our eyes: we should then call to mind the grievous nature of sin, that brought death into the world: by the woful wages, we should be reminded of the unhappy service. Had there not been sin, there would have been no death: upon the death of the soul came in the death of the body: first the soul died in forsaking God, and then the body died, being forsaken of the soul: the soul forsook God willingly; therefore it was compelled, unwillingly, to forsake the body. This is the way that death came into the world by sin, therefore let the remembrance of death help us to put out sin.

That householder in the parable, when he saw tares grow among his wheat, he said to his servants, *An enemy hath done this.* So, whensoever thou seest death seize upon any, say to thyself,—Sin hath done this; this is the wages of sin: for if man had never sinned we should have seen no such thing.

Once more, this text ought to deter us from sin, since it earns such wages. Indeed the manner of sin is for the most part, if not always, to promise a better satisfaction; but it is deceitful, and this is the wages it pays. *The wages of sin is death:* wages are paid in the evening; and though the morning of sin may be fair, yet the evening will be foul when the wages come. At the first, sin may be pleasing; but remember the end,—the end of it is death. Like to a fresh river that runs into the salt sea, the stream is sweet, but it ends in brackishness and bitterness: or like to the feast that Absalom made for Amnon, where there was great cheer and jollity and mirth for a while, but all closed in death and bloodshed and murder. Sin deals with men as Laban dealt with Jacob: it entertaineth them at the first with great compliments, but useth them hardly at the last. As the governor of the feast said:—*Every man at the beginning doth set forth good wine, and then that which is worse;* so sin gives the best at first, but the worst it reserves for the last.

This should keep us from every sin, though it seem never so pleasing and never so sweet to us, remembering that the worst is still to come. We read that when the people saw that Saul forbade them to eat, though they were exceeding hungry, yet not one of them durst touch the honey for fear of the curse: so the pleasures of sin may drop as honey before our eyes, but we must not adventure to taste of them, because they are cursed fruit, and because of the wages that will follow. Never take sin by the head, by the beginnings, as most men do; but take it by the heel; look to the extreme part of it; consider the end, and thou shalt be careful to avoid it.

Jezebel might have allured a man when, having painted her face, she looked out of the window; but to look upon her after she was cast out, eaten of dogs, and nothing remaining but her extreme parts, her skull and the palms of her hands, and her feet, it could not be but with horror. So sin may allure a man, looking only on the painted face in the beginning; but if he cast his eye upon the extreme parts, it would then affright and deter him: for the wages, the end of it, is death. What a world of people run blindly and desperately on! they turn to the race of sin as the horse to the battle, without fear; as if the Psalmist's—*Stand in awe and sin not* were rather—*Sin and fear not.* Whereas we have great cause, every one, to tremble at the least motion of sin in ourselves, to which so dreadful and woful wages is due.

Lastly, from this point those who have repented and have already left the service of sin, may learn to be humbled in themselves, considering what danger and misery they have escaped; and to be more thankful to Christ, who, by taking the whole punishment upon himself, hath freed them from so wretched wages due to their sins. For we must know, beloved, that the best of us are *by nature children of wrath, even as others:* the stipend we have earned is eternal death; and surely it had been paid to us, and nothing could have kept it from us, but for the satisfaction of Christ, coming between God's justice and us. Let us view then, if we can, the misery that we have escaped (as many of us, I mean, as be in a state of grace): we have escaped temporal death, that is, the hurt of death natural; and we have escaped eternal death too.

What is eternal death? It is a separation

from the blessed presence and glory of God—destruction of body and soul for ever—unutterable torments—company with the devil and his angels, and the rout of reprobates—darkness, blacker and thicker than that of Egypt—*weeping and wailing and gnashing of teeth* in the infernal lake—the worm that never dies and the fire that is not quenched. This is the wages of all sin; and the cause wherefore it is not duly rendered to all sin and to all sinners is only this, that the payment hath been already exacted of Christ, in the behalf of those who believe, so that in their own persons they are discharged.

How infinitely then are we bound in thankfulness to him for this great mercy, and how careful should we be to walk worthy of it—resolving never to return to the service of sin, but studying to please and honour a Redeemer who hath delivered us from such misery as this!

The SECOND thing to be considered is the reward that God giveth of free grace to them that serve him. *The gift of God is eternal life through Jesus Christ our Lord.* There is a twofold life to men: the one is natural, and is common to all, good and bad, in this world; the other is spiritual, and is proper to the faithful, being begun by the union of God and the soul, and maintained by the bond of the Spirit.

And this spiritual life hath three degrees:—the *first* degree is in this life; and it begins when we are first brought to repentance, and to a saving knowledge of God and of his Son Jesus Christ:

as it is said, *This is life eternal to know thee, the only true God, and Jesus Christ whom thou hast sent.*

The *second* degree is—from the time of death to the resurrection: for in that time the soul being freed from the body, it is withal free from all sin, original and actual.

And the *third* degree is after the resurrection, when body and soul shall be reunited and we shall have immediate communion and fellowship with God, and so enjoy a more perfect and blessed life than ever we could here.

And this spiritual life, with all the three degrees of it, is the life here spoken of, especially the last degree, the perfection of it in heaven. This is *the gift of God, through Jesus Christ our Lord,* to all that believe.

It is called the *gift* of God, because we cannot deserve it; but it is given and bestowed on us freely for Christ. The Apostle, when he hath said, *The wages of sin is death,* doth not add and say, the wages of righteousness is life eternal; but he calls that the gift of God, to make us understand that God brings us to eternal life merely for his own mercy, and not for our merits; or else surely he would have made the latter part of the sentence answerable to the former.

But here perhaps some may ask—why eternal life should not be the wages of righteousness, as well as death the wages of sin?

I answer, because there is no reason or comparison between sin and righteousness; and therefore there can be no like consequences.

For first, sin is our own — it merits punishment; but righteousness is none of our own: it is given and imputed to us, and is due to God.

Then again, sin is perfectly evil, and so it deserves death; but our righteousness is not perfectly good; it is imperfect in this life, and nothing that is imperfectly good can merit, as wages, eternal life. Yet eternal life is sometimes, yea, many times in Scripture, called a reward; and God is said to reward his children. How is that? Though the reward come originally from mercy, yet God hath tied himself by a promise to bestow this upon his people, and therefore the Lord may be accounted a debtor. How? saith St. Austin. As a promiser; for if he had not promised us this blessing, he would owe us nothing at all—much less eternal life, which is so great a thing.

Yet it may be doubted how eternal life is the free gift of God, seeing it is given for the merits of Christ, as it is here expressed,—*The gift of God is eternal life, through Jesus Christ our Lord.* Now, he that gives a thing upon merit, gives it not freely.

I answer, It is free in respect to us; whatsoever Christ hath done, we did not merit it.

If it be replied, Christ's merits are made ours, and we merit in and by him, and so it cannot be free; I answer, This reason were of force if we ourselves could procure the merits of Christ for us: but that we cannot do, therefore that also is of free gift. *God so loved the world that he gave his only-begotten Son, that whosoever believeth in him should not perish:* he gave him freely, a free gift; so that, though eternal life be due to us by the merits of Christ, yet it is the free gift of God. I will stand no longer in proving the truth of this doctrine, but come at once to the application and use of it.

First, it serves to confute our adversaries of the Church of Rome in the point of merit. They look for heaven and eternal life as wages: we see the Apostle teacheth us otherwise; that eternal life is not given in that manner, but it is *the free gift of God.* And this was the constant doctrine of the primitive church—a good life when we are justified, and an eternal life when we are glorified; all that is good in us is the gift of God, and eternal life is not a retribution to our works but an additional benefaction from him. When God crowns our merits, he crowns nothing else but his own free gift: these and many other sentences we find among the ancient fathers, plainly convincing our adversaries that in this point they swerve, not only from Scripture, but from all sound antiquity.

Secondly, to come to ourselves, this should humble us in respect of our own deservings. Do all the good thou canst, but take heed it do not puff thee up: think not to merit heaven; alas, thou canst not do it. *Is it any pleasure to the Almighty that thou art righteous?* Thy well-doing extends not to him; thou canst do him no good, therefore thou canst look for nothing at his hands. All thou dost in his service is not for his good but for thine own, and the utmost thou canst do is no more than thou art bound to do: therefore, when thou hast done all that thou canst, thou must acknowledge thyself to be an unprofitable servant. If thou hast many good works, yet thou hast more sin; and the least sin of thine, in the rigour of justice, will deprive thee of the favour of God. Therefore thy appeal must be to the throne of grace, and thy only plea must be that of the publican, *God be merciful to me a sinner.* When we have done all we can, it must still be mercy, and not any merit of ours, that must bring us to heaven.

Thirdly, here is comfort for the children of God, in that this inestimable treasure of eternal life is not committed to our keeping, but God hath it in his own charge. It is his gift; it is not committed to the rotten box of our merits: if it were we could have no certainty of it, the devil would easily pick the lock; yea, without picking it, he would shake in pieces the crazy joints of the best work we do; he would steal it from us and take it away, and deprive us of this excellent benefit. But the Lord hath dealt better for us: he hath kept it in his own hands: he hath laid it up in the cabinet of his own mercy and love, that never fails, for *with everlasting kindness he will have mercy on us;* he loveth us with an everlasting love; his compassions fail not; and whom he loves, he loves them to the end. Therefore in temptations, when we are driven to doubt of our attaining eternal life, let us cast our eye upon the keeper of it; it is the Lord, and he is wary to discern and faithful to bestow it: therefore let us comfort ourselves and say, every one of us, as Saint Paul, *I know whom I have believed, and am persuaded that he is able to keep that which I have committed unto him against that day.*

Lastly, seeing eternal life is the free gift of God, we must be thankful to him for it. Pride is a great enemy to thankfulness; and if we did think eternal life were the due reward of our merits we should never be thankful for it. Therefore we ought to humble ourselves, and to consider that we deserve no good thing at God's hands, and to take this great benefit most thankfully. And this is all that God requires of us; for, saith he, *Call upon me in the day of trouble, I will deliver thee, and thou shalt glorify me.* Glorifying God and being thankful to him is all the tribute we are to pay to this our God and King; and shall we deny him this? It is a small benefit that is not worth thanks. We set eternal life at too low a rate if we forget to be thankful. There was never a precious jewel offered at so cheap a price, as—eternal life for our thankfulness.

If we did but know what it were to want it, we should give ten thousand worlds rather than be without it. Therefore, as Naaman's servants said to him concerning his washing in Jordan, *If the Prophet had bid thee do some great thing, wouldest thou not have done it?* So, if God had commanded us a great matter for eternal life, we should have been ready to do it; how much more then, when he saith—take it and be thankful: be but thankful.

Thus have I described to you this twofold service; the service of sin and its wages, that is—death temporal and eternal: and the service of righteousness and its reward—eternal life, which is not wages, but is the gift of God. So that I may now say to you as Moses did to Israel, *I have set before you life and death, cursing and blessing.* Therefore choose not cursing, choose not sin, nor the wages thereof; but choose life, *that both thou and thy seed may live.* If we follow sin the wages will be death, but if we apply ourselves to righteousness in the service of God our reward shall be eternal life; not that we deserve it, but that it is the pleasure of our heavenly Father to bestow it upon us—*For the wages of sin is death, but the gift of God is eternal life through Jesus Christ our Lord.*

SERMON X.

THE STEWARD'S SUMMONS.

LUKE, XVI. 2.

"GIVE AN ACCOUNT OF THY STEWARDSHIP; FOR THOU MAYEST BE NO LONGER STEWARD."

IN the chapter going before, our blessed Lord and Saviour had preached the doctrine of the free grace of God, in the remission of sin and receiving of repentant and returning sinners, in the parable of the prodigal son. The Pharisees were a people that hardened their hearts, and scoffed at everything that Christ delivered: therefore he cometh now in this chapter to warn them that they must soon appear before God, the great master of the world, to give an account of their stewardship; that, by the consideration of God's proceeding in the day of judgment, they might the better know how to prize the remission of sins in the day of grace. This he doth by presenting to them a parable of a certain rich man that had a steward, who was accused unto him that he had wasted his goods, and whom he thereupon calleth to account. And to the end that the Pharisees might not think that it was a matter to be jested withal, and that such considerations as these were to be slighted, he telleth them how the unjust steward, having received this summons and warning from his master, forthwith, for his temporal good, casteth about him, that he may the better be prepared for the loss of his office; thereby teaching them, and in them the whole world, that if this steward, for his own temporal benefit, was thus careful to prepare himself, much more should they be careful to prepare themselves for that great day of account, wherein God will come to judge the world, and will bring to light all things that are hid in darkness.

In these words ye have two things considerable:—A narration or parable; and an application of it.

The narration is twofold:—Of the persons; and of the proceedings.

Of the persons, in the first verse:—A rich man and his steward.

Of the proceedings, in the second verse:—The rich man, on the information made against his steward that he had wasted his goods, calleth him to an account. *Give an account of thy stewardship, for thou mayest be no longer steward.* The steward thereupon falleth first to consult, and after to resolve, as we shall see presently.

In this verse then that I have read you see here is, FIRST, the summons or warning,—*Give an account.*

SECONDLY, The reason of that summons,—*For thou mayest be no longer steward.*

In the FIRST, the summons and calling of this steward to account, ye have clearly offered to ye these two propositions, considerations, or conclusions :—

First, That every man in the world is God's steward.

Secondly, That every one of God's stewards must be brought to a reckoning.

First, I say, every man in the world is God's steward.

If ye ask me who it is that is called a steward, the text tells ye: it is he that must give an account to his master.

If ye ask me who is the master, it is God. If then God be the master, and if every one must give an account and reckoning to God, then every man is the steward intended in this text. That every man must give a reckoning to God it appeareth by St. Paul:—*We must all appear before the judgment-seat of Christ, that every one may receive the things done in his body, whether it be good or bad. All* men,—that which is here expressed by the Apostle in plain terms is more obscurely signified by Christ in his word steward—*Give an account of thy stewardship;* so that the conclusion remaineth clear, and is gathered directly from the text, that every man in the world is God's steward. There is no man or woman in the world, but in some respect or other is the steward that must be called to an account.

For consider these two things :—What every man receives from God, and what God expects from every man. Man receiveth from God that which a steward doth from his lord, and God expects from every man that which a lord expects from his steward.

I say a man receiveth from God that which a steward doth from his master: that is, such goods and such abilities as may enable him to be of use in that place in which his master hath set him in the family. All the world is but God's great family, and all the fittings and endowments of men are the talents, the gifts, wherewith God hath entrusted them. Some have the gifts of the world—riches and places of authority: others have the gifts of the body, as health and strength, and the like: others have the gifts of the mind, understanding and wisdom and policy: and to all these, some have spiritual graces. According as men are furnished with these gifts, and according to their several qualifications and endowments, they all receive them from God, as stewards.

And God expects, in return, those things which a lord requires from his steward.

He requires that they acknowledge him to be the chief, and that they hold all from him; that they have it not from themselves, nor for themselves: this is what every master expects from him to whom he committeth his treasure; and this would God have all men do. God speaks that truly which Benhadad spake proudly and falsely to the king of Israel,—*Thy silver and thy gold is mine; thy wives also and thy children, even the goodliest, are mine.* All are his; *the earth is the Lord's, and the fulness thereof.* He is the possessor of all things, and he letteth out parcels of his possession to the sons of men. To some he committeth a larger portion than to others, yet they are but tenants at will; and tenants upon certain conditions and reservations, wherein this great Lord bindeth those that hold anything of him.

And one condition or reservation unto which he ties all his stewards is this—that they waste not his goods, that they scatter them not abroad vainly or unprofitably. Now a man that hath riches, if he relieve not the poor,—a man that hath authority, and helpeth not the oppressed,—a man that hath wisdom, and instructeth not the ignorant,—in a word, a man that hath any abilities and turneth them not to good account—this man scattereth his master's goods, and is like that unprofitable servant that hid his talent in a napkin, and therefore was bound hand and foot and cast into outer darkness. This was the accusation that was brought against this steward here: he had wasted his Lord's goods, that is, he had spent them vainly, he was no honour to his master, there came no profit to the household by him.

Another thing that this great Lord expects of

all his stewards is, that they do not scatter his goods, nor vainly waste them, nor abuse them to evil ends. There is in the world a generation of men that fight against God with his own weapons, and use all their strength and wisdom and power to maintain a faction of rebellion against him,—that side with the wicked of the world against his laws and ordinances; and this is the greatest ingratitude and presumption that can be. If a king should raise a servant to honour, and bestow offices and dignity upon him, and yet if he should raise an army against him, and set himself against all his laws, what great unthankfulness would this be! Therefore Christ, the King of the Church, shall say of all who thus rebel against him,—*Those mine enemies which would not that I should reign over them, bring hither and slay them before me.* This is the case of all those men that have wealth and abuse it, consuming it upon their lusts and their pride; that have wit, and spend it, like Tertullus, to cry down the ways of God and to harden themselves and others in the course of sin; that have greatness and authority, and misemploy it to the crushing of good persons and fair causes: these and the like are stewards that abuse their master's goods, and misemploy them to his dishonour: these Christ counteth his enemies, and he will not spare them.

Again, God expects this of all his stewards, that they should do him homage, and especially that they should present themselves before him at his court-days. God's Sabbaths are God's court-days, wherein he calleth and assembleth his servants together. He will have every one wait upon him, that they may know his will. As Cornelius bringeth his family together, and saith to Peter,—*We are all here present to hear all things that are commanded thee of God,*—so God, I say, will have his servants present at his court-days; and not only so, not only to be present there to hear his will and to understand his mind, but to submit to his orders, to yield obedience to his laws, to be governed by his rules. God hath certain rules to which he will have every man subject: there be rules for magistrates, for ministers, for masters, for parents, for servants, for children, for all; and he is a rebel, and carrieth himself not as God's steward, that doth not keep the rules that God hath set up in his own house.

Once more: God expects from all his stewards, that whensoever he sendeth his bailiffs for rent, they will return him the fruit of his own ground. Every soul is God's ground, from which God expects some fruit or other; and he sends his servants, his bailiffs, continually, to gather these fruits from men. When he sendeth a poor man to a rich, there is a bailiff sent to him to gather some fruit of his wealth. When he sendeth an oppressed man to one that is in authority, there is a bailiff sent to him to gather the fruit of his power and greatness. When he sendeth an ignorant man to one that hath wisdom and knowledge, there is a bailiff sent to him to gather the fruit of his knowledge. And so we may say of all things. Whatsoever endowments of body or mind or estate any man hath, if another need it, that other is God's bailiff, sent to him to call for his rent, to call for the fruit of his ground; and to such an one thou must return it, for thou art but a steward, and thou knowest how fearful the proceedings of the great king are: *He will miserably destroy those wicked men* who will not render the fruits in their season. So, when God shall send the poor to thee for relief, and thou helpest him not; shall send the ignorant to thee for instruction, and thou informest him not; shall send any one to thee that he may have use of thy gifts and abilities, and thou dost not employ them that way,—thou deniest the great Lord the fruit of his own ground, and art of the number of those husbandmen that must expect this at his hand, to be miserably destroyed in his wrath.

Ye see the point opened, that all men are God's stewards, both in respect of what God hath bestowed on them and what God doth expect from them. I come now briefly to make some use of this.

Are all men God's stewards? Then certainly there is some work required of every man in the world, by virtue of this title and office put upon him. It concerns therefore every one to look to his place.

There are two things required of every

steward:—a dispensation; and a right ordering of his dispensation.

A steward, ye know, is appointed to dispense for others, not for himself; for the good of the family in which he is set, not for his own benefit. God hath made every creature to be for the use of others, and not for itself. Those heavenly bodies, the sun and moon and stars, their motion and influences, are for us, for the service of the world. The earth with the fruits of it, the beasts and all, are for the service of man. So every man in his several place hath some work to do for others, some abilities given him for the service of others. Hence it is that the magistrate is said to be the minister of God for the people's good. Hence the ministers are said to be servants of the church;—*I am debtor*, saith Paul, *both to the Greeks and to the Barbarians; both to the wise and to the unwise.* Hence it is that the master of a family is said to be *worse than an infidel* if he provide not for those of his own house. And every other Christian, though he stand not in any of these relations, yet he hath some particular gifts that are to be laid out for the use and advantage of others; and every person in the world may be of some use or other in the place in which he is set. This is the cause that the name of *brother* is common to all Christians, and ye know that Joseph acknowledged that he was called to those honours and to that authority and place that he had, for the good of his brethren and of his father's house. So should all God's people acknowledge other Christians their brethren, and that whatsoever parts they have, they have them for the good of the family. Christians are rightly called *members* one of another; and as every member is of use to the whole body, so must every Christian be profitable—some by the riches of the body—some by the riches of the mind—some by the abilities of their estates—every one according to the treasure he is entrusted with and the talent that is committed to him.

This is one thing that men must make conscience to do, to be dispensers of their goodness, of whatever they possess; to be communicative, to diffuse and extend themselves to others, as occasion shall be offered. And indeed where there is any goodness in a man, he will express it this way, by doing all the good he can to others.

It is likewise required of a steward that he consider of the manner and right ordering of his dispensations. He must dispense both faithfully and wisely: *Who,* saith the Lord, *is that faithful and wise steward, whom his Lord shall make ruler over his household?* &c.

If we would be faithful in our places, God's glory must be our end, and his word our rule. Let a man consider what God commands him in such a place, in such a qualification, having such endowments, such parts, such abilities; and let him dispense these—by that rule, according to that command—to the glory of God that gave him those talents. Thus was Moses a faithful steward, *faithful in all the house of God as a servant.* His Master's glory was his end; and therefore, when he saw his Master dishonoured by idolatry, he could not then contain himself, but *his anger waxed hot,* though he was the meekest man upon earth. And his Master's will was his rule; therefore he came down from the mountain with the tables in his hand, that it might appear what was his guide and direction in all his carriage amongst the people; and we shall find that in all the doubts of the people, either in matter of command or punishment, he always sought direction from God. He is no faithful servant that doth not do this.

And as he must be a *faithful* steward in dispensing, so he must be *wise* in his dispensing too.

What is the wisdom of God's stewards? Not the wisdom drawn from the writings of Macchiavelli, nor the wisdom of the world, nor of the flesh, for that is *enmity against God*—not drawn from the rules that politicians walk by; but that wisdom that is drawn out of the Scriptures, the word of God, which is able to make us wise unto salvation. This is the wisdom that God's servants must express and manifest, in dispensing their gifts; they must be made wise by the word; they must seek wisdom from the word, the rule of wisdom, and from the example of those who were guided by the Spirit of wisdom. They must compare the precepts of the word and the practice of the saints together; see what God commandeth in such a place, in such a condition; see what God's servants that have gone before have done in such an office. Mark how Abraham and Job and others of God's saints have employed their wealth and authority for the relieving of the poor, for the furtherance of God's glory, for the help of those that were oppressed. Mark how Nehemiah bestirred himself for the sanctifying of the Sabbath, for the furtherance of God's worship. Mark again how St. Paul, as a minister, watched against the wolves, and how he would spend himself to the uttermost for the church of God. Mark how Abraham, as a master of a family, governed his household, teaching and commanding his children to walk in the way of the Lord. Mark how other of God's servants have employed their gifts, as Samson his strength, for the church, and as Solomon his wisdom; and whatsoever gift any of them had, they acknowledged that the talents that were committed to them were for God and for the service of his church, for the furtherance of his glory in the particular places in which he set them. I say, if men would be wise stewards they must do thus. But I cannot stand upon this, lest I be prevented in that which I most intend, which followeth.

Ye have heard who is the steward. It is every one that hath received any ability from God to do him service; God expects that he should employ that ability in his service.

We come now, *secondly*, to consider the reckoning which every man must make, the account that every man must render of his stewardship.

In the opening of this I will show ye two things. I will show ye, first, what time of reckoning God hath with his stewards; and after, why God proceedeth judicially in this manner, called a reckoning or account.

For the first: there are two times of reckoning that God will have with his stewards: the first time is in this life; the second after death.

Also he hath two ways, while in this life, of calling them to account; by his word and by his rod.

By his word he hasteneth every man to an account, by the Gospel and by the doctrine of repentance. This course God himself took with Adam, when he called him to account for his carriage in the garden. *Adam*, saith he, *where art thou? Who told thee that thou wast naked? Hast thou eaten of the tree whereof I commanded thee that thou shouldest not eat?* Afterwards, when God sent his prophets into the world, they took the same course; as Elijah, when he came to Ahab:—*Hast thou killed, and also taken possession?* So John Baptist, when he cometh to the Pharisees and those other hard-hearted sinners, he calleth them to a reckoning:—*O generation of vipers, who hath warned you to flee from the wrath to come?* So Peter calleth those three thousand souls to a reckoning for crucifying of Christ, whom, saith he, *ye have taken, and by wicked hands have crucified and slain.*

And because there are many that, like the deaf adder, stop their ears, and if God speak to them they pass it by (as Elihu, in Job, saith,—*God speaketh once, yea twice, but man perceiveth it not*), therefore, when the word doth not prevail, God calleth them to a reckoning by his rod:—*Hear ye the rod, and who hath appointed it:* that is, God hath appointed scourges and afflictions for men, to awaken them to hearken to the voice hat calls them to a reckoning.

Now afflictions are outward or inward, corporal or spiritual. God sometimes calleth man to account by corporal afflictions. He chasteneth him with pain upon his bed, and the multitude of his bones with strong pain. What is the reason of this, but that man may come to this conclusion with himself—that he must bring his own heart to a reckoning for his former carriage? This is that the Apostle saith:—*For this cause many are weak and sickly among you, and many sleep.* Some were taken with sickness, upon others there was a consuming weakness, and others were stricken with death. What is the end that God propounds in all this? It is this,—that we should judge ourselves, *for if we would judge ourselves we should not be judged; but when we are judged, we are chastened of the Lord, that we should not be condemned with the world.* As if he should say, God now calleth you to a reckoning in this life, to the end you may prevent that heavy and grievous one that cometh after this life.

Again, when outward afflictions prevail not, God hath spiritual afflictions to awaken men. Thus

David, when he was in a deep sleep of security, God awakened him with a spiritual judgment. See his speech in the 32d Psalm:—*When I kept silence, my bones waxed old, through my roaring all the day long.* What followed? God by this means brought him to confession:—*I said, I will confess my transgressions unto the Lord, and thou forgavest the iniquity of my sin.*

Thus God, in this life, calleth men to a reckoning, sometimes by the preaching of the word, sometimes by judgments upon the outward man, and sometimes by terrors upon the soul. But if all this prevail not to make a man reckon with himself in this life, then God hath another reckoning after this life, where every man must give an account, and cannot avoid it; and there he that would not prevent the sentence of the judge, must submit to it and abide by it for ever.

That there is such a judgment to come is evident both from the equity of it, and from the necessity; and that in respect of God, of the saints, and of the wicked.

In respect of God, there is a necessity of it, that his decree may be fulfilled and executed. *He hath appointed a day in the which he will judge the world in righteousness:* and he hath said, *My counsel shall stand, and I will do all my pleasure.*

Also, it is necessary that God's honour may be vindicated. Now things seem to go in some confusion and disorder in the world. Good men, the children of God, are often oppressed by the wicked; they are in adversity, they suffer wrong, while the wicked flourish as a green bay-tree; justice is perverted, wickedness is in the place of judgment, and in the place of righteousness there is iniquity. Therefore Solomon makes this observation:—*I said in mine heart, God shall judge the righteous and the wicked; for there is a time there for every purpose and for every work.* God hath a time to do that great work that he hath now purposed. What is that work? To bring every thing to judgment, whether it be good or evil: to set all to right again that is uneven and unjust in the world.

In respect of the saints also, a day of judgment is necessary, both that their innocency, that is here traduced, may be made manifest, and also that their works may be rewarded. For the first:—they undergo many disgraces and hard censures amongst men; the world accounts them proud, hypocrites, singular, foolish, vain-glorious, and I know not what. Now, saith Job, *my witness is in heaven, and my record is on high:* and, saith St. Paul, I care not *to be judged of you, nor of man's judgment; but he that judgeth me is the Lord.* The word in the Greek is *man's day;* as if he should say, men have their day here, but God hath a greater day after: the Lord will judge in another manner and upon other grounds than men do. And for the second, the reward of their works:—When we speak of reward, we mean not the reward of merit; we mean the reward of grace, called a reward because God is tied to it by his promise. The servants of God, though they serve him with all care, they have not the fat of the land, as sometimes the Ishmaels of the world have; they do not abound with outward things as many others do: nay, sometimes they are in the worst condition. God therefore hath a time in view when his servants shall have full measure, heaped up, pressed down, shaken together, and running over. When God shall make up his *jewels, then shall ye discern between the righteous and the wicked, between him that serveth God, and him that serveth him not.* Mark, *ye shall discern;* God will make it appear to the whole world that, notwithstanding his servants are despised and lie here under divers pressures, yet they are a people in whom he delights, whom he accounteth as *his jewels,* his precious treasures.

It is necessary in respect of the wicked, too: both that God's righteousness may be fully manifested, and that their unrighteousness may be fully punished.

The day of judgment is called *the day of wrath and revelation of the righteous judgment of God:* for then God will manifest his wrath against the vessels of wrath, and so make it appear to the world that he proceedeth in a right manner and by a right rule in judging. For we must know, that though God cannot be unjust, and though the ungodly men of this world are ever convicted by their own consciences, yet such is their corruption and the hardness of their hearts, that they would fain justify themselves among men. And again, though it be true that the soul when it is departed out of the body is under God's particular judgment, and hath such a spiritual illumination and understanding of God's actions as that it may know itself to be accursed or acquitted, and accordingly is entered already into the possession either of happiness or misery; yet all this is secret in the world till the day of God's tribunal come, wherein secret things shall be revealed, and things that have been done in darkness shall appear before men and angels. Then shall God's justice be cleared and fully manifested.

And then, also, shall the wicked and unrighteous receive their full punishment. They are not fully punished while under the sense of God's wrath in this life; nor yet when the soul is judged at their death: there must be yet a further degree for all this. For the wicked sin, not only in soul but in body too. The body hath been the instrument of the soul in sinning, and therefore it cannot serve the turn that the soul be punished while the body lie in the grave: no, those that have joined in the sin must be joined together also in punishment.

Again, though the sinful actions of the wicked are transient, and seem to die with them, yet, in respect of the contagion and evil effects, these actions work upon others and upon posterity; and thus the actions of those wicked men continue to the day of judgment. See how the

Jews revived the sins of their fathers: *We will burn incense to the queen of heaven,* say they, *as our fathers have done.* See how the kings of Israel, that succeeded Jeroboam, went on in the steps of Jeroboam *the son of Nebat, who made Israel to sin.* As long as men go on in the sins of their forefathers, the sins of their forefathers live. So that some men's sins, by a continued imitation, are perpetuated long after they are dead, even to the day of judgment. Wherefore there must be a day of judgment, that may fill up a measure proportionable to their sin.

This it was that Dives feared in hell, and that made him cry out as he did, that one might go and tell his brethren upon earth, that they might not follow him into that place of torment. Why would he have them tell his brethren? Was there in hell such love to the kingdom of Christ, that Dives would have his brethren converted? No such matter. Was it love to the souls of his brethren? No such matter, neither. What then? Certainly it was nothing else but a sense of his own guilt: he knew what evil example he had given, and what a counsellor he had been to his brethren; and if they should go on in his steps, and their children after them, all this would but add to his punishment in the great day when soul and body shall be joined together to make up the full measure of their torment. For this reason, also, I say, it is necessary there should be a day of judgment, after this life, at the end of the world.

The SECOND thing remaineth; and that is, why the Holy Ghost expresseth God's proceedings by way of reckoning, or calling to account? What need the Lord reckon with men? He might proceed to pass sentence and to execute judgment; but he saith,—Come, give an account of thy stewardship. I answer, there are four things implied in this, all showing the manner of God's proceedings at the day of judgment with his stewards, that it shall be like the proceedings of a master with his servants, in an account and reckoning.

The *first* is this: that it shall be a proceeding in particulars. God shall then proceed, not by gross sums and in the total;—ye have done evil in the general: none will deal thus with an accountant, but he will run over the particulars, and require an account for pounds, for shillings, for pence, for everything. So will God deal with all his stewards when he bringeth them to a reckoning. He will reckon on particulars: he will require an account of all things that he hath enabled them with for his service.

Those that are rich men he will ask, first, how they have *gotten* their estates; whether they have built their houses as a moth, that is, to the hurt of others, as men do that raise themselves by usury and oppression and fraud and bribery, and such-like courses.

And then again, how they have *kept* their wealth; whether to the injury of others, *withholding good from them to whom it is due*, from the poor, who in case of want are the owners of their goods, because God hath entrusted them to his stewards for their sakes.

And again, how they have *spent* what they had, whether on their lusts or no. *Ye ask and receive not*, saith St. James, *because ye ask amiss, that ye may consume it upon your lusts.* So ye lay out amiss; ye spend it on your lusts. When men, for pride in apparel, for excess at their tables, for vain buildings, for sinful upholding of wickedness, for unnecessary and injurious proceedings in law-suits, or in whatsoever indirect course lay out their estates, it is a mis-spending of their master's goods. And as he that hath got his wealth unjustly and he that keepeth it unjustly shall give an account, so he that layeth it out in a confused, sinful, profuse way, shall be called to give a reckoning for that.

And not only for matter of estate, but besides, for matter of place and authority. Moses knew this well enough; and therefore, when he was to go out of the world, he first clears all reckonings with the people of Israel:—I have been a ruler thus long; let any man come and stand up and say, I have done him wrong: let every man come and clear me this day, before the Lord. This was the account that Moses made with the people of Israel before he died, that he might lift up his head with comfort in the day of the Lord. Thus it must be with you: ye must give an account of your places.

And so for the state of your bodies. The

health thou hast had, how hast thou spent it? Mark the speech of Solomon to the young man. *Rejoice, O young man, in the days of thy youth; but know thou that for all these things God will bring thee unto judgment.* Now thou hast a great deal of health, a great deal of strength; but hast thou been the better for God's service? hast thou employed it for God's glory or no?

And so for the members of thy body; thou must give an account for thy employment of those instruments. Thou must give an account for thy tongue, *for every idle word* that thou speakest. And if for every idle word, what then for thy swearing and cursing and lying? What for the abundance of filthy, obscene, and rotten communication that cometh out of thy mouth? Thou must give an account for thy tongue, and so for every other member and for every sense that thou hast.

Thou must give an account likewise for the gifts of thy mind, how thou hast employed thy wisdom and learning and experience.

For all thy passions; *Whosoever is angry with his brother without a cause shall be in danger of the judgment.*

For all the dispositions and inclinations of thy heart; *for out of the heart proceed evil thoughts, murders, adulteries,* and many other things *which defile a man.*

In a word, whatsoever ability thou hast, whereby thou mightest have been beneficial and serviceable to the church and commonwealth, thou must give an account of it in particular unto God. He will call thee to a reckoning of every parcel of it by itself. The master in the Gospel that gave the talents to his servants, he called them to an account for every talent he gave them. So there must be a particular enumeration to God of all those several abilities wherewith he hath fitted thee for his service: how thou hast behaved thyself in matter of health, strength, and time; in thy senses; in the members of thy body; how with thy mind; how with the dispositions of thy soul; how in all the gifts and endowments he hath entrusted thee with, for the service of the church and commonwealth.

Secondly, it is called a reckoning, because in this reckoning, God will go by a method, keeping an order, such an order as men do in reckoning with their accountants—everything being taken in its due place. God will proceed to give every one in the day of judgment his due place, and ye shall find that many sins that ye have accounted the lightest of all will be the heaviest and grievous at that day. *I will reprove thee*, saith God, *and set them in order before thine eyes.* God will observe such an order, that everything shall have its due place, its due head.

In the first place shall be that apostasy whereof all Adam's posterity are guilty. This David saw; and therefore when he judged himself, he judged himself as one born in sin. *I was shapen in iniquity, and in sin did my mother conceive me.*

In the next place shall be that concupiscence, that depravity of nature from whence all actual sins proceed. This St. Paul knew, and therefore, in the 7th of Romans, he bewaileth it, as the original and root of all other actual sins. God will begin first with the sins of the heart, because thence come all the outward actions of the whole man.

Then he will judge the outward works themselves. He will begin with those against the first table, atheism, infidelity, profaneness, contempt of God and his service, neglect of his glory and of the opportunities he hath given us.

And when the Law and the Gospel come together, he will proceed more severely for the sins against the Gospel than the Law. Therefore our Saviour telleth us it shall be easier in the day of judgment for *Sodom and Gomorrah,* that had the Law only, than for *Capernaum* that had the Gospel too. And, saith the Apostle, *If he that despised Moses' law died without mercy, of how much sorer punishment shall he be thought worthy who hath trodden under foot the Son of God!* how much worse shall it be for him who hath disobeyed the Gospel of Christ—the law of faith! Thus God will proceed.

And therefore, when ye would exercise repentance, follow God's order. Mourn more for impenitency and infidelity than for other things. Be more humbled for sins against the first table, for profaneness, for atheism and neglect of God, than for sins against the second; though these, too, must be repented of. Again, be more constant in lamenting the inward sinful disposition of thy heart than thy outward sinful actions, and forget not the original root of all, which we brought with us into the world. I say, mark God's method and his order: that which he takes most notice of in the day of judgment, lay that to thy thoughts, and take greatest notice of it now.

It is a grievous thing for a man to be born in sin, but to add actual sin to that is still more grievous. For a man to sin in thought and in heart, this is very grievous.

It is a grievous thing for a man to sin against righteousness and to deal unjustly with men; but to deal unrighteously with God, in point of his worship, is more grievous. It is a grievous sin for a man to disobey the law of God; but to disobey the law of faith, to delay repentance, to despise the mercy and forgiveness of God, this is far more grievous. Thus, we should mark God's order that he will observe in calling us to a reckoning.

Thirdly, it is called a reckoning, because God will proceed with men at that day as a master with his servants, by writings, by books. In Daniel—*the book was opened*, and in Revelation there is mention made of *the books that were opened*. There are two books: the book of the law, that shows what we should have done—*The word that I have spoken*, saith Christ, *the same shall judge you in the last day*;—and the book of conscience, that shows what we have done. God will put the memories of men to the task, as Abraham did Dives. *Son, remember that thou in thy lifetime receivedst thy good things.* So remember that thou in thy lifetime hadst riches: how didst thou employ them? Remember that thou hadst authority and office and place in the commonwealth; and what service didst thou do to God? Remember that thou hadst wisdom and learning and knowledge; what good had the Church thereby? God, I say, will put every man's memory to the task; what opportunities he lost carelessly; what occasions he avoided wilfully; how, when he might have done God better service, yet, lest he should be disadvantaged in his bye-respects in the world, he baulked them. Remember this: *The sin of Judah,* saith God, *is written with a pen of iron and with the point of a diamond: it is graven upon the table of their heart.* God hath the sins of men graven upon the table of their hearts. Little dost thou, that art an old man, think of a thousand things that God will bring against thee that were done in thy youth. Job little thought, till the day of his affliction, when God made him possess the sins of his youth, that there was such abundance of guilt against him as there was. God will remember all that thou hast forgotten.

God will proceed by books, and this will clear God's justice in his proceedings, and make everything appear righteous in the sight of men and angels; because every man's conscience shall testify against himself, and therefore the mouth of all ungodly men shall be stopped at the day of the Lord: they shall have nothing to say for themselves why justice should not proceed against them. Here, will God say, I find so much given to usury, so much gotten unfairly, so much spent in vain, so much kept injuriously from the furtherance of God's worship and from planting the Gospel where it was wanted, so much kept from benefiting the Church and commonwealth in public and private, so much from helping the poor: here I find it; how comes it here? was it not written with thine own hand? was it not thyself that made this impression upon thy conscience by thine own guilt? What wilt thou say for thyself? Hath any one accused thee wrongfully? hath any one written it by mistake? No, all is done with thine own hand, and thou canst not deny thine own handwriting when it is brought to thy face. Hath any one else had the keeping of this book of thy conscience? Hast thou not always had it in thine own possession? What canst thou allege for thyself?

I know, beloved, that there are many other ways whereby ungodly men shall be accused at the last day. God himself shall accuse them, and be a swift witness against them: the saints shall accuse them: wicked men shall accuse them: the devil shall accuse them. But the main proceeding, and that that shall clear God's justice and stop the mouths of all ungodly men, is this, that the accusation by their own handwriting, their own book, shall accuse them, that they have wasted their Lord's goods and mis-spent them.

The *fourth* and last thing wherein this proceeding at the last day shall be like a reckoning, is this: that there shall be an account made in measure and in proportion to the trust committed to men. The master, when he reckoneth with his servant, he calleth him to account, not for some lesser sums, or for some one or two things, but for all that he hath entrusted him with; and if one servant have more than another, his account shall be greater than another's: according to the greatness of that that is committed to him, so shall the largeness of his reckoning be. *Unto whomsoever much is given, of him shall be much required.* When the master, in the Gospel, called his servants to an account for the talents, he that had ten talents made account for ten; and he that had five, for five; and he that had one, but for one; every one for so much as he had received. He that hath received bodily abilities of health and strength shall account for that. He that hath had wealth and an estate in the world shall make account further for that. He that hath had all these, and authority and place wherein he had power to do right and to glorify God amongst men, he must make account for so much the more.

Alas, beloved, if men considered that the more wealth they heap up and the more places of authority and preferments they have in the world, their accounts shall be greater at the day of the Lord, certainly it would make them more sober and to walk more humbly and watchfully; it would make them so much the more industrious to improve their talents to the best advantage of their Lord that entrusted them with them.

So much for the opening of the point. I will conclude, briefly, with a few uses of it.

Ye see, beloved, not only that all are God's stewards, but that all God's stewards shall be brought to a reckoning—brought to it in this life and in another. The first use then shall be, for confutation of those atheists that put far from them the fear of the day of judgment.

Is it possible that there should be a generation of men in the world that should doubt of the judgment to come? Nay, shall we go further and say that there should be, not only in the world, but even in the Church, such as doubt of the time and day? Do but try men's courses. What sins do they most fear and most avoid? They fear only such sins as, in the course of justice, men and their laws take hold of: such as are only a breach of the second table. Men will not be injurious to men, lest man's justice be brought against them: but how comes it to pass that there is so little regard of God, so little reverence of his name, so little of his worship in their houses and in their hearts? Certainly men do not think that God will be as exact in his judgment, as men are in cases that are brought before them. Again, do not men fear those outward actions that expose them to the censure of their neighbours? Yet, at the same time, they fear not evil affections and the motions of sin in their own hearts. A man would not be taken with open theft; yet, nevertheless, he useth fraud when men cannot discern it. A man would not be charged with murder; yet, nevertheless, he is full of malice and envy and repining. Why is this, but because men acknowledge not a judgment to come? They fear not the judgment of God wherein he will bring the breaches of the first table to an account as well as those of the second, and the secret thoughts and sins of the heart to a reckoning as well as outward actions.

Yet God will assuredly call all men to judgment; and let no man think that he will fail in this because he now deferreth the promise of his coming. The time may be long with us, but it is not long with God; and in that he deferreth, it is that some men may be brought to salvation and others made inexcusable.

Secondly: it serveth for instruction. If there shall be such a judgment to come — if God will have such a time of reckoning with all his stewards in the world — then it teacheth us not to busy ourselves in judging one another, since God shall judge us all; but to turn judgment on our own hearts; to be more in judging ourselves, that we may the less be judged of the Lord. Will God call thee to a reckoning? Then begin to call thyself to a reckoning first.

Reckon with thine own heart. Doth God

awaken thy conscience by the preaching of his word: descend into thine own heart and ask thyself, What have I done? How have I followed this teaching and these commandments of God? If God smite thee with afflictions and losses, reckon with thyself how thou hast gained and how thou hast employed thy wealth. If with disgraces, reckon with thyself about thy pride and ambition and vanity of heart. If God smite thy body with sickness, consider how thou hast employed thy health and strength, and for what object. Every evening, call thyself to an account: What have I done this day; where have I been; in what company; how have I carried myself there; what good have I done; what good have I received? In the matters of thy calling, reckon with thyself, with what heart thou hast followed it, with what care to conform thyself to God's word, the rule of righteousness: if thou hast been in pleasures, whether they were lawful; and if so, whether they were lawfully used. Thus must every man reckon with his own heart, as the Church in Lamentations,—*Wherefore doth a living man complain, a man for the punishment of his sins? Let us search and try our ways, and turn again unto the Lord.* There are many that think to outface God and man in their sins; but know this, whoever thou art, that if thou forbear to reckon with thine own heart, God will assuredly reckon with thee: thou must reckon here with self, or hereafter with God. Therefore, saith David, *Commune with your own heart upon your bed:* that is, be sure to take time from your sleep, rather than neglect this business of reckoning with your own hearts.

Reckon also with others.

Let masters reckon with their families, their servants and children, whether they have done their duty towards them faithfully, in furthering them by instruction and by example to all good.

Let those who are in a way of traffic reckon with those that they deal withal. If thou hast wronged any by unjust gain, thou must reckon with him by restitution: there is nothing thou hast gotten unjustly, but if thou dost not reckon for it now, at that day, saith St. James, *it shall eat your flesh, as it were fire.* Therefore, Zaccheus, when salvation was brought to his house, restored fourfold all that he had gained by unjust dealing. Doubtless there are many that now clothe themselves in satin and velvet, and abound in all variety and bravery, that would be houseless, and moneyless, and apparel-less, it may be, if they should make restitution of their unjust gain. Well, but let them do it as they love their souls. They must reckon with God, as stewards, how they have come by every penny they have in the world, and therefore let them go about it now.

Reckon with others, also, for works of mercy; in what thou hast been wanting to thy brethren. Thou hast lived thus long in a plentiful estate: what good hast thou done with it? Josephus reckons up three several tenths that were expected and exacted from the Jew. Wouldst thou be less liberal now, in the time of the Gospel, than they were under the law?

Is God less merciful, or hath he less interest in thy estate? You cannot, if you look about you, want objects of mercy, and means to further your reckoning at the day of the Lord; and if you would be faithful stewards to God, say thus: I have been thus much behind-hand in paying the due I owe to the poor, to the church, &c.; but I will now pay it while I live, and while I have the means and opportunity to do so. Let every man reckon thus with his own heart.

Again, if you would stand at that great day of judgment, when there shall be such an exact reckoning, interest yourselves now in Christ. There is no way to escape the judgment to come but by making peace with the Judge now. *There is no condemnation to them that are in Christ Jesus.*

Once more: seeing that ye must thus account to God for all that ye do, *what manner of persons ought ye to be in all holy conversation and godliness?* Alas! brethren, little do ye know whether this be the last sermon that many of you may hear, whether this be the last day wherein God will ever call upon you to repent and amend your lives. There shall be a fearful dissolution and destruction of all things that you see. There shall be a naked appearance made before the Judge at that day of reckoning; let every man, therefore, say within himself, How shall I stand at that time, at that judgment? All our care should be that of the Apostle Paul; because, saith he, *there shall be a resurrection from the dead, both of the just and unjust*, therefore, *herein do I exercise myself to have always a conscience void of offence toward God and toward men.* Look to it in your places and in your hearts, that you may have a good conscience, for the time shall come that nothing in the world shall stand you in stead but this; and if then, when the books are opened, it be found that your reckonings are even, and the accounts clear between you and your Maker, by repentance, by faith, and by obedience, happy shall that servant be whom his Master shall find so doing.

The last use is a use of comfort to all the servants of God. Let them quietly and cheerfully suffer that portion of misery and affliction that the Lord dealeth out unto them. Let them not grudge at the prosperity of ungodly men, nor at the variety of changes that themselves are exposed to; because there is a day of reckoning and account, when all things shall be made even. The Apostle, St. James, exhorteth Christians to patience upon this very ground, because *the coming of the Lord draweth nigh.* If, therefore, you see wicked men prosper, and bring their enterprises to pass, be not troubled at the matter. Yet a little while, and they and we shall all be called to account for the things committed to us: then all shall be righted; the wicked shall be cast out and condemned, and the good and faithful steward, he who has held his account right before God, who has got repentance and obedience and hearty faith in the merits of Jesus Christ, as a set-off against his debts and deficiencies, shall be called to enter for ever into the joy of his Lord.

SERMON XI.

SPIRITUAL HEART'S-EASE;

OR,

THE WAY TO TRANQUILLITY.

JOHN, XIV. 1, 2, 3.

"LET NOT YOUR HEART BE TROUBLED: YE BELIEVE IN GOD, BELIEVE ALSO IN ME. IN MY FATHER'S HOUSE ARE MANY MANSIONS: IF IT WERE NOT SO, I WOULD HAVE TOLD YOU. I GO TO PREPARE A PLACE FOR YOU. AND IF I GO AND PREPARE A PLACE FOR YOU, I WILL COME AGAIN, AND RECEIVE YOU UNTO MYSELF; THAT WHERE I AM, THERE YE MAY BE ALSO."

IN the 33d verse of the former chapter, our Saviour Christ told his disciples that he must now go away from them: *Little children, yet a little while I am with you. Ye shall seek me, and as I said unto the Jews, Whither I go ye cannot come; so now I say to you.*

This message of the departure of Christ from the earth, of his being taken from them, did exceedingly sadden their hearts and very much perplex and disquiet their spirits. They knew what a comfort they had in the presence of Christ; they knew what a faithful Teacher he was, what a mighty Protector he had been, how gracious and full of heavenly comfort he had manifested himself to them at all times; and they could not now think of parting with him without much anxiety and trouble of spirit. Therefore the words that I have now read are the speech of our blessed Saviour to comfort them, strengthening their hearts against those disquiets under which they were exercised.

In which words you may observe, mainly, these three things:—

FIRST, a duty whereunto they are exhorted,—*Let not your heart be troubled.*

SECONDLY. The means whereby it may be performed,—*Ye believe in God; believe also in me.*

THIRDLY. Some instruction and encouragement in the use of these means.

FIRST, the duty that is to be performed is this, to stablish and comfort the heart: to confirm it against fear and trouble.

The word that is here translated *trouble*, signifieth such a trouble as is in water when the mud is stirred up, or when the waves and surges are raised by some tempest or storm. It signifieth such a trouble as is in an army when the soldiers are disranked and routed; and it shows us that those distempers that are in the hearts and affections of men do exceedingly hinder their judgments, so that they can see and discern no better than a man can do in muddy water. All the affections are as so many soldiers in an army that is disordered, that keep not their due subordination to their leader and guide, by reason that the understanding, that should govern the will and affections, is led captive by them.

And this distemper of spirit, arising from the inordinacy of the affections, doth so affect the soul, that no faculty can perform its own work, but it is deceived and misled, and disabled from judging of things according to truth. It is with the mind in sorrow, as with the eye in tears; it can see nothing clearly, it can judge nothing correctly.

But that which our Saviour aims at here hath a particular respect to the affections of fear and grief. When these are in excess, when a man overfeareth anything, or yieldeth to overmuch grief, then is the soul *troubled* and (as it were) disjointed: it suffereth pain and disquiet, as a bone that is out of joint: therefore, by all means, keep your hearts in a right state, in that order that God hath set them. *Let not your heart be troubled.*

Men are wondrous prone — even the very best men — to be *troubled* when sorrows and afflictions come upon them. You may see the malady in the medicine. Every prohibition in the word supposeth a corruption, and an aptness in the natural heart and spirit of man, to transgress in that particular against which it is directed: therefore, when Christ speaks to his disciples and tells them not to be troubled, it shows that even the best men are subject to excess of passion and affection, and to be disturbed through immoderate fear and grief.

And this trouble that is sometimes upon the spirits of even the best men, it ariseth partly from God's providence and hand upon them, partly from Satan, and partly from themselves.

First, It ariseth many times from the hand of God. The Lord is to his people a sun and shield; but, as with the earth, when the sun withdraweth his light, it is all dark and cold and dead, so with the soul of man; when God withdraws the light of his countenance from the soul, it is as the earth at midnight. And as it is with soldiers in the battle, if their shields be taken from them they are exposed to every dart and danger; everything may annoy and wound them; so it is with the soul: if God withdraw himself from it, and do not support it as before, and do not fence and strengthen it as at other times, the fiery darts of Satan will pierce deep into the soul, and the spirit will not be able to uphold itself against these assaults.

Now God withdraws himself sometimes from his servants in special wisdom, and that either in respect of the time past, of the present, or of the time to come.

In respect of the past, he doth it by way of correction. In their former wantonness they have abused the expressions of his love, and now, as a father takes away the light from his child when he sees that he makes no better use of it than to play with it, so God withdraws the light of his countenance: that is, he casts clouds before himself; he doth not manifest himself in his wonted loving favour, when his servants neglect the reverence and fear that he expects from them in the midst of his mercies. He doth it also, sometimes, as a correction of their negligence; when God hath called on them from time to time, and they have not waited upon God. He hath called upon them for duty and for the leaving of such particular evils, and they have neglected it; and now, because they will not hear his voice when he calls, he will make them feel it, by not hearing their voice when they pray. Sometimes he calls to them, as he did to the Church in the Canticles; *Open to me, my sister, my love.* The Church is negligent and careless; *I have put off my coat; how shall I put it on? I have washed my feet; how shall I defile them?* Now he withdraws himself from the soul; and what is the end of it? *I sought him, but I could not find him: I called him, but he gave me no answer. The watchmen that went about the city found me, they smote me, they wounded me: the keepers of the walls took away my veil from me.* So the soul is left to trouble and perplexity when Christ absenteth himself, whom she would not entertain when he was present.

And farther, God doth it sometimes to correct that carnal confidence and security whereunto men are wondrous prone when they go on in a clear way, with much comfort, with wind and tide. *In my prosperity,* saith David, *I said, I shall never be moved: thou hast made my mountain to stand strong.* But what followeth? *Thou didst hide thy face, and I was troubled.* Trouble came upon him, trouble of spirit, because he rested too much on that outward mountain to which God had exalted him: he placed his hope too much on this, and thought it should be always thus; therefore God now turns his face from him, and David is troubled.

And in respect of the time present, God hath this further aim,—to inform all his servants where their strength lies, that it is not in themselves nor in any creature. God will have them seek it only in him, and that they may do this, he draws them to it by sense, depriving them of comfort, in respect sometimes of outward conveniences, and sometimes of the light of his countenance shining upon their souls.

How do we know that the moon shines but with a borrowed light? Because we see it is not always alike in its light; sometimes it hath a full light, sometimes it is enlightened but by half, and sometimes only by a very little part. We know by these changes and variations that the light of the moon is not its own, but is borrowed from somewhat else, from the sun. And how do we know that the heart of man is fed, and relieved, and supported with comfort from without itself, with comfort borrowed from a foreign source? By this—that the state of God's servants, in respect of their spiritual quiet and satisfaction and contentment of heart, is not always alike. Sometimes they have abundance of joy, and seem to be in heaven: sometimes they are perplexed with many disquiets and griefs, and are cast down to the deep: what is the reason of this, but that no flesh should glory in itself, that every man may know that, whatsoever he hath to make his life comfortable and pleasing to him, he hath it only from God, who dispenseth it to men in such proportion as seemeth good to his wisdom? God will have us know that all the happiness of our spirits is in their union with himself—the chief of spirits; and that when they are but a little separated from him, when he doth but withdraw himself from them, they are as if dead. How shall we know that the branches have sap from the root, that it is the root that makes them to flourish and grow? By this—that if you do but cut them off from the root, they wither presently. So with the soul of man. Let sin make a separation between God and the soul, and man becomes as a withered branch: he hath nothing now to revive him, because he is separated from the root. At the least it is with him as with a tree in winter, when the sap remains in the root; so that, though he be still in union with the root, yet he getteth no moisture from it: for the servant of God that is once united to Christ shall indeed never be separated; the union is now, and always shall be; but the sap and comfort of the Spirit may for a time be cut off; our life may be hid in Christ and not appear in us; and we are then in that estate as if we were branches cut off: whereby it may appear that, whatsoever life and comfort and strength of heart we had, we had it only from Christ, and by the influence and work of his Spirit.

And then, for the time to come,—God doth it to prevent some distempers that might grow in the hearts of his servants if they should always be in a state of spiritual joy. God doth it to prevent pride. A man would begin to ascribe somewhat to himself, to his present condition, if it were always well with him. Paul was apt to be lifted up with those revelations that were made to him; therefore a messenger of Satan was sent to buffet him: and he himself saith, *We had the sentence of death in ourselves, that we should not trust in ourselves, but in God which raiseth the dead.* To the same end God's faithful servants sometimes receive the very sense of death, and the sense of the destitution and want of all spiritual comforts for a time, that they may not trust in themselves, nor in those comforts and habits of grace that they have, nor in any creature whatsoever. The comfortable work of God's Spirit in the regenerate soul, it is but a creature, a work of God; and God will not have men trust in any such thing, but in himself; not in the effect, but in the cause. God will bring them to such a state that they shall seem as dead men, that they may trust in him that is able to give life even to the dead body, and to raise them from the very gate and shadow of death.

Secondly, this trouble of which we speak proceedeth many times from Satan. Satan wonderfully sets himself against the seed of the woman, especially against the promised seed, Christ; he will always be at his heel; and in his opposition against Christ he sets himself against the very glory of Christ, and that is his kingdom among men. Now the kingdom of Christ consists, as the Apostle speaks, not in meat and drink, but is *righteousness and peace and joy in the Holy Ghost*. Therefore if Satan cannot keep a Christian from righteousness, he will labour to interrupt his peace; and if he cannot keep him from the condition of peace, yet he will keep him from the exercise and effects of peace, from joy, that he may not have the sense of his blessedness. He knows that spiritual joy strengthens a man to all spiritual duties, and his endeavour is to weaken all the servants of Christ in all their services; and therefore he labours with all his might, that if they will needs go on, he may at least propound and occasion as many things to trouble and disquiet them as he can.

And there are two principal ways whereby Satan wondrously prevails in this particular.

The one is by stealing out of our hearts those precious promises, those comforts, whereby the word of God revives the soul. And the devil meets in man two advantages to help in effecting this. One, is that aptness of the mind to turn towards new objects and to entertain a constant variety of thoughts, which God hath given for the ease and relief of the spirit of man; this very disposition, intended for his good, Satan turns against him. He leadeth a man on into a world of business and temptations and distractions, that shall draw him from the thought of those things that he hath heard for the relieving of his spirit and wherein God spake comfort to his heart, and so he fasteneth on him more easily those discouragements that he desires.

The other advantage he hath for this end is—the careless neglect that is in man. Every man loves ease; there is such a spirit in man that he ordinarily avoids the things that require much labour; so, when a man hath come from hearing the word and reading the Scriptures, whereas he should now be exercised to fasten those things on his heart by meditation, he passeth by this easily. Now the seed that falleth upon the highway, the fowls of the air come and take it away, and it is gone presently; and when there is no labour bestowed upon the heart, as there is none upon the highway, every motion, every direction, every spiritual instruction lies lightly there, and is soon carried off. This is the advantage that Satan makes of a man's love of ease.

Thirdly, trouble cometh from ourselves, from that general corruption that is in our natures.

Sometimes we see the soul subdued with

lusts and corruptions: some strong lust, some grievous sin or other prevails; and then, as it is with the fowl that now flieth in the air, when there is birdlime cast upon the wings of it, it presently falleth down and can fly no farther, so it is with the soul when it is pressed down and entangled by sin, and encompassed about with evil thoughts and desires. Therefore saith the Apostle, *Let us lay aside every weight, and the sin which doth so easily beset us, and let us run with patience the race that is set before us.*

And sometimes the soul is disturbed by inordinate passions, arising from that general distemper that is diffused through every faculty, so that the understanding looks upon things as through a mist, and sees nothing clearly, but in most things is blind, and is led by blind affections too; and when the blind leads the blind, both shall fall into the ditch: and so the memory that should retain the precious treasures, the promises of the gospel, to relieve the soul in all cases, it is like a leaking vessel that lets these things run out; it lets them *slip,* as the Apostle saith, alluding to that metaphor. And the very conscience itself, that should be conclusive, it now rests in generals and uncertainties. Conscience should determine what my case is, whether I be a child of God or no, whether I be in a state of grace or no: but for the most part, by a man's own neglect, all this remains in doubt; and because he cometh not to that resolute conclusion that may determine of his own particular case, therefore every thing troubles and disquiets him.

Thus, beloved, you see the causes which bring trouble to men's hearts. We will briefly pass it over with a word of application.

And first, it should teach us compassion towards those whose spirits are troubled. Our Saviour saith here to his disciples, *Let not your hearts be troubled.* He considereth of them in their weakness, and doth not much upbraid them for it, but helpeth them, in much mercy and love, to bring them out of it; and so should we. There is such a disposition among men, arising from the pride and cruelty and uncharitableness of their hearts, that they are apt to add to the burden of the afflicted, and to make their troubles greater, by contempt and reproach. You know the speech of old Eli (a good man, and yet he failed in this) when he saw Hannah in great trouble of spirit, pouring out her heart before the Lord: *How long wilt thou be drunken?* said he; *put away thy wine from thee:* he thought she was drunken, and reproved her; and in that manner he rather added to her grief than eased her. So Job's friends, you see what they said; they judged that God had cast him off for pride, for hypocrisy, for covetousness, or for some other thing, and they cast this in his teeth. And Christ himself, the censure of all men was upon him: *We did esteem him stricken, smitten of God, and afflicted.* So you see the inclination of the heart of man, so uncharitably judging of those that

God hath cast down, and suffereth to be exercised under many afflictions and troubles. Let us learn then spiritual wisdom, let us learn love and spiritual mercy, and judge more favourably of the state of those whom we see troubled in spirit.

Many times God enfeebleth and distresseth the spirits of his best servants, to abate the pride of men, that they may not exalt themselves before God; nay, in that very thing wherein they have excelled, he sometimes abaseth them. Abraham was called the Father of the Faithful; his excellency was in his faith: yet faithful Abraham so doubted of God's providence, that he could expose Sarah to danger, to save himself. *You have heard*, saith the Apostle, *of the patience of Job;* yet who would think that Job, whose very excellency was in his patience, should utter such complaints as he did, cursing the very day of his birth! David was a man of a cheerful spirit, a man full of the praises of God, a man wondrous large when he comes to speak of the glory of God: one would think that his fortitude and courage should be invincible; yet you shall have David so cast down as that he thinks God hath forgotten him, that the Lord will show no mercy upon him, that he hath hidden himself from him, and will never regard him more: who would think that David, who abounded so in the comforts of the Spirit sometimes, should ever be so dejected or in such a conflict?

Why doth God do this? To show that the

very best of his servants, in the chief of their excellencies, are dependent still on him; that they have nothing in themselves nor from themselves: therefore they sometimes seem to want that they have, that the very having and using of it may be ascribed to his glory. Then let us reason thus, when we see the servants of God in trouble, exercised under disquiet. Let us conclude,—Now God is glorifying himself. This the Apostle infers in that passage—*I will rather glory in my infirmities, that the power of Christ may rest upon me.* And for ourselves, let us learn therefrom to labour, above all things, that our hearts may be kept in that blessed plight of spiritual joy, that we may be strengthened with freeness of heart, to serve God in our inward man.

The SECOND thing that we have to notice is, the means whereby we may observe the former precept. *Ye believe in God, believe also in me.*

As the words are read in the translation, they seem to be uttered by way of concession,—*ye believe in God;* as if Christ had said, You already believe in God, therefore believe now also in me. The Syriac expresses it otherwise, and renders it by way of command, *Believe in God; believe also in me;* propounding a twofold object whereabout faith should be exercised, that the heart may be quieted in the time of any trouble.

The first is God, considered in the trinity of persons, in the unity of essence. Believe in God, saith he; rest upon God.

The second is Christ the mediator, God and man: believe in me also. So the second part seems to be the prevention of an objection: for when he saith, *Let not your hearts be troubled; believe in God;* they might say, Alas, shall we that are sinful men believe in God! *Our God is a consuming fire: who shall dwell with the devouring fire?* Therefore saith Christ, *believe also in me:* that is, know that God will be your God; for my sake he is reconciled and well pleased with you: therefore, in all your approaches to God, take me with you; look up to God; pray to him; depend upon God through me; keep me as a mediator between God and you, and this will preserve your hearts in peace. Faith in Christ, a humble, constant dependence upon God's providence and mercy through the Saviour, is a special means to quiet the soul under all troubles, and this we shall see throughout the Scriptures. David found it thus,—*Why art thou cast down, O my soul, and why art thou disquieted within me? hope thou in God.* Jehoshaphat too, in that excellent speech to his soldiers that were troubled for the multitude of their enemies,—*Believe in the Lord your God, so shall ye be established; believe his prophets, so shall ye prosper.* It is written of Moses that *he endured, as seeing him that is invisible.* And those three companions of Daniel, that were in such an extremity that they must either worship the image or be cast into the burning fiery furnace, this eased them of all trouble and disquiet:

Our God, whom we serve, is able to deliver us; therefore, *we are not careful to answer thee in this matter.* They knew in whom they had believed, and were persuaded that he was able to keep both their bodies and souls which they had committed to him.

On the other hand, the want of this faith hath been the cause of all that trouble and perplexity that hath at any time been upon the hearts of God's servants. Moses was wondrously troubled when the Lord bade him go to Pharaoh and deliver Israel out of Egypt. *O my Lord,* saith he, *send, I pray thee, by the hand of him whom thou wilt send. I am slow of speech, and of a slow tongue.* Saith the Lord, *I will be with thy mouth:* he bids him quiet his heart in that perplexity, and rest on him that made man's mouth, and that would revive his heart, so that he should not fear to speak. So in other servants of God, this was always the reason of any indirect course they took. Why did Rebecca use that device in getting the blessing for Jacob? Because she failed in her trust in God; and so, through her own foolishness and unbelief, she got many sorrows. And you know what a hard service it cost Jacob, and how many evils he endured, because, through fear and disquiet of heart, he cast not himself upon God in His way, but would find out ways of his own for the gaining of those things which were promised him.

This should teach us, in all disquiet of spirit, to look principally to the strengthening of our faith. This is called a shield, to preserve a man when all the darts of temptation, that fire the soul and perplex it many ways, are cast upon him: faith is a shield to keep him safe; therefore let us have this for our use, whole and sound. You shall find that all the servants of God have so far been in a comfortable estate as they have been in the exercise of their faith.

Take David for an example, when Ziklag was burnt, and his wives and servants and goods and cattle were all carried away, and the soldiers in their rage and disappointment began to think of stoning him: saith the text, *David encouraged himself in the Lord his God.* When there was no comfort in his soldiers, nor in any that were near him, still David comforted himself in God. So Job; see how quiet his heart was, and well satisfied, when he rested on God in his great afflictions: when his goods were carried away, his sons slain, and himself utterly destitute, he cometh only to this,—*The Lord gave, and the Lord hath taken away; blessed be the name of the Lord.* He is able to look above the creature to God, and settling his heart upon that rock he finds comfort in it.

On the other side, the servants of God are never out of trouble and disquiet when they neglect this. The disciples, in the tempest on the sea, they cry out that they are utterly undone: *Save, master! we perish!* Saith Christ, *O ye of little faith!* It was only the not exercising of their faith that did so perplex and disquiet them.

And if you look upon all the complaints of men—for the loss of such friends, for the decay of their trade, for the ill-dealing of their customers, and for whatever else—you will surely find this to be the cause of their uneasiness: they place too much hope and confidence in the creature; they look not above these things with the eye of faith; and if the outward means be taken from them, they have no confidence in God that hath all the means and opportunities in his own hand.

They that would have their hearts quiet by believing in God should especially exercise faith in resting on Christ: *Believe in me,* saith Christ; for the heart of man fears and flies off from God. Alas, the Lord is righteous, and I am a sinful man: the Lord is holy, and I am vile; what am I that I should stand before God? But when faith can look upon Christ and set him between God and me, and look on God through him; when the soul looks on Christ as my husband, my head, my Lord, that hath taken me under his protection, then it beholds God in all his attributes of love and mercy, wondrous comfortable to the soul. There is no ground of reposing the soul upon God but by believing in Christ. He is the mediator. Therefore, saith Christ, *If ye believe not that I am he, ye shall die in your sins.* The Jews, they did believe God; they were the children of Abraham, and worshipped the God of their fathers: but saith the Saviour, Except ye believe in me,—that I am he whom the Father hath sent as mediator,—*ye shall die in your sins.*

And so in this chapter,—*I am the way, the truth, and the life; no man cometh unto the Father but by me.* As the high-priest, under the law, was between God and the people in all things pertaining to God, so Christ our great High Priest is, in all things that concern the glory of God, the salvation of man, and the acceptance of the sinner, between God and us.

And yet Christ, when he uttered that precept, was despised and abased, and about to die a cursed, shameful, cruel death upon the cross: he was then made subject to man that we might have acceptance with God. This showeth us that they who believe in Christ must believe in Christ abased and crucified, as well as in Christ in glory. This is a thing that flesh and blood despise. All the world speaks well of the profession of the faith and dependance upon Christ, when Christ is in triumph—*conquering and to conquer;* but when Christianity is cried down in the world, when Christ is crucified, those who followed him before are apt to forsake him and flee. But faith must be exercised no less when Christ is abased than in the time of his glory; and to obey a crucified, scorned, despised Christ in the sight of the world, to rest on him in the midst of his adversity, this will comfort the heart of man in the times of his greatest trouble.

For Christ is the same Almighty, glorious God, in the midst of his abasement; his divinity was not a whit abated, nor his divine excellencies diminished, by all his sufferings. You see Christ, in the days of his flesh, was able to cast out devils and to heal all manner of diseases; nay, on the cross he saved the thief that confessed him in the sight of his enemies: he triumphed at that instant, and saved a sinner who believed on him, to show that he was as mighty on the cross as he is now at the right hand of the Father. Therefore I say, if Christ's power and glory were not a whit diminished in his abasement, why should our belief be abated for all the scorn and spite of the world that is cast upon the profession of the faith of Christ?

Now, briefly, some application of this, and so to conclude without more amplification.

It should teach us, in all disquiet, what course is to be taken. Some one will say, I rest upon God; there is sufficient to make me happy. But how shall I come to have interest in God? The well is deep, where is the bucket? What means are there to relieve my soul and to supply my wants? *Believe in me*, saith Christ; let the soul look immediately on Christ as the mediator between God and man.

You will say, What is it to believe in Christ?

The first thing that is done in this is—receiving Christ upon God's offer of him. God offers Christ in all his offices: as king, priest, and prophet, and he would have men take whole Christ, or no part of him. Now if the soul answer to this offer of God, He shall be my Lord to rule me, my prophet to instruct me, my Saviour upon whom my soul shall rest for salvation; that is a true receiving of Christ by faith.

We must receive him as a prophet; as one that will instruct us in the truths that are contrary to natural principles in the corrupt understanding of man. He will not lead us through the broad road, but in the way of the wilderness, in bypaths, in crooked, rough ways. He will teach us to deny ourselves: he died to pull down the old frame and to set it up again: for what is the understanding of man, but a frame of false principles, whereby every man perisheth in his own delusions? The first work of Christ is to dissolve this frame, and to blot out those rules whereby men walk, when they are led by sense and natural reason, and observation of the world: these must all be taken away, and a man must resolve all into the authority of Christ speaking. A word of Christ is enough against a thousand examples in the world, and against a thousand corrupt reasons of a man's own heart. This is to receive Christ as a prophet,—when I will not walk by the rules of my deluded reason and corrupt mind, but the word of Christ shall carry me in all things: this is the obedience of faith in matter of doctrine.

And, for receiving Christ as a king, would you know what a king he is? He is a holy king, whose laws are all right and just. The law of faith is a righteous law, and the obedience of faith must be obedience to righteousness; that is righteous obedience, wherein a man labours more and more to perfect holiness in the fear of God.

Hence comes all that care to mortify corruptions and to frame the inward man to conform to those rules that are taught by Christ as a prophet: the soul, receiving Christ as a king, gives itself to obey all the rules and directions that Christ, in his word as a prophet, hath left: and this it doth in faith, looking upon the authority of him that hath commanded it; believing it to be his will, and acknowledging it as a duty for that reason. Thus the soul resolves all to Christ as a prophet and a king.

And then it rests on him also as a priest. If a man want comfort he must not separate the offices of Christ, and say, I will rest on Christ in this character or that: shall a man be saved by a half faith—by a piece of faith? As Christ is entire in all his offices, so the faith of a believer must be entire: we must receive him as king, priest, and prophet, that he may be to us wisdom, righteousness, sanctification, and redemption, that he may be all in all, for present and for future happiness, to the believing soul. For, if Christ be not all, he will be nothing: men must not please themselves to regard one office of Christ and neglect the rest; they must give him the glory of all his attributes, or they can have no part with him.

But a man will say (I speak of a weak Christian, or of a Christian that is weakened by temptations), Alas, what hope have I in Christ?

though I be never so careful to receive him, yet Christ is in heaven, and I am upon earth! I answer—Did Christ, when he was upon earth, so tender the hearts of his servants, that though himself about to suffer, yet he took care to comfort them,—Be not you troubled, but believe in me; as if he should say, Though I be exposed to a world of trouble, and at this time my soul is troubled even unto death, yet be not ye troubled—and will he not care for them now that he is in heaven? Certainly the soul that hath recourse to Christ shall not return empty: for though he be in heaven, yet in respect of his Church he is below: he hath not put off the bowels of love to his people, and he will be the same to thee, if thou receive him as a Lord and Saviour, as ever he was to the disciples.

But it may be objected, We are exposed to many uncertainties, and though we believe in Christ yet we find not the comfort of it here.

Therefore Christ saith, Rest not upon things present: here you are in tents; but you shall come by and bye to your father's house: *I go to prepare a place for you,* between which and this there is as much difference as between a house and a tent, between a man's own mansion and an inn; and though you have sorry entertainment in the world, yet there you shall have an abiding place for ever.

But you will say: Indeed there are mansions, but there are abundance of good men to receive them: what shall we do?

There are *many mansions,* saith Christ. As there are many children to be brought to glory, so there are many places to receive them into glory, and to settle them there. We see what vast bodies the sun and the stars are, yet they seem but little specks in comparison of the heavens above us; but what is the heaven of heavens that contains all these? *There are many mansions.*

But how shall we reach them? How shall we ascend up into heaven?

Christ hath promised, *I will come again, and receive you unto myself:* I will come in glory at the day of judgment, and you shall be caught up to meet me, *that where I am there ye may be also.* As if he should say, All that I have done is for your sakes; I die and ascend and sit at the right hand of God for your sakes; *I go to prepare a place for you,* and though *ye cannot follow me now, yet ye shall follow me afterwards;* and I will lead you to those heavenly mansions in my Father's house in which ye shall dwell with me for ever.

All that Christ did when he was on earth, and all that he doth now as God-man in heaven, as mediator between God and us, is for our sake. Therefore saith he, whatsoever affliction or adversity may befall you, care not for it; look beyond these things; remember all that I have done and suffered for you: be settled and comforted in this, and *Let not your hearts be troubled; ye believe in God, believe also in me.*

SERMON XII.

THE DESTRUCTION OF THE DESTROYER;

OR, THE

OVERTHROW OF THE LAST ENEMY.

---

1 Cor. xv. 26.

"THE LAST ENEMY THAT SHALL BE DESTROYED IS DEATH."

Death is a subject that a Christian should have in his thoughts often, and neither the hearing nor thinking nor speaking of it can be unseasonable for any place or person. We have heard that the life of philosophers is nothing but a meditation of death; and certainly the life of a Christian should much more abound in such meditations. No man can live well till he can die well. He that is prepared for death is certainly freed from the danger of death, neither is there any so fit a way to be made ready for it as to be often reminded of it. Therefore I have made choice at this time to speak of this verse.

Wherein ye see the Apostle leadeth us to treat of four things.

First,—That there is a death;

Secondly,—That this death is an enemy;

Thirdly,—That this enemy is the last enemy;

Fourthly,—That this last enemy shall be destroyed.

A word or two of each of these parts; and then to make some use and application of the whole.

First, *Death is:* Ye know that well enough, your eyes show it you every day; your senses declare it so plainly that no man that hath any sense at all can be ignorant of it: it is agreed upon by all men. Only, to make use of this point for your better furtherance, let us acquaint you first with that which *nature* will teach you concerning death, and secondly with that which *Scripture* will teach you, above and better than nature.

First, Nature showeth us concerning death, both what it is and what properties it hath.

It teacheth us this, that death is an absence from life, a ceasing from being, a being thrust out as it were from this present world, and cast somewhere. This is all that nature informeth us concerning the essence and being of death. Death is a dividing of us from this life and from the things of this life, and a sending of us abroad, we know not whither.

But concerning the properties of death, nature telleth us of these three:—it is universal, it is inevitable, and it is uncertain.

It is *universal;* it hath tied all to it—high and low, rich and poor. Death knocks at the prince's palace as well as at the poor habitation of the meanest man. It is a thing that respects no man's greatness; it regardeth no wealth, nor wit—nothing. Death takes all before it.

It is *inevitable:* if a man would give all the world he cannot thrust it out of doors. It takes whole armies as well as one man. It scorneth to be resisted by the Philistines; there is no word, no persuasion, no might that can prevent it. It is such an enemy as we must grapple with, and it will conquer.

It is *uncertain:*—A man knoweth not when death will come to him, nor when it will lay hold on him, nor by what means it will fetch him out of the world. It may carry him away at any time or in any place, and by such an occasion as no wit can possibly think of or foresee. This is in substance all that nature teacheth, and the knowledge of this is good for use, as well to remember and consider it as to know and understand it.

But now I go on to tell you, *secondly,* what the SCRIPTURE teacheth concerning death; for that giveth a larger and more perfect information of the thing than the dim light of nature. It showeth better what it is; it showeth whence it cometh and what are its causes; it declareth the consequences that follow upon it; and it telleth us what is the remedy against the ill of death. In all which nature stumbleth, and can do little or nothing.

Scripture telleth us of the nature or being of

death; how that it is the dissolution of mankind and not the annihilation: it doth not make him cease to be, but takes asunder for awhile the soul from the body: it carrieth the one to the earth, and the other to a different world; so that both continue to exist though they be not united as before.

The word of God teacheth us that he hath created man as it were in a house of three stories. The middle is this present life wherein we be; there is a lower place, the dungeon, a place of unhappiness and destruction; and there is a higher place, a palace of glory. According as men behave themselves in this middle room, so death either leadeth them down to the place of unhappiness, or conveyeth them up to the palace of glory and blessedness. This, nature is ignorant of, but the Scripture is plain in. The rich man dieth, and his soul is carried to hell; the poor man, when he dieth, his soul is advanced to heaven. So that death is nothing but the messenger of God to take the soul out of the body, and to convey it to a place of more happiness or more misery than can be conceived.

The Scripture acquaints us further with the cause of death. Philosophers wondered (since nature desireth a perpetuity and continuance of itself) that man should be so short a time in the world: the Scripture endeth this wonderment, and tells us that man was made immortal and should have continued for ever; but sin came into the world, and by sin death. Sin is the mother of death, and of all misery that by little and little draweth to death.

I say sin—the first sin of our first parents, whereby they transgressed that most easy and equal mandate about eating the forbidden fruit: that transgression that was the treading under-foot the covenant of works and the disannulling of it, that sin let in death at a great gap; and now it triumpheth and beareth rule over all the world.

Nature cannot tell which way in the world a man should die so soon, and that he that is the lord of all creatures should be inferior to a great number of them in length of life. But the word of God unriddleth this riddle, and telleth us that God made man that he might live for ever: but sin coming, and coming in the person of the first man, it brought death and made all men mortal; and when sin entered, God's curse came, and that, working upon us poor and miserable creatures, is the cause that we cannot continue long here. It was just that death should follow sin, for since God made man to obey his will, when man had unfitted himself for God's service, it was reason that he should have a short continuance of life; for the longer he endured the more he would abuse himself.

Ye see, then, two things that the Scripture teacheth concerning death: there is a third, and that is—what followeth after death. *It is appointed unto all men once to die, and after that the judgment.* Judgment, what is that?

Judgment ye know, among men, is the calling of a man before an authority, a looking into his ways, a considering of his actions, a finding out whether he be a sinner, an evil-doer, and if he be found so, a passing of sentence according to his evil deeds. When God hath taken the soul from the body, he presents them both before his own tribunal, and there searcheth into every man's life, ransacks his conscience, looks deep into his conversation, inquireth into his secrets, openeth his actions and his whole carriage from his infancy to his last breath, and passeth sentence upon him according to that he hath done. This judgment hath two degrees. First, as soon as a man dieth :—No sooner is the soul separated from the body, than instantly it is presented before the Lord Jesus Christ; and there he passeth sentence—either that it is a true believer, a godly liver, a person united to Christ, that hath walked according to the Gospel of Christ,—and then it receiveth glory and joy more than tongue can express; or else it findeth against him that he was a sinful man, a hypocrite, a dissembler, one that named Christ with his tongue but did not depart from iniquity nor live according to the Gospel of Christ,—and then he is delivered up to Satan to be hurried down to hell, and there to suffer the wrath of God according to the desert of so great wickedness. This particular judgment passeth upon every soul as soon as it leaveth the body.

Then followeth the great universal judgment,

when soul and body shall be re-united and stand before God. Every particular man that ever hath been, is, or shall be, shall appear in his own person, his whole life shall be laid open, and all secret things shall be made known; for God, saith the Apostle, *shall judge the secrets of men by Jesus Christ, according to my gospel.* This is the third thing that Scripture informeth us concerning death.

The last and best is, it giveth it us a remedy against the ill of death. It is a pitiful thing to hear of mortality and sickness, when there is no good potion or physic prescribed to destroy the ill of it: to hear tell of death, (and so tell as the Scripture doth,) that it is a going to another world of weal or woe, and not to hear of a remedy, these are woful tidings and would wring tears from a hard heart. But the Scripture report maketh death not only tolerable and easy, but comfortable and gladsome to a Christian heart; for it showeth by whom and by what means we may infallibly and certainly escape all the hurt that death can do; nay, by what means we may so order ourselves that death may become beneficial to us.

What is that? In one short word, it is Christ:—*I am the resurrection and the life: whosoever liveth and believeth in me shall never die.* Again,—*This is the record; that God hath given to us eternal life, and this life is in his Son:* and *He that hath the Son hath life.* Our Saviour Jesus Christ came into the world, as the Apostle telleth, us, *that he might destroy him that had the power of death, and deliver them who through fear of death were all their lifetime subject to bondage.* And St. John saith, *The Son of God was manifested that he might destroy the works of the devil* —which works are sin and *death.* So that now death hath lost his sting, because Christ hath overcome it: in dying he slew death, and was the death of death: the man Christ Jesus offered himself to his Father as a sacrifice for the sins of the world, and dying a cursed death upon the cross, so satisfied the justice of God on the behalf of all those that are in him, that death can now do them no harm: it is nothing else but a passage to eternal blessedness.

Oh, blessed be the name of God, that hath been pleased to provide so perfect a remedy against so mortal an enemy, and to lay it open so plainly in the Gospel!

I have done with the first point.

The SECOND is—that death is an enemy. It is an armed enemy, for the Apostle Paul telleth us of a certain sting it hath—*O death, where is thy sting?* It cometh as a serpent, with a sting that entereth into a man's soul and putteth it to extreme danger if he be not armed against it. An enemy, ye know, is a person that setteth himself wilfully to hurt and injure another. A man may hurt his neighbour, either (through indiscretion or unadvisedness) against his will; or he may lay wait to do him hurt, intending mischief, and seeking to perform somewhat that shall be injurious to him. We call not him an enemy that doth us a little hurt by accident, against his will, but he that studieth and desireth beforehand to be an enemy. Now death (as we may say) studieth our hurt in all extremity, beforehand.

There are but two sorts of hurt that can come to a man. The first is to deprive him of that which is beneficial and comfortable, to rob him of all that is contentful to him in this life; as when a company of foes break into a nation, they burn their goods and spoil their houses, and rob and take away all that is comfortable to them so much as they can. Death is such an enemy: it seeketh to bereave a man of that necessary contentment he hath. When it meeteth with a learned man, it takes away all his learning at one blow; as soon as he is dead, he ceaseth to be a scholar—*the dead know not anything.* It cometh to a rich man, and robs him of all his goods in a moment: though he have millions, death taketh them all away and giveth them to another. When it cometh to a king, it pulleth him down from his throne, taketh off his crown from his head, and casteth both him and it into the dust: he is a king no longer when he is dead. And so in all the contentments of a man: it takes away the husband from the wife and the wife from the husband: it divideth children from parents and parents from children: all the benefits that this life affords, death strippeth a man of them all and turns him naked out of the world:

just as he came he must go, and carry nothing in his hand; death will not permit him to take one farthing nor anything else with him; he is a formidable enemy, for he spoileth us of whatsoever is desirable in this life.

But death is an enemy also in inflicting a great deal of ill upon men. It bringeth torment for the present; it is a terrible thing to wrestle with; it maketh a man bleed and sweat as it were: no man can encounter with death but he feeleth anxiety and distress of mind and body, and unless he hath comfort from above to enable him to wrestle with it, it will not cease till it hath dragged his soul into the presence of God, and after into the torment of eternal fire in hell. Death proceedeth from sin and is a fruit of sin; and therefore of its own nature it tendeth to the destruction of man and to the perdition and overthrow of the soul. For sin makes God angry with us and separateth from him and, by consequence, from all manner of comfort; and in regard it separateth from him, it bringeth all manner of ill upon us. Death, properly and of itself, seeks to draw all those that it lays hold on to a state of everlasting unhappiness: therefore it is an enemy. So you see the second point opened.

The THIRD is, that death is the last enemy, after which there shall be no more. But I must tell you to whom it is the last; for it is not so to all. There is a generation of men that shall find death to be in a manner the first of enemies, the enemy that openeth the way and exposeth him to the injuries and attacks of many others: but to the saints, and to those that are prepared for death, and those that will use the remedy, to these and these alone death is the last enemy: after they have once grappled and fought and encountered with this enemy, they shall be at peace and rest for ever:—*Blessed are the dead that die in the Lord, for they rest from their labours.* There is no more toil and labour for a good man after death; and why? because death separateth sin from the soul as well as the soul from the body, and so, taking away the cause of unrest, it must needs take away misery and unhappiness itself.

Indeed, properly, it is not death that doth this, but the Lord Jesus Christ by death; for it is by his mercy that those who serve him are made fit, when they leave this world, to enter into a place of happiness in his own kingdom, which they could never be, except they were freed from sin. Death is the daughter of sin, and with a happy patricide, as it were, it at once destroyeth itself and sin; and therefore it takes away all misery, because it takes away all sin. Therefore it is the last enemy, because it killeth the worst of our enemies; for when we are dead there shall be no more enmity between God and us, and so no more enemy than we need care for. This is the third point.

The LAST is that this enemy shall be destroyed. A thing is destroyed and abolished when itself ceaseth to be, and when all the ill effects that it did or would produce are removed. So the Lord Jesus Christ abolisheth death; he destroyeth it, that it shall never again be known in the world nor felt by his servants; and he preventeth all those evils that it would work in the soul for eternity, and removeth all the ill effects of it that it hath wrought on their bodies for the present time. Death takes away a man's goods for the present—Christ taketh away death and giveth everlasting substance in heaven. Death takes away friends—Christ abolisheth death and sendeth us to heaven, where we have more friends and better. Death brings the body to rottenness and corruption, it layeth it in the dust and turneth it to putrefaction,—Christ restoreth it to a better condition; at the resurrection it shall rise again in glory. How that is done the Apostle telleth us in the end of this chapter: the body shall be laid in the grave, a weak and feeble, a mortal and natural body, but it shall be raised in strength and clothed with immortality: *this corruptible must put on incorruption, and this mortal must put on immortality; and then shall be brought to pass the saying that is written, Death is swallowed up in victory.* Thus death shall be destroyed: but to whom? to all men equally? No; but to those that use the remedy, that partake of Christ, that have put on him who is the Resurrection and the Life.

Thus have I laid before your eyes briefly these four things that the Apostle leadeth us to treat of concerning death:—That it is; that it is an enemy; that it is the last enemy; and that it shall be destroyed. Now I desire to apply this and to make use of it.

First, I shall be bold to play the examiner, and to search each of your consciences as you will allow me. Brethren, let the word of God enter into your souls. Ye hear that there is a death, and that this death is a sore and bitter enemy; and ye hear that to some sort of men it is the last enemy that ever they shall encounter with; and that then it shall be utterly destroyed and they freed from all the hurt of it. Now do so much as descend, every one into himself, and inquire what care there hath been to prepare for death and to make use of the remedy against death,—what time and pains hath been bestowed in getting that that is the only means to escape the dart of this enemy, and that is the only cause to procure the enfranchisement of the soul from the evil that will else destroy it.

A man hath not fitted himself to encounter with his enemy when he looks after wealth, and followeth the pleasures and contentments of this life. These things will do no good, they will be rather a burthen to the heart, and vex the soul, and increase the mischief, laying more sin upon the soul, and giving death darts to pierce the soul with.

But when is a man fit for death? and who may encounter with this enemy with safety?

I will tell ye. The man that takes the

greatest care to disarm death of his weapon and to arm himself with defensive weapons against death. If an enemy with good weapons in his hand come upon a man and find him altogether unweaponed, it is hard for a naked, unarmed man to deal with him; it is hard for a man that never thought of it before, to fight with one that is skilful at his weapons. Death, I have told ye, is an enemy, and one that is skilful in his weapons, and the worst weapon he hath it is our own sin. Death bringeth nothing of his own wherewith to do us hurt,—it findeth in us and with us that whereby to hurt us. As many corruptions as are in the heart, so many weapons in the hand of death: as many idle words and bad deeds, so many swords to pierce the heart. Death makes use of those weapons it findeth in ourselves, and with them he destroyeth and killeth us and bringeth us to perdition.

Now what have ye done, beloved, to disarm death? What care have ye taken to break sin to pieces, that it may not be as a sword ready drawn for the hand of death when it cometh, as arrows in a bow to shoot at you when death maketh his assault?

That man that hath taken no care to overcome sin in the power of it, and to get himself free from the guilt and punishment of it, is unfit for death. If death come upon him and find his offences unrepented of, unpardoned, unsubdued, he will so order those offences that he will thrust them into his soul as so many poisoned darts, that will bring sorrow and anguish and vexation and destruction, to all eternity.

Ye may see then whether ye have any fitness to meet with this enemy, whether ye be in case to fight that battle, that of necessity ye must; for death, as I told you before, is inevitable. If ye have not, get alone between God and thyself, and there call to mind the corruption of thy nature, the sins of thy childhood, of thy body and of thy mind; bring thy soul into his presence, confess thy sins with an endeavour to break thy heart for them, mightily crying to him through the mediation of that blessed advocate Jesus Christ, that died on the cross to pardon thee and to wash thy soul in his blood, and to deliver thee from the pollution of thy sins. Beg for the Spirit of sanctification to bear down those sins and to subdue thy corruptions; bestow time to perform these exercises daily; carefully present thyself before God, thus to renew thy repentance and faith in Christ and to make thy peace with God. Labour to purge away the filthiness of thy sin, and then, whensoever death cometh thou shalt find in thyself sufficient power to resist it, for thou hast altogether disarmed it.

But if ye spend your time in pursuing profits and pleasures, and follow the vanities of this life, and either do not think of death, or think of it no otherwise than as an heathen man would do, to no purpose; if ye think of it only to enjoy the world while ye live, because ye know not how soon death will end the world and you; if ye play the epicure in the thought of death, using it only to animate you to enjoy the outward benefits of this life; if ye think of it only in wantonness, idly to talk and discourse of its doings now and then as occasion serveth—then death will find your souls laden with innumerable sins that repentance hath not discharged, and undoubtedly it will bring you to eternal perdition. Have ye thus disarmed death?

But again, a man's self must be armed, or he cannot encounter with his enemy: what is your armour then against death to ward off his blow?

The Apostle in one word showeth us these armours when he saith, *Stand, therefore, having on the breastplate of righteousness; above all, taking the shield of faith, wherewith ye shall be able to quench all the fiery darts of the wicked; and take the helmet of salvation and the sword of the Spirit, which is the word of God.* If a man have got faith to rest on Christ alone for eternal happiness—and his soul filled with the hope of glory and salvation through him—and then with love to him, and to his servants for his sake—these three virtues will secure him against all the hurt that death can do. Faith, hope, and charity, the cardinal virtues that Christian religion requires and commands us to seek, these are armour of proof against all the blows of death,—he that hath them shall never be hurt of death, because he shall never taste of the second death; he hath only to wrestle with the first death—and there is no terror nor terribleness in that, if a man's heart be secure by these graces.

Faith, whereby we depend on Christ, and on him alone, for grace and salvation,—bringing hope whereby we expect and look for salvation of our souls by his blood, according to his promise,—and working charity, whereby we love him for his goodness, and his servants for his sake—this makes us that death cannot separate us from Christ, but the farther we are from life, the nearer we are to him: *for we know, that if our earthly house of this tabernacle were dissolved, we have a building of God, an house not made with hands, eternal in the heavens;* and therefore death is but the opening of the door to let us out of the middle room, the earthly tabernacle, and to place us happily in the palace of eternal bliss.

I pray enter into consideration how ye have behaved yourselves in the course of your lives, whether as heathens or as Christians. A man that takes no care to prepare for death, though he come to the church Sunday after Sunday and partake of all God's ordinances, yet if the consideration of death be not so imprinted in him that it become a motive to him to labour for faith and hope and charity, and to endeavour to edify himself in these graces, he liveth as an heathen or an infidel; and when death cometh to him it will do him more hurt than it will an infidel, because, by how much God hath given him means to escape, by so much is sin greater, and so shall his punishment be.

Secondly, I will speak somewhat by way of reprehension. Now be ashamed of it, and sorrow for it; let your hearts now smite you and ache within you—Say to thyself, O foolish man that I am, I have lived twenty, thirty, forty, fifty years; I have laboured against other enemies; if men had anything against me I would be sure to make ready my defence; I have laboured for the things of this life, for riches and friends, and have given myself leave to enjoy pleasures, and taken pains to do good to my body; but all this while it never came into my heart seriously to think I must die, and after that comes judgment; that I must stand before God's tribunal and give account of my ways: I have not laboured to beware of death and sin, nor to kill my corruptions; I have not laboured to increase in faith and hope and charity; I have left myself unarmed against the last and worst enemy. Oh what folly is this, to live in the world many a long day, and never to consider that there will be an end of all these days, and that the end of them will be the beginning of another life—a life that will be eternal and infinite in misery, unless I be armed against death!

If this, beloved, have been any of your faults, to be carelessly forgetful of your latter end, not to consider of your departure hence,—if the world have so tempted you, and pleasures have so enamoured you that you have forgotten your latter end, blame yourselves and spare not, it is the greatest of all follies.

And that I may disgrace this folly and make you ashamed of it, consider a little, that this is to be like children: the Apostle biddeth us not to be children in understanding, but to be men; but he that forgetteth death and is careless to prepare for it is a very child. A little one never thinketh he shall some day be a man himself, and maintain himself and live in the world by his own labour; he careth for nothing but meat and drink and sport and pastime, and would never prepare himself for more serious matters: we blame this folly and laugh at it as ridiculous, and therefore by our diligence we restrain them and prevent that ill that might else come upon them. Is it not thus with many of you? Ye live and build houses, and raise your names to be glorious and to make a fair show in the world; but to get grace, and to get repentance and faith and hope and love, your thoughts run but little in that way, scarce any of your care is so bestowed. Is not this to be children in understanding?

Again, he is a foolish man that knoweth he shall meet an enemy and will not prepare for an encounter. If a man should hear of twenty or thirty thousand soldiers gathered together against his city to besiege and destroy it, he would not be so foolish and so simple as to bestow himself then in his trade, and to follow his business, and to give himself to merriment; but he would look about him, and get his weapons and help to arm the city and to make it strong. Why do ye not consider that your soul is as a city? Death will come against it and batter your outer walls with sickness and pains, and at the last will certainly seize upon your soul if it be not prepared, and carry it prisoner to hell fire. Why will you be so reckless and senseless as to eat and drink and to bury yourselves in earthly labours, and toil still after riches, and never think how to escape the enemy — how that death may be kept out, that will else destroy both soul and body for ever?

I presume you are ashamed of this folly by this time, and I hope you will go away with remorse and sorrow for so carelessly neglecting a thing of so great importance.

In the third place, therefore, I entreat you, begin this great work without delay. Consider, O man or woman, if thou hast not begun, the enemy lieth in wait for thee; be thou never so young, thou mayest meet with him before night; and if thou be old thou must encounter him ere long: prepare for him betime; think what an enemy may suddenly stand out and oppose thee in the way. If a man be to travel, though he be not assured to meet with an enemy, yet he will strive to get good company, and will weapon himself and carry his sword, that if a thief come to attack and rob him, he may be able to prevent the danger. Beloved, think—there is an enemy that waylays us as we go along in the world, and one time or other he will be sure to come upon us; therefore stir up yourselves—begin this very day and prepare for your enemy.

How shall I prepare for death?

I told you before, but it is not amiss to repeat it; in a word,—Get faith in Christ, and repentance and charity and hope: these will be a means to prepare and help thee against death. Therefore lament and bewail more and more the sinfulness of thy nature and life. As soon as thou art out of this place, get thee into a solitary room, fall upon thy knees, lament thy sins, weep for the evil of thy nature and carriage, rehearse thy ways as much as thou canst, condemn thyself before God, mightily cry for pardon through the mediation of his Son, and never leave sobbing and mourning till he hath given thee some answer that he is reconciled. And then strive to get faith in Christ; call to mind the perfection of his redemption, the excellency of his person and merits, that thou mayest repose on him, that thou mayest say—Though my sins be as the stars for number, and as the sand upon the sea-shore for multitude, yet the merit of my Saviour and his satisfaction to the justice of God, it is full: in him God is well pleased, and for his sake reconciled to me; I will stay on him. Lord Christ, thou hast done and suffered enough to redeem me and all mankind; thou hast suffered for the propitiation of the whole world; and though my sins deserve a thousand damnations yet I trust upon thy mercy, according to the covenant made in thy word. Thus when a man laboureth to cast himself on Christ—to lay the burden of his salvation and to venture his soul upon him — then he hath a mighty shield before him that death shall be unable to thrust through.

And then labour that this faith may work so strongly that it may breed hope—a constant and firm expectation, grounded on the promises of the word, that thou shalt be saved and go to heaven and be admitted into the presence of God, when thou shalt be separated from this lower world. He that is armed with this hope hath a helmet; death shall never hurt his head; it shall never be able to take away his comfort and peace; he shall smile at the approach of death, because it can do nothing else but help him to his kingdom.

And labour further for charity, to inflame thee to him again that hath showed himself so truly loving to men as to seek them when they were lost, to redeem them when they were captives, and to restore them from that unhappiness that they had cast themselves into. Oh that I could love thee and thy people for thy sake! Thou didst die for me and for them; shall not I be at a little pains and cost to help them out of misery?

If ye thus labour to be furnished with these graces, you will be armed against death; these will do you more good than if you had gotten millions of gold and silver. As you have understanding for the outward man, as you have care to provide for that, to preserve and comfort life while you are here, so have a care for the future world and that boundless continuance of eternity. If a man live miserably here, death will end it; and if he be prepared for death, he shall live happily for ever: but if a man live happily (as we account it) and die miserably, that misery is endless. Ye mistake, beloved; ye account men happy that abound in wealth and honour, that have great estates, that enjoy the good things of this life, that can live in prosperity to the last time of their age, possessing what they have gotten. I say, ye mistake in this; for if such a man be not prepared for death, death makes way for a terrible and never-ending woe: for the more sin he hath committed, the more misery shall betide him; and the natural life of man is nothing but a continued chain of wickedness and rebellion, one link upon another, till he settle upon a preparation for death.

And, in the last place, here is a deal of comfort for those who have laboured to prepare for death: though death is still an enemy to them, it is one that is utterly destroyed. The philosopher* said that death was "the most terrible of all terrible things:" and it is so to nature, because it doth that that no other evil can do; it separateth from all comfort and carrieth us we know not whither.

Death is terrible to a man that is unarmed and unprepared to meet it; but to the poor

* Aristotle.

saints that have bestowed their time in humiliation and supplication and confession, that have daily endeavoured to renew their repentance and faith and hope, death hath no manner of terribleness in the world; and if it be terrible to a Christian at first sight, it is only because he hath forgot himself a little,—he doth not bethink himself how he is armed and protected.

If God hath fitted his servants for death, he hath done for them all they can need: if they have not riches, yet they are ready for a great store of blessings; if they have not an estate among men, it mattereth not a whit, so they be fit for death; if they be miserable here, in torment and in sickness, while others have health, it is no matter: all these may increase their repentance and make them labour more steadily for faith and hope and charity, whereby they may be armed against death.

Nothing can save us from the hurt of death but the Lord Jesus Christ put on by faith, and that accompanied by hope and charity. If God give a man other things and not these graces, death is not destroyed to him; but if he deny him other things, and bestow these graces, he doth enough for him. His body indeed falleth under the stroke of death as other men's; but his soul is not hurt. Death layeth him a-rotting as the common sort, but the soul goeth to the possession of glory and remaineth with Christ: it departeth and is absent from the body, that it may be present with Christ. Nay, when the last day shall come, death shall be utterly swallowed up; and the poor, frail, weak body, that sleepeth in corruption and mortality, shall be raised in honour and in immortal beauty and glory—a spiritual body, free from all those corporal weaknesses that now vex and corrupt it: it shall be made most glorious and blessed, even as if it were a spirit; and it shall enjoy as much perfection as a body can in a spiritual nature:—*it is sown a natural body, it is raised a spiritual body:* therefore I beseech you, for your present joy and comfort, if your souls tell you that you are armed against death, rejoice and give thanks to God evermore for so great and admirable a benefit.

THE END.

London:—Printed by G. Barclay, Castle St. Leicester Sq.

www.ingramcontent.com/pod-product-compliance
Lightning Source LLC
LaVergne TN
LVHW020223110826
845151LV00003B/808

* 9 7 8 1 4 2 5 5 3 3 3 9 7 *